Openings & Outings

David Pryce-Jones

Openings & Outings

An Anthology

Criterion
Books

First American edition published in 2022 by Criterion Books, an activity of Encounter for Culture and Education, Inc., a nonprofit, tax exempt corporation.
Encounter Books website address: www.encounterbooks.com

Manufactured in the United States and printed on acid-free paper. The paper used in this publication meets the minimum requirements of ANSI/NISO Z39.48–1992 (R 1997) (*Permanence of Paper*).

FIRST AMERICAN EDITION

LIBRARY OF CONGRESS CATALOGING-IN-PUBLICATION

Names: Pryce-Jones, David, 1936– author.
Title: Openings & Outings: An Anthology / by David Pryce-Jones.
Other titles: Openings and Outings
Description: First American edition. | New York: Encounter Books, 2022. | Includes bibliographical references and index. |
Identifiers: LCCN 2021052097 (print) | LCCN 2021052098 (ebook) | ISBN 9781641772570 (paperback) | ISBN 9781641772587 (ebook)
Subjects: LCGFT: Essays.
Classification: LCC PR6066.R88 O64 2022 (print) |
LCC PR6066.R88 (ebook) | DDC 828/.91409—dc23/eng/20211213
LC record available at https://lccn.loc.gov/2021052097
LC ebook record available at https://lccn.loc.gov/2021052098

CONTENTS

For Clarissa, as always

PUBLIC OPINION is a constant tug of war with those of one mind attempting to influence rationally or irrationally those of another mind. Most of us grew up with the belief that our forebears got things right more often than they got things wrong. Some are now so sure that our forefathers were wrong in pretty well all respects that we have to atone for them and make amends. The issue, then, is what we are to think of ourselves and the history and culture that have made us who we are.

Credit for this anthology has to go to the editors who commissioned its various contents. In 1964 I was invited to spend a year at the Writers' Workshop of the University of Iowa. At the end of it, I wrote a series for *The Daily Telegraph* about my experience of the United States. So I met John Anstey, the editor of the paper's weekend color magazine. Always courteous, he was marvelously inscrutable. Reluctant to speak on the telephone, he wrote long letters. It was known that he had returned something Graham Greene had written with suggestions for improvement. If anything, he was amused when a record number of 3,000 offended readers protested about my depiction of Benidorm. He sent me without ado to cover the Six-Day War of 1967. Afterwards, I traveled widely in the Arab world. Marty Peretz, then the owner and editor of *The New Republic*, printed a good many articles from me about the difficulty Arabs have in deciding what purpose the past is to serve. Our forebears may have been wrong in Middle East matters, but those setting the pace today are worse.

Mel (Melvin, that is) Laski was a New Yorker who made his life in London because *Encounter* had its editorial offices there. Always on the lookout for contributors and topics, Mel could never be got off the telephone, and he smoked a pipe with the same determination. Every issue carried fiction and poetry. He made it seem an honor to be published by him. Militant, he stood on the frontline of the Cold War, and his opponents thought it was scandalous when the CIA was revealed as the magazine's secret sponsor. The Agency ought rather to be congratulated for leaving posterity a heritage of much of the best writing of the period.

Like *Encounter*, *Commentary* stood (and still stands) at the center of American intellectual activity, and there was occasional overlap between the two monthlies. The tone is firm, the moral clear. Norman Podhoretz and his successor Neal Kozodoy have never been afraid to take a position and defend it. Neither of them was prepared to take no for an answer. Norman was the first American publisher to accept a piece of mine. Once when he was about to take an extract from a book of mine, he said, "Add a few Beethoven chords," as though this were child's play. Neal gave me my head, though he once reversed the two opening sentences of something I'd written and we argued about it for days.

Contributions to *National Review* and *The New Criterion* form the greater part of this anthology. There is something idiosyncratic and personal about both, old-style if you must. At the time managing editor of *National Review*, Jay Nordlinger happened to have read me in *Commentary* and thought well of it. Roger Kimball turned up at my house one day in the company of Hilton Kramer, bringing a good idea, the first of many. In both publications, ideas are current coinage. *National Review* also has a voice of its own on the issues of the day, while in Roger Kimball's hands *The New Criterion* has a mission. In 1940 in the face of being overwhelmed by an irreconcilable enemy, Cyril Connolly, a highbrow critic at the best of times, launched *Horizon*, a monthly that was to uphold for ten crucial years the highest artistic and literary standards. What might seem a small and even marginal step proved to be a successful defense of identity and freedom. *The New Criterion* has taken over from wherever *Horizon* left off. I like to think this anthology will help keep barbarians at bay.

David Pryce-Jones
December 2021

Postscript: The temptation to make some point a little sharper in the light of later experience was strong. Occasionally I have corrected the odd mistake or put a wayward comma in its place. The retaining of American and British differences of spelling and punctuation only goes to show how far superior authenticity is to consistency.

AS RUINS GO, Royaumont is as good as any. French roads
also being what they are, Royaumont is about 45 minutes
from Saint Denis, the cathedral in Paris where the kings of
France are buried, and perhaps 20 minutes from Chantilly,
where as much English as French is spoken on the race-
course. Beginning his reign in the 13th century, King
Louis IX chose Royaumont as the site of one of the Cistercian abbeys he was building. Dying while on crusade in
North Africa, he probably never saw what was reputed to be
the most magnificent of all Cistercian abbeys in the whole
country, the rival of Mont Saint-Michel or Fontevrault. Royalty notwithstanding, the Vatican singled him out for
canonization.

Thousands of Cistercians took the vow at Royaumont,
and one among them was Abbé Prévost, whose novel *Manon
Lescaut* was an 18th-century bestseller, later turned into
operas by Massenet and Puccini. In the 1780s, the worldly
abbot of the day commissioned Louis Le Masson to build
him a palace, a *palais abbatial*, presumably paid for out of
Abbey funds. An example of Palladian architecture with
nothing ecclesiastical about it, the house is a huge symmetrical cube with steps up to a terrace on three sides, a main
door adorned with pillars and five upper stories.

The work was finished just in time for the French Revolution and the expropriation of church assets. A local aristo-
crat, the Marquis de Travanet, had the church pulled down
by teams of oxen, and then he sold the stone. What's left are
the indestructible bases of the supporting pilasters and one

surviving tower rising to its full former height, like a gigantic finger pointing straight to the heavens. Right next to these remains still stands what was once the Abbey, set around an inner garden in the formal Cistercian style with box hedges, trees and a surrounding cloister around which I and my first cousin, Elena, used to roller-skate. In honor of Saint Louis, the founder-king, anything that can be counted, for instance columns and windows, comes nine at a time. Off the cloister are refectories, a chapel and concert rooms, while at upper levels are the cells and a roof, magnificently medieval, at a pitch so steep that it looks as if it will slide away any minute now.

After it was disestablished, the Abbey remained in private hands. In the First War it was turned into a hospital. The owners that I knew were Madame de Ségur and Henri and Isabelle Gouin, members of a family successful in industry and the arts. My grandparents, Eugène Fould from Paris and Mitzi Springer from Vienna, bought the Palais from them in 1923, largely because Eugène did not want his son, my uncle Max, to have to serve one day in a German-speaking army. The Abbey now belongs to a foundation that is given over to music and the arts, and the Palais is a conference center. Private property has gone public.

A year or so ago, I went back to Royaumont, together with Helena Bonham Carter, the actress and the daughter of my first cousin Elena. A film company had selected Helena among others to make the point that their grandparents had lived in more dangerous times than they did. I was part of the family wartime story of escape that Helena was about to tell. The sun was shining when we arrived, and it seemed improbable that I could ever have lived in this grandiose and genial setting.

The Phony War lasted for the first five months of 1940. Nothing was happening: perhaps tomorrow there'd be no war. My father, already in the British intelligence services, had to attend a course at Cambridge, and my mother wanted to be with him. She had been brought up by a nanny who had stayed on at Royaumont. Born in 1872 in the village of Horspath, now virtually incorporated into Oxford, Jessie Wheeler had been my mother's nanny and took charge of the four-year-old me. She had much the same determined look as Queen Victoria in old age, and her opinions were the same as Churchill's.

Also in the house were its owner, my uncle Max, and my mother's elder sister Helene, and Helene's husband Eduardo Propper de Callejón, a secretary at the Spanish embassy in Paris. Their two children, Philip and Elena, were a little older than me.

In the middle of the night, Max arrived with dramatic news. As I describe in my autobiography *Fault Lines*, we had to leave. There was no time to lose, the Germans had broken through and would soon be here. The government had fled from Paris to Bordeaux. In a car flying the Spanish flag, we joined what came to be known as the "great exodus," as most of the population from the north of France took to the roads in cars, on bicycles, even on foot carrying suitcases. For a while afterwards, mothers were advertising for their child that had gone missing. The nation had collapsed. Quite why the French proved unwilling to fight is still unclear, but the shame of it conditions the national psyche.

Helena hardly knew her grandfather Eduardo. It was strange – to say the least – to be sitting drinking coffee in one of the downstairs rooms of the Palais in order to analyze what sort of a man he must have been, just as we might have done if there had been no war and we were only gossiping.

Once we were in Bordeaux, Eduardo went to the Spanish consulate. Orders had come from Madrid that refugees with exit visas to the United States could have a transit visa

4

across Spain, but they had to apply for it from Madrid – obviously a move designed to grant no visas. A crowd of some 1,500 would-be transiters had gathered outside the consulate, and not wanting to be compromised either by granting or withholding the visas, the consul had disappeared. Eduardo took his place. The researchers for the film had traced a lady from Slovakia who still had her father's passport with Eduardo's official stamp and life-saving signature in it.

Thanks to Eduardo, I could get out, too. While England was preparing to be invaded, we spent that summer at Zarouz, a resort on Spain's Atlantic coast. The beach there had a bench on which Jessie liked to sit while I played around. German soldiers in Franco's Spain were allowed to wear uniforms but not to carry arms. One of them one day in uniform sat next to her, whereupon she drew herself up and said, "Do you think I am going to sit next to you? Get off this bench at once." Her anger must have made him think he was doing something wrong, and in any case most likely he couldn't distinguish English from Spanish. He saluted and left.

Madrid was quick to demote Eduardo for his disregard of regulations, posting him to be vice-consul at Larache, then a fishing village in Morocco, now a tourist destination. People as old as Jessie were allowed to travel, but Eduardo could get me into Spain and out again only on false papers as one of his children. As though nobody would notice, General Franco had taken over Tangier, and that cosmopolitan city was close enough to Larache for us to live in it. After France, Morocco meant food and sunshine and something exotic as well. A witch doctor worked spells at the entrance of the house, and close by there lived a Berber chief, whose presence was announced by loud tribal music.

Thanks to Eduardo, a Spanish flag flew on Royaumont to protect it from the occupying Germans. Marcel Vernois, the factor, and his wife, Renée, the housekeeper, looked after the property as if it were theirs. Both of them were well below average height and red in the face with goodwill. Marcel belonged to the generation of Frenchmen who wore breeches and leather gaiters. His moment came when an RAF bomber was shot down and the navigator was able to parachute into the Royaumont woods, breaking his leg in the process. Marcel hid him on the farm. When the Germans couldn't find this man, a firing squad put Marcel up against the wall, but he managed to talk his way out of being shot. Flight Lieutenant Tony Vidler writes in the Palais visitors' book how he came to Royaumont the first time unwillingly by parachute, but in 1946 willingly for the second time.

I used to spend school holidays there. The granaries where Marcel had concealed Tony Vidler occupy the whole length of one side of the old Cistercian farmyard, and the way of life was still immemorial: in the French idiom, here was *la vie de château*. A fast-flowing stream ran past the farmyard, and the women would wash the sheets in it, beating them against a wall. Carthorses would come clattering over the cobbles to drink at that stream. When the season was right, Renée and Marcel laid a table outside their house and served buckets of snails to everyone from the farm and the Palais.

The Palais has a basement room with a column at its center that gives the impression of carrying the whole weight of the world. This was the library of my grandfather Eugène Fould and a refuge as well. Get that boy out into the fresh air, was Jessie Wheeler's plan of action, he's always got his nose in a book. I owe it to Royaumont that I became a writer.

The Spectator *US Edition*
October 2020

6 *Tangier*

ON FRIDAYS the Mons Calpe ferry from Gibraltar carries Moroccans home for the weekend. No less than 1,500 people from Tangier are filling the jobs available as a result of the Spanish embargo measures against Gibraltar. The numbers have been rising as the Moroccan government discreetly relieves its unemployment problem. Our crossing is rough. The Moroccan women take off their black veils to be sick: they slump across the tables.

Docking at Tangier, the ship will have to be scrubbed out. Distastefully, the Europeans wait beside their baskets bursting with duty-free stuff. In the customs-shed the Moroccans are jostling and pleading for attention. At last one of the customs officers opens a suitcase of the workman next to me and chalks a pass-sign on it. The surrounding crowd sighs. Five minutes later he sees that this same man has another suitcase, and in it are revealed several packets of sugar and cream-crackers and other paper bags. Shouting begins. The customs officer throws this small cache of food over the floor, he treads on the crackers and spilt rice. He takes a shirt from the suitcase, spits on it and wipes out the earlier chalk mark. The crowd gasps. Noticing the Europeans suddenly attentive, the officer salutes with the verve of a French gendarme, and pushing aside the waiting Moroccans, he waves us all through unchecked into the blue half-lit night of Tangier.

More than 20 years ago, food had dominated another impression of Tangier. It was at night too, but we had come out of wartime Europe where we had been hungry. The

Minzah Hotel glowed with luxury. At midnight a tray of boiled eggs was brought up to our rooms by the lift attendant, a jelly of a man weighing 25 stone. We ate three, four, even five eggs while he watched. For weeks afterwards we laughed all the time at this liftman who was obliged to push sideways into his own lift. It was a relief that the world in those days still contained fat men. He laughed with us, chins and *tarboosh* wobbling. The lift has been automated now, the Minzah has new owners. Sir John Lavery's Academy portrait of the English adventurer Caid Maclean, who once organised the Sultan's troops, still hangs in the ornate bar. "We had Mick Jagger and Marianne Faithfull here" the manager says, pointing to the swimming pool. "In public they were very correct."

Already in the 13th century St Francis of Assisi was calling Tangier "a city of madness and illusion." For a long time I have kept alive a fantasy of returning to the villa where we lived, at the end of what the enamel street sign calls the Rue Shakespeare (in Cairo a professor has published a thesis that Shakespeare was really the Iraqi Sheik Subir). Everything clicks into familiar shape on this clear morning, the exactness of the cobbles in the entrance, the exotic flowers under the wall of the palace of the Mendoub, the Sultan's former representative who lived next door in impenetrable grandeur.

Mohammad Driss, the gardener, is still there. Excitedly he hugs me, giving bristly kisses. Toothless, in traditional baggy trousers he has no idea of his age, except that in 1926 he learnt gardening for no pay from Lord Bute. His daughter Malika, younger than me, is dead: his son is with a fishing-boat at Larache. Down the path we go to the roses and bamboos, with the spacious view beyond of the sea and the Straits of Gibraltar. During the war these secret thickets would be rustled by strangers with binoculars who would then run away as we approached to play at soldiers too. Sometimes grey convoys were to be seen slipping past, and those out shopping afterwards would pretend to have inside information. At nights the raids on Gibraltar were far-off displays.

Driss makes spearmint tea, and we sit. Plenty of *Inshallahs* and *Hamdulilahs*. He laughs, he has forgotten nothing, not even the colour of the shirts we bought for our scratch football team. Out on the kickabout ground Phoenician tombs have been discovered. Beyond them is the house of the Sherif of Ouezzane whose family would come to play volleyball. When they walked home, people would kiss their hands because they were holy. On the streets squatted the witch-doctor, the *fqih* whose feet were dyed with henna and who worked with crow's feathers and other more indefinable things. It is still common to hear that the *fqih* is preferred to penicillin.

Past the tombs, garbage is thrown openly down the rock cliffs to the seashore, piling up next to a growing huddle of shanty huts. Kick a ball here now and hundreds of children would run after it. Driss insists on as many photographs as possible, to add to his collection – Spanish dukes, English ministers and Moroccan Moulays and boy scouts, he carries them all in a plastic wallet somewhere in his clothes.

Tangier ceased to be an International Zone in 1960, four years after the rest of Morocco had won its independence. Nationalism made it certain to happen, just as one day the remaining Spanish coastal enclaves of Melilla and Ceuta will be handed back – even Ceuta which has in its fortress a protective monument, the imprint of Franco's neat little feet in cement. That Tangier, so sweetly soporific, should now be unpainted, its famous dazzling whitewash a range of shabby pastels, yes, that was to be expected. But not that the trees of the Socco should have been cut down and part of its garden concreted over to make it a proper Arab square. Specially not when the Moroccans have adopted the old European habit of promenading each evening along the boulevard.

Outside the city the road climbs up the mountain. The Diplomatic Forest begins, of soft-scented pines and eucalyptus. Rapists were always thought by the picnicking ladies to lurk in its depths. The trees have caught some disease and their bark hangs off like untied old bandages. Many enormous houses are deserted (like the Glaoui's) or closed up, their shutters broken and peeling. The last administrator of the International Zone is still living here, a Belgian whose first decree in office was that live chickens should not be carried head-downwards to market (he has something to reflect on if he ever goes shopping now). At rock bottom prices, the rich from Casablanca and Rabat have bought these houses as investments. The best villas belong to the King and his family who come for the summer. The Golf Club has added the word Royal to its title. The game has become a craze: the royal family presents trophies.

The road on to Cap Spartel passes Donabo Park, a very large stretch of unspoilt scenery. Foreign developers hoped to build here the most expensive holiday resort of the Mediterranean and they finished two villas before the Suez crisis of 1956 stopped them short. A wire gate creaks with rust. The road is private, curling through olive and broom to the sea. In the overgrowing wild flowers, white lilies and red montbretia and mimosa, nestles a superb swimming pool. Earth is falling into it. A bar is already hidden by shrubs. The restaurant is lived in by two young caretakers, wandering in these relics of the past, camping like Bedouins. Above their bedding-roll is an order from the Governor, dated 1953, that it is forbidden to serve alcoholic drinks to Muslim Moroccans. It is ten years now since the pumping equipment and all the pipes were stolen. Ten years, and this beautiful place has sunk into its surroundings, a ruin from the start.

Europeans still live in their fastnesses, reservations almost, on the Mountain, the Marshan, or the Charf with its pointed cypresses. But the consuls are all too familiar with the prayerbook Order of Burial. St Andrew's Protestant cemetery is virtually full and the knot of widows coming to matins may have to be handed over to the Catholics up the hill. A few of the same kind of people still retire here, civil servants and diplomats and planters from Indonesia, Africa, the Far East. Men with an interest in the Arab world come for a short time each year, like Anthony Nutting, or General André Beauffre, commander of the French forces at Suez, or Colonel McLean, supporter of the Yemen royalists in their civil war. Continuity lingers – the nickname of the old Tangier character, the Black Baron, has been appropriated by a Swede in the Casbah.

Tea-parties are followed by the round of drinks at which there are no Moroccans except the five or six smart ones, men like the chief Customs Inspector. Charities take up time. Dogs catch distemper. The People's Dispensary For Sick Animals flourishes, the headstones of the animal graveyard are spreading. In the Cheshire Homes the cripples have passed the age of puberty and are a scandal to their benefactors. The Europeans complain – the telephone is never working, the Butagas containers are sold half-full, the black market whisky is unreliable. Every three months most of them go to Gibraltar to re-enter Tangier as tourists. For that is what they have become, tourists on extended stays. "Bond Street in Africa" the small English haberdashery may say, but it is for the Arabs. And as for the former British Post Office, closed as it celebrated its centennial – it is inexplicably daubed with swastikas.

Independence for Tangier means that these Europeans matter only as a source of hard currency. Where once Moroccans had to oblige, they can exploit (indeed the wiser of the

Europeans are surprised that the Moroccans continue to be so tolerant). They used to despise those they abuse. I remember as a child being driven into the Casbah in the back of a big black car. We rolled up the windows. A face loomed up and spat so that a gob of phlegm slid slowly down the pane. I asked why he did it and was told that he was dirty. I knew there was more to it than that. Well-connected Moroccans now have what they want out of Tangier, and they protect it with every venality and with the secret police. Nationalism was a pretext which served their purpose. Tentative probes are still directed at Europeans, such as curtailing missionary schools or putting a 45 per cent tax on yachts and seeing if the owner will pay up or sail away. But the pressing majority can get no bargains out of the Europeans, and if they cannot ride in the black cars, then they would rather there were no cars at all. Now as then, they can only spit.

Eid-el-Kebir, the Muslim Feast of the Sheep, commemorates the ram caught in the thicket. All over the city sheep are dragged or carried home or pushed by the legs like a wheelbarrow. The head of the family will cut the animal's throat and for a few days fleeces will be hanging to dry on balconies.

For the Europeans this means no servants. They talk of their fatimas going home, the word being used as if one name would do for every maid. *Chauouch*, the word for concierge and odd-job-man all in one, has acquired the tones of wog and is dropping into disuse. So off they go to the sheep market, these European householders, to buy a sheep for their servants. After bargaining they pay a third as much again as an Arab would pay.

If they were to continue down the road past the market, they would come to Beni Makada, one of the appalling fresh slums of lean-tos made out of cardboard and corrugated iron and palm-leaves. Peasants from the countryside are pouring into Tangier looking for work which does not exist. Children throng round every passer-by. Three-quarters of the Moroccan population is under 18, and exploding.

When Eid-el-Kebir comes, ladies and gentlemen are invited to eat a bit of the sheep they have bought. They visit tiny concrete rooms and sit on divans and ask questions. Folklore without tears.

A new Governor has been appointed by the King. He is 32 and is held to be energetic in pursuit of his career. "What can he do, there's no budget," says the dry French administrator who has been filling my ears with tales of bribery and extortion. One enterprise would have shown a profit of three million francs, half of which would have to be given to local officials. What can you expect, he asks, of a system which required the endorsement of fortune-hungry bureaucrats right up to the top? Like most Frenchmen in Morocco he is depressed, he chooses his words carefully; he sees communism approach.

The industrial zone has been under construction for eight years and has a high grey, enclosing wall to show for it. In the clay soil the conduits which have been laid down have burst three times. Who knows? Everyone shrugs, perhaps they will never work. It's the same at the docks where attempts are made to start a free port again. The young official who takes me round points to empty hangars. Soon he hopes to publish a brochure.

The damage goes back to 1951, when a mob swarmed out of the Casbah. The Spanish probably inspired the riot for their political ends, but the great families who had the money market – Pariente, Cohen, Bendrao – discreetly moved out to Geneva, to Madrid. When independence came and 80 banks abandoned Tangier in three weeks, there was nothing left but the formalities – and no money.

"Banknote?" The touts suggest it even before "Girl, boy –

what you want"? Talk to the touts and you get a picture of self-hatred. They like to call themselves students but in fact are living with a Mr Christopher or a Mr Robin or whoever it is – and Mr Christopher will keep up a pretence that this boy is really his servant. They need the money. Pickups finish in half-hidden hotels often run by Europeans who have an eye for the trade. Among them one notices the Hotel Colon. Homosexuals are the last colonisers of Tangier. They chalk up credit at the Parade Bar, run by a lady who was once a lion-tamer. Male strip-tease for them can be found, and at Michel's the Englishmen dance with Arab boys – those particular Englishmen whose faces all the year round are greedily sunburnt and whose cheques are bouncy. Every so often one of them has his throat cut and the police scarcely bother to investigate.

In the Casbah the touts will, as a matter of course, point out Barbara Hutton's house, explain how much she is supposed to have paid for her most recent husband to call himself a prince, describe her parties and so on. Until recently there was a small *bidonville* at the bottom of the street. The discrepancy of wealth fascinates them. Where once it might have been Allah's will, now there is a growing mini-skirted-and-transistor set who know perfectly well what the score is. These *évolué* have been educated to be as French as possible; all their standards are European. Once Moroccans were among the best-dressed people in the world. Now under their *djellabahs* are blue jeans, a perfect symbol of what has happened. Traditional values are a slight cloak to their aching adoption of all things Western. They imitate European civilisation, yet the examples of it which they have before their eyes make them cynical. Hear what they say about Barbara Hutton. They chase what they reject.

Once upon a time the American presence was William Burroughs with his syringe in a room as white as a cell. Paul

Bowles still lives here, eminent among a troupe of cultural beachcombers. "We see only other writers," one of the wives said to me. The annual play at the American School is their big event. These Americans will make trips into the interior in search of Berber music, they will tape it and talk academically about the names of Arab wind instruments, and for that they may receive grants from back home. One of the local characters has invented a dream-machine, which even St Francis of Assisi might think a kind of parody. *Kif* or Indian hemp, is smoked everywhere, although illegally – I saw a policeman near the crowded docks take a pull at one old man's pipe which was being passed round. The smell of *kif* wafts like a sweet, smouldering bonfire in the large apartment buildings where Americans live. Smoking is called by them "enlarging your experience." The wives also know how to bake hashish cookies. You can tell the *kif* addicts because they have liver complaints. How appropriate it is that a whole new suburb of the town is called California.

Some people think that the lotus-men are part of a Great American Plan. Out on Cap Malabata a site has been chosen for an American university which will institutionalise them all. Recently a delegation of sponsors from the United States was taken out to see the headland and a Moroccan army officer with them pointed out that the university would command the approaches to the Mediterranean.

I came across an American girl who rented a room in the Casbah and lived there with first one, then two, Moroccans. No furniture. Going away, she would leave her baby on the floor with opened tins of milk. Perhaps she would come back, perhaps not. Her friends sit in droves in the cheap café in the Petit Socco where the menu offers *poison* or *buftik*, fish or steak. But they also crouch here and there, huddled forms on steps or in alleys, sometimes asking for money or a lift. In summer the consuls are heard complaining about the smell in their offices as the beatniks wait to be sent home. "They fall out of the sky," is the odd phrase the Moroccans use about them. They fear them in the way they would the first breaking spots of some incurable disease.

I went back to the Lycée Regnault, passing on the way the new premises of a famous *pâtisserie* kept by Madame Porte. Her support of Vichy during the war deprived us of her cakes, for the Free French would cross the road to avoid compromising themselves. It was the last day of term but the director assured me that he was always pleased to see old boys.

The lycée is like a quadrilateral castle between the Rue Tolstoy and the Rue Jeanne d'Arc. The gravelled courtyard and hard bell are as evocative as ever. There is a new building and a new war memorial but the atmosphere of French pedagogy never changes. Twenty nationalities attend this school. The proportion of Moroccan children has risen from a quarter to over half, but standards have fallen, some subjects are no longer taught and the lycée could take many more pupils.

My old teacher has heard that I am back in Tangier and he comes unexpectedly to my hotel. Because of his pupils, we cannot spend much time together. Like Driss, he remembers more than I do, he has photographs and is touchingly pleased that I have become an English writer. He volunteers to drive me out to my friends for dinner, but as we approach the Old Mountain, someway out of Tangier, he grows nervous and slows down the car. It turns out that he is Jewish, that for this reason he thinks it is unsafe for him to be out here in the dark lanes of the country. From a stall lit by an oil-lamp comes a young Arab, and my teacher hysterically pushes me out of the car, saying that without him I shall be quite safe. He accelerates away and the young Arab politely escorts me to the house where I was invited. And there my teacher telephones to ask if I am safe.

A few weeks before, the Chief Rabbi of Tangier was

stabbed in the neck as he was leaving a little synagogue in a passage just behind the street where once the money-changers had been. General Oufkir, strongman and Minister of the Interior, was in Tangier that day, and he visited him in hospital before the rabbi was flown to Paris for treatment. In Meknes two similar knifings occurred and the Saturday after my incident with my old teacher, a Polish Jewish lawyer, a refugee practising at the Tangier bar since 1938, is stabbed in the street. No mention of it reaches the papers but the news spread at once.

One last Jew, a very old man, is living in the *medina*, the ancient Arab town. Outside his bolted and barred house knife-grinders are at work in the hubbub of the narrow passages. When he opens up, I see that he has let himself go completely. In the international days he ran his prosperous shipping offices in this mansion, now so dramatic a ruin, with its skeleton remains of paying counters, ledgers and desks. Pictures and books are piled everywhere, damp and stained with filth. "I am happy with my memories of the past." So he says, but the tears pour down his face. In his scrap-book which has a range of letters from minor royalty and assorted celebrities, I find the signatures of my aunts, from 1942, and their tribute to his house: "To admire beautiful things is to believe in God." If he goes out, he says, the older Arabs are decent but the young ones throw stones.

Men like him will stay. The rest, even if they cannot take their savings with them, will emigrate. All the time Jewish property is being sold. Bargains can be made and there must be handsome commissions for anyone who knows how to get money out of the country. The Government is distressed, officially. But the Jews are leaving, leaving in a far repercussion of the war those thousands of kilometres away down the Mediterranean.

An American hostess in a red and gold caftan describes

how June 1967 struck her: "My gardeners are usually so sweet but they were all muttering over the radio. I had the Cadillac run me over to Tetuan to fetch some flowerpots, but the penny didn't drop until I found that nobody would speak to me." Another lady says that she looked at her husband in their drawing-room. "We're going to have to leave all this." First the Jews, then the Europeans ...

One night the bedroom shakes with a rumble like a train. It is an earthquake which shivers the whole country and reaches as far as Lisbon. A second tremor and the windows are open and everyone is swarming and shouting in the streets. They race off, cars drive away pell-mell. For the next couple of days everyone in the *souk* is talking of Allah's will but they prefer to sleep outdoors just in case. Yet the only casualty proves to be an Englishman who jumped off his third-floor balcony.

"It'll go on for five years, maybe ten," says the young man with the nationalistic opinions. Educated in Cairo, he thinks the world of Nasser and wishes Moroccans were more like Algerians.

We walk together in a sea of Moroccan red and green flags. The King's accession to the throne eight years ago is being fêted. The newspapers are sycophantic, the radio carries his message, the television shows him live. Hoardings depict his 22 forebears in portraits of the fiercest realism. "Only women like the King," says the young man, and by way of an answer I quote St Francis of Assisi to him. Everywhere public rejoicing is heard. I go to a Berber dance, of a boy dressed up as a woman. The audience sits on sacks of American aid with the Hands Across The Sea badge. A Yugoslav couple are there, he is under contract to the government and explains that technicians from communist countries are the cheapest. Next to us is a schoolmaster who tells us that he takes two daily classes of 50 children. And what is communism, he wants to know. The Yugoslavs do not mince words. "You don't know what a paradise your country is," they tell him, "may it never change."

18   The dancing goes on for 24 hours. Outside places like the Khalifa's offices all over the town gather tribesmen with muzzle-loading muskets which they volley off intermittently. In Tangier it is the custom to hold receptions in the King's honour. I attend one given by the Association of Arab Musicians and another by the Jewish Community. The Governor turns up, in his blue uniform with gold braid, his waiting car ringed by security men who are being presented with cigars. He is called Excellence. Jewish children sing for him in Arabic before he makes a nice speech. He goes on to another reception at the Casino and is heard saying that Tangier needs tourists, and conditions which will attract them. May the hotels be full next year as they were not last year. Everybody applauds. And the dancing goes on, and the music. Tourists everywhere and facilities for them, speeches from the Governor, holidays, everything held in suspense for the package tours – and who knows, now that the past has been laid aside, perhaps the future of Tangier really is with them.

The Daily Telegraph Magazine
October 24, 1969

By EIGHT O'CLOCK the Hotel Eden in Piest'any was full. I crowded into the small entrance, which was steamy with drying mackintoshes – it had poured with rain all day. At the reception desk twelve square-shouldered men from a football team were shouting that they would not share rooms. Twenty minutes later the team was sulkily dragging the luggage upstairs. Earlier in the afternoon I had telephoned from Brno to make a reservation. My room was at the top of the hotel, up flights of narrow, concrete stairs overlaid with heavy matting.

On the first-floor landing was the restaurant, its plate-glass swing doors misty from the heat inside. A band was playing dance music, and groups of people sang as they waited for the tables. There were only two or three waiters, though, so nobody left these tables and the singing had a steady continuity about it. The members of the football team were already beginning their soup.

I drove to the Thermia Palace Hotel, which before the war had been one of the most famous hotels in Slovakia, built for those who wished to take the mud baths and the medicinal waters of this secluded spa in the foothills of the Carpathians. In those days members of my family had stayed there, but when I asked about the hotel, I was told that, except for its bar and restaurant, the Thermia Palace was closed to casual visitors: it was the whole cure or nothing, and then only for trade unionists. Against the dark, rainy sky the late-Imperial architecture of the hotel provided a top-heavy silhouette. The entrance up a flight of terraced steps was boarded up, but I found a side door overhung by a single naked bulb against which the rain drummed and sizzled. The interior of the hotel was under reconstruction, and the unlit salons and halls were shuttered behind improvised draping and a makeshift scaffolding of planks. It was nine o'clock as I entered the huge dining room, once resplendent with Edwardian gilt and fashionable frescoes, and the lights were being turned out. The last guests, mostly elderly, were sitting in a little reading room opposite, knitting and playing cards.

There remained the bar, secreted in the hotel's heart, an artery independent of the big lifeless limbs – a contrast of gaiety with angled lights, streaks of stained glass set against the Prussian-blue walls, white-clothed tables, a dapper orchestra. The cook had not yet arrived, and the headwaiter left me to drink Czech wine while around the room the women in black dresses with beehive hairstyles sipped orange juice and the men drank cognac.

There was polite dancing, at arms' length, to American tunes. At the next table sat a party of ten young Germans, all blond, ungainly figures except for a dark, pretty girl. The strap shoes, clean shirts, and gaudy ties made me fidget self-consciously and reach for a nonexistent comb. Behind me some Czechs were being animated by a thick-set man doing tricks with matches and putting on sunglasses. Turning around, he tried to bring me into the jollity over his shoulder.

Then the cook arrived; the headwaiter bowed and busied off; he had been in the hotel for thirty years, he said non-committally. I asked him if he remembered my family. "Your uncle, a bachelor? He came regularly for the season. Of course." After nearly an hour the food came, a steak and thin-sliced chips, the best I ate in any Czech restaurant.

The next morning, in the spring sunshine (a night wind had cleared away the rain and clouds) Piest'any looked like any provincial town spruced up for a festival. For every

Czech flag there flew a Russian one alongside: the streets had been decked out with banners, wide strip-slogans: "*Nech zije 1 Maj*" – Long Live the First of May.

I walked down to the square where the procession would march past, and where bystanders were beginning to gather listlessly. A couple with a stall of plastic ties was doing quick business. Over the people the ubiquitous loudspeakers began to crackle with patriotic songs and an anthem, its tune punctuated with repeated gunshots, which aroused the old men slouching against the sunny wall opposite. At first they had failed to recognize the music. Now they shame-facedly crept their hands up to sneak off their hats and then stiffened them into attention. Above their heads, two boys on a balcony were pulling grimaces until someone shouted at them gruffly and they too stood still. More music and at last the inevitable propaganda speech.

People began to circulate in the square again as the inter-national words hissed out at them, hissed because there was a faulty connection in the electrical wiring: "Front … prole-tariat … Marxism-Leninism … collective … revolution …" The grey vans of local party headquarters buzzed up and down the waiting streets, setting out from the *Agitacni Stre-disko*, or Agitation Centre, which had an ostentatious dis-play of posters and charts. Organisers were coping with the last minute work, the crowd was thickening.

I made my way to the rallying point, where several bands thumped away in the background to keep spirits up, most appropriately a brass band in traditional Slovakian costume. Slogans, pasteboard doves, floats, banners, waved above the crowd until at ten o'clock the parade set off on the slow wind around the town, and I followed to one side. I caught sight of the Germans striding under a banner proclaiming their solidarity: the dark girl was wearing an enamelled red star on her impeccable suede jacket.

Suddenly I came across the burly Czech, still the life and soul of his group as he pranced ahead like a bear leader. We shook hands. The marchers passed the tribunal where the local pressmen were taking it all down. The youth movement group stopped in front of them to smile and wave patriotic flags. Up the streets went the parade and into the square with the blaring music: then marchers and spectators crowded into the cinemas, the Mir and the Moskva, for the speeches. I walked away, eyed at a distance by a volunteer policeman, a PS-VB with his yellow armband.

Buses and lorries clubbed together in the open spaces on the edge of the town. Empty roads led out of Piest'any, giving way to lanes, angling and curving through the meadows and the orchards now heavily in blossom. Through the countryside there were few signs of the festivities, although on the wide village greens the Maypole rose, tall and skinned bare except for its decorated top.

Cachtice was outwardly no different from any other of these attractive somnolent places, but I was visiting it because my family had once lived there and I had grown up familiar with the name. Along its single street the farmhouses were strung side by side, each enclosing an interior courtyard behind the whitewashed walls and iron-studded doors, on the Slovakian pattern which has remained unchanged for centuries.

At the end of the village I found someone to ask about the pre-war days: he was bald, although he had a young face. Who remembers my grandmother? He would find out, there was a woman here who knew everything. Before he disappeared I asked him the way up to the castle, and he pointed it out.

It followed the irregular remains of a ramped mediaeval road which climbed through flowering apple trees and hayfields speckled with wild flowers. The ruin surmounted a slow rise, although on the far side the ground unexpectedly fell away for hundreds of feet to open up a valley, hitherto concealed, with a view across to the far Carpathian Mountains. Here in the sixteenth century the notorious Elizabeth Bathory was reputed to have cut the throats of her serving maids to provide baths of blood for her white skin.

In the castle precinct a group of teen-age girls giggled around a loud transistor radio. Below, on a buttressed ledge, some boys had stripped to their underpants and lay in the sun. In front of the fallen barbican stones, I recognised a free-standing arch: in the family photograph album this bit of the ruin had served as a proscenium for the posed and picnicking uncles and aunts. And now here were two elderly women carrying bundles of firewood, both of them barefoot.

On leaving, I met the bald man pushing his bicycle uphill, the sweat trickling on his shiny head. Having realised who I was, he explained, he wanted to give me a message. Of course he remembered the Frau Baronin. Yes those were different days, he said and after a pause. "You will come back, you'll see," but when I began to talk, he hurried on to the castle outskirts, trundling his bicycle.

Back in Cachtice, I met another man who had already heard that I was here on a visit. Only last month he had been asking a former bailiff for news of the family. "Oh it was just three weeks ago." He slapped his temple, and his face wrinkled with pleased surprise. He remembered those days well, when he had stood in a reception line for the Frau Baronin, but he had only seen her that once. He looked at me and said reflectively, "Now we have everything which used to belong to Springer, Horvath, and Széchenyi. It is one of the biggest collective farms." I asked him what it was like and he answered quietly: "Well, some are worse off and they are unhappy, and some are better off, but for nearly everybody it is much the same as it always was. They work, and how they work."

In Bucany, the next village, I was directed to a former family accountant and his wife who lived in the collective. As soon as I had introduced myself, I was made at home in their two small but spotless rooms, a kitchen with a modern refrigerator and a big stove, and a bedroom beyond it. Half of the latter was occupied by an old-fashioned bed with eiderdown and lace counterpane, while the wall above was fitted with the portrait of some great-aunt in Edwardian *grande toilette*. On another wall was a wooden crucifix overlooking us as we sat together drinking glasses of a rum-and-raw-egg drink.

The man was dejected, the woman energetic, with an energy all the more ferocious in that her face and hands were covered with acute eczema. They were both of German extraction, and they complained that they were victimised because of their Sudeten origin, that they could never buy meat, that they were deprived of fuel; a long catalogue of complaints which it was plainly a relief to unfold to a stranger.

They said that they had no friends except a baptized Jew who had returned after the war, although he need not have taken the trouble to get baptized because the authorities had driven the priest into the factory and shut down his church. In their eyes the rest of the village was worthless, and the young were the worst, no respect, no discipline. "*Sie sind ein Schweinsgesindel*" the wife said, a rabble of swine.

After a final glass of the rum egg-nog, the husband put on his shoes to accompany us around the farm. At the far end of the yard a one-storey building which had been the family office and the home of the former bailiff framed three sides of ruined ornamental garden. The man talked of thirty years spent book-keeping for the family in this very house; every morning he came across just to remind himself, to get the feel. As we wandered around the arcade, women and children from these converted rooms came out to smile and to pose for photographs.

Finally he took me to see what had been my uncle's house, an unimpressive period piece set in the middle of the village. Thirty-five people were now living there, he said. The front door was hanging off and the shutters had mostly vanished: laundry was out to dry on lines between the windows. I walked up the steep stairs, noticing the dusty buzzard's head still in place as a hunting trophy. Outside I was confronted by a blaze of overgrown rhododendrons, pink and scarlet in the sun.

There were other villages on this pilgrimage to the past, Bory, Kostolany, Konopiste, but I had nothing in my stomach except the rum-and-egg drink, and I did not want to miss the evening celebrations in Piest'any. On the way back I passed the buses and lorries delivering home the marchers. As the buses stopped, groups got out and dispersed, the children holding their flags; everywhere the fields were cheerful with these blobs of colour.

Piest'any itself had settled down to a quiet holiday mood. The footballers were out in the sports ground. People sauntered about or lounged in the sun, dating boys and girls were window-shopping, the couple selling plastic ties slept under the barrow. The speeches were over, the slogans had disappeared, the loud-speakers would be silent for a few more hours.

In the last puddles of yesterday's rainwater lay the paper streamers and the bunting, now flaccid in the gutters, the running dye staining the pools red.

Vogue
May 1965

When the Nazis Stole My Painting: And the Austrians Didn't Much Care

IN THE FINAL YEAR of the 20th century, my family, or to be precise my aunt Liliane, received notification from authorities in Austria that they would be returning a picture stolen from us by the Nazis. Since the end of the war, it appeared, this picture had been on permanent exhibition in the Belvedere, Johann Lukas von Hildebrandt's architectural masterpiece that has become a museum in the center of Vienna. Now a change in the law obliged those in possession of such stolen art to restore it to the rightful owners.

Plain sailing, you might think. They knew who we were and how to reach us. In a masterly display of bureaucratic obstruction, though, the Austrian authorities resorted to one delaying tactic after another, succeeding in spinning out their response to this obligation for eleven years. At times, I felt that since they wanted so badly to keep this picture, we should let them have it. But my cousin Elizabeth, Liliane's daughter, rightly maintained that in principle theft should not be condoned, however much frustration and indignation this might arouse in us.

The picture in question, titled *Hungarian Shepherd Boy*, is small, a mere eight by ten inches, painted in oils on a piece of board. A barefoot ragamuffin is shown sitting on the ground, intent on eating from a blackened cooking pot that rests on his knees. This may have been a study for some larger work, because the detail of the figure is very full but the background remains unfinished. Living in the Habsburg

Empire in the 19th century, the artist, Johann Gualbert Raffalt, tended like many others of that period to idealize his subjects. A slight coating of sentimentality does not detract from the genuine pity Raffalt evidently felt for the poor Hungarian boy. An expert from Christie's puts a value on the picture today of $3,000; in the light of this estimate, the tenacity shown by the Austrian authorities to retain it is all the more extraordinary. Eleven years of defensive bureaucracy will have cost them many times that amount.

The picture used to hang in Meidling, the house Gustav Springer built in Vienna for his daughter Mitzi, his only child. The reddish stonework, the mock Renaissance details of roofs and windows, the immense wood-paneled staircase that rises through the center of that house are a celebration of opulence; visitors would have to make of it what they liked. Born in 1842, Gustav was the kind of character captured in the novels of Balzac, Musil or Joseph Roth. In surviving photographs he is usually shown wearing formal clothes and a top hat. In old age he was bald, the skull like ivory. The expression on his face is serious but sensitive, as befits a self-made man who became one of the great magnates of the day, an industrialist with railway concessions all over Europe, owner of prize-winning racehorses, someone who earns a worthy mention in the history books. At the entrance to the musical institutions and museums of Vienna are stone tablets recording the principal donors who made their foundation possible, and his name is to be found there as well. Himself descended from an orphan, he built and underwrote what was called the Springer Waisenhaus, the city's Jewish orphanage.

After Gustav's death in 1924, Mitzi became responsible for Meidling. The life that she and her four children lived there now has the aura of a fairy tale. My mother, one of her daughters, was born in a room on the first floor of the house.

In 1934 she married my father, an Englishman, and in due course I was born in that same first-floor room. Mitzi was by then a widow, and around that time she too married an Englishman. Becoming a British national, Mitzi liked to be known as Mary. Those of us with foreign passports were free to come and go, but by chance everyone in the family was away in March 1938. Meidling stood empty when the German army invaded the country and incorporated it into Hitler's Reich.

Adolf Eichmann had overall responsibility for the measures put in place to rob and destroy the Jews of Austria, and one of his men had charge of everything to do with Gustav Springer and his descendants. The staff of the Springer Waisenhaus and all the children in their care were deported, first to Theresienstadt, and later to Auschwitz, where they were murdered. The only one who returned was Frau Margoulies, daughter of the director of the orphanage, and a distinguished elderly lady by the time I knew her. The orphanage itself, its buildings and grounds, were declared abandoned property, and expropriated by the municipality whose blocks of subsidized housing today occupy the site. Years ago I enquired into this, and was told that everything had been done according to the law.

Official documents in my possession bear the stamp of the Nazi eagle at the top of the sheet and the typewritten greeting "Heil Hitler!" above the signature at the bottom, which is often illegible, as though the writer wished to be protected from identification. In a letter dated December 1, 1939, one of these illegible signers describes himself as the Head of State Collections and draws the attention of the authorities to what he calls the "rich inventory" and "outstanding things" to be found at Meidling. In his opening paragraph he makes the all-important point that the owner is a "Jewess with English citizenship." Six weeks later, on

January 14, 1940, the Gestapo duly expropriated the house.

Gustav Springer had conventional tastes when it came to art, and bought what was fashionable in his day but is now of interest mainly to specialists in nineteenth-century painting. An exception, however, is a Van Dyck of Saint John, one of that artist's favorite subjects. The Head of State Collections was particularly disappointed that this picture had gone missing. Within 24 hours of moving into Meidling, he was already recommending an investigation into its whereabouts. It is still unaccounted for, and the only plausible explanation is that one of these Nazis had been quick enough to lay hands on it for himself. The Head of State Collections was also eager to have several pictures by Rudolf von Alt, and one of these also could not be found. One memorandum in the correspondence accuses my father of having taken it to England, which he had indeed done.

A full list of the pictures stolen from Meidling comes to 57, all carefully inventoried by the Gestapo. Someone then made a further selection of 22 and on a separate sheet of paper penciled in values for them. The Raffalt is estimated at 300 Reichsmarks. Scrawled in huge handwriting on yet another sheet of paper is the name of my grandmother Mary née Mitzi, with an exclamation mark after it and a total value of 33,000 Reichsmarks given for the pictures. In a final document in June 1941, an outside expert confirmed this valuation.

Meidling became a school to train senior Nazi-party officials. At some undetermined point, as defeat approached, the remaining possessions of the house were packed into numbered containers and stored in the Salzburger salt mines of Alt Aussee. The Nazis intended to assemble there some ultimate repository of treasure that would escape the Allies and finance their own comeback. In 1947, an American officer by the name of James A. Garrison authorized the release to my grandmother of her containers. Having escaped to Canada in the war, she was by then living in Paris. A coercive law of the time forced owners to relinquish some of their valuables in order to obtain export permits for others. An official from the Belvedere museum immediately claimed that the Raffalt and two Rudolf von Alts were such outstanding examples of Viennese painting that they could not be sent abroad. Our family registered complaints in January 1949 against this refusal to return the pictures, but the Belvedere staff now claim to be unable to find them. The museum has also claimed that our family made a written promise in March 1949 to donate the Raffalt, but the Belvedere staff cannot find that either. On July 18, 1949, the director of the Belvedere put out a declaration that the Springer family had made a bequest of the Raffalt to the museum; and that is how the theft was regularized. The Belvedere's inventory stamp in black ink on the back of the stretcher then simply registered the picture as state property.

These subterfuges have to be seen in the context of a decision taken at about that time by the Austrian government. A cabinet meeting on November 9th, 1948, had discussed what should be done about restoring stolen Jewish property. Oskar Helmer, then Minister of the Interior, laid down what became the official position, "Ich bin dafür, die Sache in die Länge zu ziehen," which translates "I am in favor of dragging out this matter for as long as possible." He is further on record telling his cabinet colleagues at that meeting, "Ich sehe überall nur jüdische Ausbreitung," or again in translation, "All I can see are Jews spreading out everywhere."

After the matter had been dragged out till the end of the 20th century, a historical commission was set up to examine the state's role in the expropriation of Jewish assets. By that time, Helmer had died, and death had also whittled down the number of those with a claim. His strategy had been rewarded. My grandmother was dead, and so were three of her four children who had known Meidling in the old days. My aunt Liliane lived long enough to receive the letter that the Raffalt would be returned, but not long enough to see the picture again.

The Jewish community of Vienna has a Department for Restitution Affairs, and it acts as a go-between with the relevant ministry. The Department for Restitution would pass our documentation to the ministry and, after a lengthy pause, convey back to us the ministry's dissatisfaction and its further demands. This dual mechanism prolonged obstruction. The heart would sink as every new communication on the computer screen from the Department for Restitution extended the workload for some further unspecified duration. Family members in the several countries where they had come to live had to be briefed to dig through their records and contact lawyers, notaries and registrars. Death certificates had to be obtained. Legal succession had to be established for all my grandmother's descendants. This involved wills. The civil servant who had first written to my aunt retired. Nobody now answered letters; correspondence went into abeyance. Switching the focus from the Department of Restitution to the ministry itself, I would telephone to ask how things stood, and what documentation was still required, but the secretary took to hanging up at the sound of my voice.

On one or two occasions my cousin or I got through to the Herr Doktor seemingly in charge of this dossier in the ministry. He was never less than charming, making sure to admit and regret the Kafkaesque delay we were experiencing, and offering to conclude the business by next month. Next month would come and go; he would be away, travelling, on vacation. Then they wanted proof of probate in legal form – the extremely efficient French lawyer who had handled my uncle's estate had experienced this process of restitution and sardonically wished me the best of luck. Then they raised the question of liability. We had once more to provide documentation of our identity as descendants of my grandmother and provide assurance that in the case of a future dispute over ownership none of us would sue, and further that we accepted responsibility should other heirs or as yet unidentified descendants of my grandmother appear. And so the eleven years passed.

This whole procedure, I came to understand, has nothing to do with righting a wrong or making amends. Those eleven years served quite a different purpose. Nazism set in place a huge transfer of wealth and the question became how to keep possession and enjoy it. Oskar Helmer's original determination to play for time implicitly conceded that Austrians are war profiteers and know it. Psychologically, they could rid their consciences of residual guilt by making themselves out to be deprived of what they convince themselves by now is theirs. The bureaucratic obstacles to restitution have the purpose of making Jews out to be the kind of grasping and vindictive people who will go to the most extreme lengths in pursuit of their property, casting aspersions on others in the process – spreading out everywhere, in Helmer's disdainful expression.

The same morning that a messenger finally delivered the Raffalt to my house, I received a letter from the present director of the Belvedere museum. She expresses pleasure that what she calls mischiefs are now being rectified "even though it is with a considerable delay." I cannot expect her or any Austrian to make the connection, as I do, between a Hungarian shepherd boy in an old painting and the children of the Springer orphanage. The Raffalt, she goes on to say as though this were quite natural and would surely bring Mitzi's descendants to their senses, is an important national masterpiece and she would like to have it back for an exhibition next year. This is how to turn 70 years of illegal possession into a claim for more.

33

National Review
April 4, 2011

BYRON HAS HIS MEMORIAL among the honored national poets in Westminster Abbey. How this would horrify him! He mocked fame and society, and accused everyone respectable or ordinary of cant and hypocrisy. A cynic through and through, he particularly loathed enthusiasm of any kind, or "entusymusy" as he called it. It amused him to think of poetry as "poeshie" or even "brain-money" and he downgraded *Don Juan*, his masterpiece, into "Donny Jonny." Southey, the poet laureate of the day, was the butt of Byron's satire at its most savage; Keats, he thought, wrote "piss-a-bed" stuff; and "Turdsworth" was his name for Wordsworth. His own life was short, dissolute, and ultimately broken – a cautionary tale of how not to live. Yet to read him is still to be struck by the ease of his writing, its conversational tone and immediacy, the unexpected and unforced rhyming of his poetry, and the brilliance – no other word is right – of his enormous correspondence. Indisputably this casual monster had his share of genius.

There was one thing he took seriously, however, and that was his rank. In letters to anyone who might be mistaken on the matter, the profession "peer of England" appeared under his signature. A capital B with a coronet adorned his bed. Byron assembled a group of friends with whom he kept in touch all his life, and one of them was John Cam Hobhouse. When these two went on their travels in 1809, Hobhouse reported, Byron "gave me a lecture about not caring enough for the English nobility."

It was Byron's good fortune to have been born in 1788,

at a moment when England was on the threshold of riches and imperial power, and a British peer could take for granted the respect of the rest of the world. Byron was ten when he inherited his title, as well as Newstead Abbey, a huge but dilapidated house and 3,000 acres near Nottingham, and a property in Lancashire with valuable coal mines. The outward show was misleading: The Byrons had "bad blood," in a phrase of the era. The previous Lord Byron, the poet's great-uncle, had murdered his neighbor at Newstead in the course of a quarrel about how to hang game. The poet's father married for money, destroyed his wife's fortune, and died alone in poverty and exile. Byron never knew his father, and was brought up by a fond, feckless and financially ruined mother.

Another in the group of close friends was the Irish poet Tom Moore, and he wrote the first biography, deliberately out to romanticize whatever had gone wrong. Reviewing it in 1831, Macaulay, the historian, wrestled with the paradox that a man as gifted as Byron should have had "so dark and sad a story .... He was truly a spoiled child, not merely the spoiled child of his parent but the spoiled child of nature, the spoiled child of fortune, the spoiled child of fame, the spoiled child of society." Intellectual power and moral depravity combined in him to produce a system of ethics, Macaulay judged, "in which the two great commandments were, to hate your neighbour and love your neighbour's wife."

This spoiled Byron never questioned his privilege to do as he pleased, and everyone he encountered was to defer to him. He resisted formal education, learning at Cambridge only how to strike a pose, for instance by having a tame bear as a pet. At the time he could write, "I consider myself as destined never to be happy, although in some instances fortunate. I am an isolated Being on the Earth, without a Tie to attach me to life." Here was the self-dramatization

characteristic of the whole Romantic movement then capti-
vating Europe. His adult life was to prove an obsessive sexual experiment with men and women. "I am tolerably sick of
vice, which I have tried in its agreeable varieties," he was to
confide in one of his letters. At age 23, he could inform Hobhouse that he had already, on his travels, "had a number of
Greek and Turkish women, and I believe the rest of the
English were equally lucky, for we were all *clapped*."

London society and the press were soon to resound with
the scandal gathering around him. "I will never live in
England if I can avoid it. *Why* – that must remain a secret,"
he wrote to his man of business. According to modern biog-
raphers, all this hints at a homosexual relationship with a
choirboy in the university whom Byron claimed to have met
there every day. A suggestive letter to a friend mentions that
he was writing a treatise titled "Sodomy simplified or Pæder-
asty proved to be praiseworthy from ancient authors and
modern practice." A good-looking page, Robert Rushton,
accompanied him on a number of journeys, and in Greece at
the end of his life Byron spoke and wrote of his unrequited
love for a 15-year-old Greek boy to whom he was to bequeath
money.

Childe Harold's Pilgrimage, published in 1812, was the
long poem inspired by Byron's journeying in the Ottoman
Empire, especially Greece. Byron recorded that he awoke to
find himself famous. One line in it, "I have not loved the
world, nor the world me," again summarizes Romanticism,
and Byron himself affirmed that "the poem hit the taste of
the age." In 1814, his new long poem *The Corsair* sold 10,000
copies in a single day, and seven editions in four weeks. The
blend of melancholy, bravado, and exotic storytelling gave
Byron the sort of international celebrity that film stars and
pop musicians enjoy today. Madame de Staël in Switzerland, Pushkin in Moscow, the Frenchmen Stendhal and

Lamartine – all read him with admiration. Schumann was to burst into tears at a reading of one of Byron's later plays. Mazzini acknowledged his genius. "Byronic" became an adjective recognizable internationally. In Weimar, Goethe, the most eminent literary man of the period, was almost alone in singling out critically Byron's political radicalism: "Lord Byron is only great as a poet; as soon as he reflects he is a child."

Suddenly London was full of hostesses inviting Byron, and young women throwing themselves in paroxysms at his feet. Among the latter was Lady Caroline Lamb, the wife of William Lamb, later Lord Melbourne and Prime Minister. Passionate and unbalanced enough to stab herself with a penknife and to send Byron some of her pubic hair, she nonetheless earned immortality with her description of him as "mad – bad – and dangerous to know."

While coping with Lady Caroline, he was having an affair with Augusta, his half-sister four years older than he. The daughter of Byron's father by a previous marriage, she was the wife of a somewhat colorless Colonel Leigh. Long after Byron and Augusta were both dead, her daughter, Medora Leigh, continued to assert that Byron was her real father. As though his love life were not complicated enough, Byron decided to marry yet another young woman, Annabella Milbanke. Far from courting her, he seems to have been brutally inconsiderate. The story goes that he did not speak to her in the carriage taking them on their honeymoon, and that he ravished her on a sofa and then told her to find another bedroom as he did not want her to see his deformed foot. A few days after his wedding, he could write to his confidante Lady Melbourne – the mother-in-law of the now-rejected Lady Caroline, and also a relation of Annabella – "I got a wife and a cold on the same day – but have got rid of the last pretty speedily."

A year or so of marriage, and the birth of a child, was enough for Annabella, who walked out without warning, the first person ever to stand up to Byron. For the rest of their lives, Augusta and Annabella obfuscated whatever had really happened, but it was generally believed that Byron had committed incest with Augusta and had forcibly sodomized Annabella, which explained her leaving him so abruptly. Ostracized, condemned where previously he had been applauded, he tried to recover by writing his memoirs, and these were presumably confessional. His friends, including Tom Moore, Hobhouse, and the publisher John Murray, are known to have read them. In a notorious act of literary vandalism that points to a conspiracy to protect Byron, they burned the manuscript. Edna O'Brien, the novelist, is the latest author to examine the available evidence in her new and objective book, *Byron in Love: A Short Daring Life* (Norton, 256pp, $24.95); and her conclusion is also that the charges of incest and forcible sodomy are justified.

"I was born for opposition," Byron said and may well have believed, but he was standing on the privilege of being an English peer only to pose as though he were no such thing. His radical politics were all of a piece with his sexual license. Living through the French Revolution and the Napoleonic Wars that followed it, he declared himself a Jacobin and sighed for a republic. He took advantage of his hereditary seat in the House of Lords to speak for men so frightened of the Industrial Revolution that they were engaged in breaking machinery – an ignorant mob, of course, rather than real rebels. In poems and epigrams, he incessantly ridiculed favorite hate-figures of his, such as the Prince Regent and the foreign minister, Lord Castlereagh. The "freedom" for which he was agitating so strongly remained conveniently abstract, a mere slogan. Bertrand Russell, of all philosophers, pointed out that Byron's concept of freedom was the same as that of a German prince or a Cherokee chief: the pleasure of doing as one pleases and not having to account for it.

In the course of the prolonged struggle between the nations, Napoleon could have destroyed conservative England, and this was Byron's wish. In the days leading up to the decisive battle of Waterloo, Byron was writing of Napoleon, "All seems against him; but I believe and hope he will win." British victory then made Byron "damned sorry." *Don Juan* has a sarcastic couplet addressed to the Duke of Wellington, victor in that battle: "And I shall be delighted to learn who, Save you and yours, have gained by Waterloo?" That poem characteristically makes fun of Wellington's nose as the hook on which to hang the whole of Europe. Wellington, the archetypal high Tory, repaid Byron with some finality: "There never existed a more worthless set than Byron and his friends, for example – poets praise fine sentiments and never practice them." Revealingly, Byron ordered a copy of Napoleon's travelling coach, costing £500, an immense sum at the time. Adopting the name Noel for financial reasons, he took to signing himself "NB," the initials he shared with his hero.

In 1816, Byron left England in a swirl of gossip, controversy, and disgrace; and he was never to return. First in Switzerland, then in Italy, he played the Milord on a permanent Grand Tour. At times, debauchery appeared his sole purpose. One of the women who threw themselves at him was Claire Clairmont, of whom he wrote: "A man is a man – & if a girl of eighteen comes prancing to you at all hours – there is but one way .... the next question is, is the brat mine?" In two years in Venice, he confided to a friend, he had spent £5,000, more than half of it laid out on women: "I have had plenty for the money, that's certain – I think at least two hundred of one sort or another – perhaps more, for I have not lately kept the recount." "In Italia mille tre" was the boast of Mozart's Don Giovanni.

Reassembling on the Continent, the set of friends now included Shelley, a genuine rebel. Admiring Byron, he also observed in him the "canker of aristocracy," evident in the daily circus of Byron's numerous servants, his ten horses, and his menagerie of dogs, cats, and birds. Building a boat in emulation of Byron, Shelley set sail in a storm and was drowned, paying the price, like so many others, for having been caught up in Byron's life. In a scene that ever after symbolized the Romantic age, a funeral pyre was lit on the beach for Shelley's washed-up corpse, whereupon Byron wandered away and swam out to his own yacht, in the water for so long that he became sunburned. His mistress saved a piece of his blistered skin.

In Italy, Byron was one day introduced (though in French) to Countess Teresa Guiccioli as "a peer of England and its greatest poet." She was yet another neighbor's wife to be seduced and she too was unable to hold him. Revolution against Austrian occupation and the Bourbon local rulers was in the air. Imagining that his idea of freedom was coming true, he went out riding in the woods with loaded pistols and a sword, met up there with would-be revolutionaries, offered them money, and arranged for them to stack arms in the country house of Teresa and her husband. The despised authorities had no trouble dispersing these amateurs and moving Byron away.

Back in London the Greek Committee was established to fight for Greece's independence from the Ottomans. Here was a more rewarding cause than anything in Italy or South America, where Byron also thought of venturing. Several of his friends were members of this committee, and they arranged for him to be their official agent in Greece, well aware of the publicity he was bound to attract. He spent a fortune on specially designed helmets and uniforms, and on the costs of the voyage. Eventually he established himself on the Greek mainland at Missolonghi, more a mud-patch than a proper town.

There he subsidized Greeks and wild Albanians, irregulars who valued his money far more than freedom. He imagined himself at the head of Byron's Brigade, leading a charge and driving the Turks out. Reality overtook this fantasy when he caught some sort of fever and suffered mysterious and fatal convulsions. A lonely and untimely death followed; he was only 36.

The Greek Committee and his friends were quick to build the legend that Byron had sacrificed himself in the cause of Greek independence, a hero and a martyr for the sacred ideal of freedom. So he entered history. Nationalists everywhere have perceived him as a model. A Communist leader in the Spanish Civil War asked for a poet as famous as Byron to come forward and volunteer to die for that cause.

Successive generations ever since have accepted the Byronic myth in full. Byron opened the way for men and women everywhere to indulge in whatever they like without moral judgement or acceptance of responsibility. Conduct that was once offensive has become commonplace. The outrage and destructiveness that surged around Byron have long dissolved into a sense that his poetry is a full and complete justification of the man. Radical politics like his have become a standard intellectual property, and transgression in personal relations and matters of art is considered perfectly normal, altogether in the order of things. Where once this singular English peer staggered the world by abusing the privileges of his class and his times, now innumerable demotic copycat Byrons feel born to opposition of their society, and they too have no idea that they are spoiled, abusing the very things that have protected them and made them what they are.

42

National Review
June 18, 2009

FOR SEVEN WEEKS last November and December, England relived the Abdication Crisis which had amazed, moved and baffled the nation 42 years ago. "Edward and Mrs. Simpson," a television series, aroused as much partisan feeling as ever, as though time had stood still and the Duke of Windsor had not been dead these seven years.

That the Duchess is still alive, 82 and far from well, accounted for some of the outcry. *The Daily Mail* and *The Daily Express* have run a series of articles, and letters to the editor have been unusually heavy in response. Although many letters have been hostile to the Duchess on the grounds that she damaged the monarchy, some of her friends, notably Lady Alexandra Metcalfe, have come to her defense in print. Thames Television received hundreds of letters saying that the Duchess ought to be allowed to spend her last years untroubled by publicity. The most vociferous of the Duchess's defenders is her lawyer, Maître Suzanne Blum, who is the same age as the Duchess. On November 20th she released a statement that the series is "largely and essentially a fable based on an incorrect or distorted interpretation of the facts." She spoke of a "wave of calumnies." She stated that a historian holding private papers of the Duke's might publish them soon. In particular, "the complete correspondence in 1936" between the Duke and Duchess "will make known everything that was said" between them at a time when "they were linked only by friendship." Her final complaint was that Thames Television had ignored her request for advance copies of the scripts.

Some newspapers reported that there were a score of letters in this 1936 correspondence; others reported as many as several thousand. On November 27th The Times of London quoted Maître Blum further: "People will be amazed to discover how seriously they have been fooled. Mrs. Simpson, the Duchess of Windsor, has been portrayed [in the television show] as a cheap adventuress, determined to get hold of the Duke of Windsor, determined to marry the King and destroy the King. The reverse is true. She was the reluctant partner. What has particularly distressed her – and myself – has been the allegation that she was Edward's mistress. This was quite untrue. The King did not want a mistress, and if he had, no doubt he would not have abdicated. He wanted a wife and the support of this one woman for the rest of his life."

By this time, however, only two of the seven episodes has been screened, and they had done little more than introduce Mrs. Simpson. The final episodes had not yet been edited. Since Maître Blum had not seen the scripts, how could she be sure what overall portrait might emerge?

Maître Blum's intervention built a record audience for the drama – 13 million viewers. As Verity Lambert, controller of drama at Thames, said, "We could never have bought such publicity." Day after day, acquaintances of the Windsors were interviewed in the press and on television. Editors and publishers searched for the historian who reputedly had the Windsors' private papers. If he exists, he has not surfaced.

About a year ago, Lambert began to develop a project with Andrew Brown, a freelance producer who owned the film rights to "Edward VIII," a serious study by Frances Donaldson, published in 1974. Brown wanted to dramatize the abdication chapters. "We thought of the abdication as a political situation," Lambert says. "They had met, fallen in love and created a constitutional crisis, and it was in this, as in the attitude of the press, that the drama lay."

Buckingham Palace was informed as a courtesy. Brown and Lambert both say, "We had no intention of being tasteless." Cooperation was not sought from the royal family, though the costume department was given the correct tartan for the Prince of Wales's kilt, with permission to use it.

Last May, Lambert met with Maître Blum in Paris, not to ask for help, but to inform her that the novelist Simon Raven would be the scriptwriter, and that Edward Fox and Cynthia Harris would play the star roles. Recalls Lambert, "She took up her stance from the beginning and wasn't going to move. She had read Frances Donaldson's book and disliked it, but she admitted that the Duchess hadn't read it. She had an axe to grind, commenting on what she hadn't seen, indeed on what hadn't yet been written. We felt there was no point having the scripts read by people who were already predisposed to think it a bad idea to have the series made at all. I don't feel we libeled the Duchess. I don't feel we have infringed her privacy, either."

Infringement of privacy is a grave charge. In 1976, some photographers had flagrantly intruded upon the Duchess. Maître Blum took legal action, and the Duchess was awarded heavy damages against a French newspaper and the state television. But dramatizing the abdication is something else. In 1956, the Duchess published her own story, "The Heart Has Its Reasons," and sold the film rights. She and the Duke appeared in a documentary about themselves, and the Duchess has been interviewed repeatedly for articles and books. Like many who are accustomed to being in the public eye, the Windsors resented its absence.

Raven's scripts observed the proprieties. Bad manners and unlikely language from such characters would have been preposterous. Frances Donaldson was historical adviser for the series, and, as it turned out, nothing was seriously wrong or jarring. There were few, if any, criticisms. As for improprieties, there were none – no bedroom scenes, not a single negligee. Instead, there was cut-and-thrust conversation about constitutional and parliamentary procedure.

Rather than titillate, the series aimed to illuminate many of the unresolved political and moral questions. Had Edward VIII been right to give up his throne for Wallis Warfield Simpson? He told the nation that he was unable to live without her – could that have been a considered judgment? In the words of a contemporary calypso song, "Mrs. Simpson she no fool, she make her aim the big Crown Jewel" – was that possibly so? Lord Beaverbrook, press lord and Edward's dubious champion, always maintained that the King "thought he could get away with it." Was this a great love story, or a tale of idiotic illusion and bungling?

Nightclubs, safaris, yachts, parties: the television series acknowledged the playboy in the Prince of Wales. His popularity was unprecedented. He was more accessible than any member of the royal family before him. Good-looking, he was known for those much touted plus fours and sporting caps and tweeds.

The strongest influence on him in the dance-floor years after the First World War, for 17 years all told, had been Freda Dudley Ward, who only lately burned her correspondence with him. She remains the soul of discretion. When asked by a recent interviewer if she had ever loved him, she remarked, "Oh, no, he was much too abject," a surprising adjective, but one which suggests deeper insight. Among others who followed in his affections was Lady Furness who, in turn, introduced him to Mrs. Simpson.

The Prince was 38 by the time Wallis Simpson acquired her full hold on his emotions. Unusual in an heir to the throne he had about him people who were divorcées and social climbers, some of them vulgar and philistine. The British upper class could not fathom it, nor imagine that Mrs. Simpson might be diverting. Raised in Baltimore in a most respectable family, she was first married to an American naval officer. Her second husband, Ernest Simpson, though a First World War officer in the exclusive Brigade of Guards, was a business man, a little too Galsworthy to be quite *comme il faut*. The television series remains faithful to all this, as American viewers will see when it is shown here, probably in January 1980.

"The Prince of Wales is engaged to be third mate of an American tramp" – this gag, in circulation at the time, recalls the naughty, hush-hush spirit of the royal romance. That no good would come of it was evident to those in the know. However, nobody seems to have spelled out to the lovers that constitutionally the King is Defender of the Faith and as such prohibited by Act of Parliament to marry a divorced woman. Neither of the pair came to grips with this irremovable stumbling block. "Getting away with it" – marrying her and making her Queen – was never a possibility. But, in essence, Edward listened only to himself, and Mrs. Simpson left to him the handling of the affair. Whose country was it, anyhow? By January 1936, when Edward became King on the death of his father, George V, the die had been cast. He would see to it that Wallis obtained a divorce from Ernest Simpson, and he would then marry her.

The divorce was granted that October; then the impact of the King's infatuation struck those around him. "Here's a pretty kettle of fish," his mother, Queen Mary, said to Prime Minister Stanley Baldwin. Edward's brother, the Duke of York, due to succeed him as George VI, felt unprepared; the Duke of York's wife (now Queen Mother) was so angry that she is said never to have forgiven the Windsors. The paternal efforts of Baldwin to save the King were not appreciated.

Baldwin's final verdict: "It is almost as though two or three cells in his brain had remained entirely undeveloped .... There seemed to have been no moral struggle at all."

The Duke believed that a more sympathetic Prime Minister would have enabled him "to get away with it." Baldwin wanted to limit damage to the institution of monarchy, for fear of the unforeseeable consequences on parliamentary government. A King's party did form. Encouraged by the King, Lord Beaverbrook did what he could to hobble the press so that British papers carried no information of the mounting crisis; eventually, the public was all the more disgusted to learn about the duplicity. Beaverbrook's king-making cynicism was revealed when he conceded defeat with the words, "Our cock won't fight."

Winston Churchill's motives for supporting the King were more mixed. A romantic, he would have wished to be chivalrous always. But, at the time a backbencher, he was almost alone in urging maximum rearmament against Germany, and here was perhaps a vote-catching opportunity to rally against the complacent Baldwin, who was not prepared to rearm wholeheartedly. But Churchill was shouted down in the House of Commons and feared that his career might never recover. During the war, he admitted ruefully that the prospect of Mrs. Simpson as Queen of England would have been "too horrible to contemplate."

A few days before the abdication, Mrs. Simpson fled London for Cannes. In her book, she recalls her thoughts at the time: "There is no one to speak up for me. I am sure there is only one solution: That is for me to remove myself from the King's life." But Frances Donaldson, in her book on Edward, notes that the Duchess did not intend anything of the kind, for if she meant what she said, by then the King risked losing both her and his throne. Rationality had long since been jettisoned by the would-be royal couple. It was in the King's temperament to believe that some conjuring could still be performed. To that extent, he misled Mrs. Simpson. On December 10, 1936 the King signed his abdication and quickly left for Enzesfeld, a friend's castle near Vienna, for he had to spend six months by himself while Mrs. Simpson's divorce became absolute. (The strict divorce law of the time granted only a conditional divorce at first; this could be overturned if one of the divorcing parties consorted with a member of the opposite sex during the first six months.)

Thames Television has reconstructed these events faithfully. Those like Maître Blum, who search for "cheap adventuress" touches, may find them, but plain bias is absent. Besides the Queen Mother and Duchess herself, the only other living person represented in the series is Lady Diana Cooper. Well into her 80s, she is a *belle époque* marvel, heroine of Evelyn Waugh novels. In the summer of 1936, with the abdication imminent, she and her husband, Duff, were on a cruise on a yacht, the Nahlin, as guests of the King, who was visibly in adoration of Mrs. Simpson at his side.

Lady Diana, of course, watched the television series and told me, "Simon Raven made her too tender and too dull. Cynthia Harris [who plays Mrs. Simpson] wasn't high spirited enough. I have been asked constantly if I thought they went to bed together on the Nahlin and so on. I tell them all, 'I haven't the least idea. How should I know?' Though I am perfectly sure they did. But I don't think she was scheming from the start. She was enjoying it, and then it got beyond her."

Another witness is Lady Alexandra Metcalfe, daughter of Lord Curzon. Her late husband, Major Edward Metcalfe – "Fruity" to his friends – had accompanied the Duke to Enzesfeld. As described in Fruity's letters to his wife, the Duke was pathetically lonely and dependent on Wallis, ringing her up for mammoth telephone sessions day and night. This is the period, says Maître Blum, when the correspondence which "will make known everything that was said" is supposed to have taken place. Fruity makes no mention of any correspondence.

"He was like a child in her hands," Lady Alexandra told me. "Poor little man, he was given hell; it was a stranglehold she had over him." When the Windsors briefly returned to England in 1939 at the beginning of the war, they stayed with the Metcalfes. "There was never any sign of rows then … only of him being driven round the bend with worry by her. After he came under her influence, he disintegrated. If you stayed with them, though, as we often did after the war, you could not help being aware that he would do it all over again. I don't think he did have regrets."

After the Windsors' wedding in June 1937, their story should have receded toward a happily-ever-after ending. The trouble was the Windsors themselves. It was beyond the Duke to perceive the enormity of what he had done. When the Duchess was refused the courtesy title of Her Royal Highness, the Duke was incensed, and said so often and loudly during his life, including in his memoirs. This pique lasted till his death, unbecomingly, after he had left his family to continue the institution of monarchy as best they could.

The Windsors did themselves lasting damage by visiting Hitler at Berchtesgaden in the summer of 1937. Two years previously, as Prince of Wales, he had made a speech saying that war between England and Germany was unthinkable. In consequence, he became a popular figure in Germany and Joachim von Ribbentrop, then German Ambassador to England and later Hitler's Foreign Minister, was encouraged to get in touch with him.

In the summer of 1940 the Windsors were living in France, but after the Dunkirk evacuation they sought refuge in Lisbon. There the Duke compromised himself by remaining in contact with German representatives. There was more to this than the Duke's love of the German language and his feeling that through the Battenburgs and Saxe-Coburgs he was a German prince. To the end of his life, he did not hide his opinion that English appeasement of Hitler should have been carried into an alliance. Throughout the war, Hitler entertained hopes of exploiting the naïve Duke, while regretting that "so fine a pillar had been toppled."

Appointed Governor of the Bahamas in 1940, the Duke was out of harm's way for the duration of the war. Here was another grievance: A better job in a more befitting station was what he felt himself entitled to. Unfortunately he had had such a job already, and neither George VI nor Churchill, now Prime Minister, was inclined to give him a second chance. In 1945, he returned to France. His house had been scrupulously maintained by the occupying Germans. From 1953 on, the French Government, for no very clear reason, put at the Windsors' disposal, for a nominal rent, a house in the fashionable Bois de Boulogne. State security guards are provided there to this day, and – a further tremendous concession – the Windsors have always been exempted from French taxes.

After the war, and for the succeeding 27 years, the Windsors were a couple killing time. The Duke had stockbrokers and a Swiss banker to telephone; he played as much golf as he could, usually on the course at St Cloud; he enlarged his wardrobe. He liked to show that he could talk to the Spanish gardener in his native tongue: "'*Usted hable la lengua de Cervantes?*' How many times have I heard him ask that!" one of his private secretaries exclaimed to me. Some of the year was spent traveling, mainly in America. The Duchess also enlarged her wardrobe and saw that the household was meticulously run. Several pug dogs had to be cherished. Every evening at 7:30, the hairdresser would attend to her –

a high point of the timetable. The Windsors entertained or dined out often – nightclub regulars, attenders of balls and dances, integral members of café society. Among hundreds of acquaintances were few friends.

A former private secretary of theirs told me: "Their life was essentially a life of entertainment. It was really empty as far as I could judge, but it was what they enjoyed. He would have liked to have had some kind of official appointment. He had begun to tire of social life, but that was her great thing. She loved anything to do with a party. She had to make sure she never missed one. Was it enough? How could it be? They were wretched personalities. They were completely egocentric. I don't think they ever outgrew the abdication. I always felt that if they had let down this business of being royalty, they'd have had a much better time. The Duke would never touch a drop of drink before 7 in the evening but that is no guarantee of what can be drunk after 7, and sometimes the sound of their drunken bickering was unbearable. She was a dominating woman, no question of that but he was certainly sincerely in love with her."

Having no children set the seal on the all-round lack of achievement. One way or another the crown would have been bound to devolve upon the present Queen, and this added to the illusion that the Windsors had counted for nothing, had never been quite real. But at least relations within the royal family could thaw gradually. Just before his 78th birthday in May 1972, the Duke was visited in Paris by his niece, the Queen, and Prince Philip. It was timely. Within days, the Duke died. His funeral was on June 5, at Windsor Castle, where he was buried in the royal cemetery. By special concession, the Duchess will one day lie alongside him, the only commoner admitted. For the funeral she was also invited to stay with the royal family. Photographs showed her looking out of a Buckingham Palace window with a curiously forlorn yet energetic expression.

Since then, Prince Charles is reported to have stayed in touch with his aunt. In addition, Lord Mountbatten, who is the senior statesman of the royal family, and Prince Philip's uncle, (and who Maître Blum says is persistently on the telephone to her) is thought to have advised the Duchess on behalf of the royal family about disposing of her fortune, for she has no heirs at all, no close relations, nobody. It was always said, and never denied, that the Duke had received from George VI in 1936 a settlement of £2 million with an additional income of £60,000 a year, against the crown and family properties which he handed over on abdicating. He took with him some personal possessions, certain of which were extremely valuable. Although the Duke bought the Duchess splendid jewels, he was always careful about money, not to say stingy, and the Duchess is under no financial strain.

Since becoming a widow, the Duchess has been increasingly ill and isolated. For some time, she has been suffering from arteriosclerosis. According to Maître Blum, in order to prevent blood-pressure complications, her physician has forbidden her to receive visitors. She last went out two years ago. She remains alone all day except for three nurses from the American Hospital who are in constant attendance. I spoke to one who had looked after her five years ago, and she told me that even the drinking that the Duchess, too, used to enjoy, has been stopped by doctor's orders. Last month, at the American Hospital, she had an operation for an intestinal blockage and was reported to be recuperating well.

The Bois de Boulogne house is closed up and shuttered, the gateway padlocked, burglar alarms everywhere. Although Georges, the butler, and his wife are still there, many of the old servants and staff have been dismissed, notably the

Duke's valet, Sidney Johnson, always called Mr. Sidney, who was hired in the Bahamas during the war and remained with the Duke for almost 30 years; he works now for a Chilean émigré in Paris. "You must ask Maître Blum for permission to speak to me. I've signed a paper about it," he says. The social secretary for the last seven years was Joanna Schultz and last April she was asked to leave; like Mr. Sidney, she would not comment. The Duchess's hairdresser for 18 years was in some panic lest Maître Blum should find out that I had contacted him. Incapacitated, alas, the Duchess is now beyond coherent conversation, but a kind of fortress has been created around her, which makes her plight that much the more stark and dreadful.

So rumor breeds. A golfing companion of the Duke's told me, "I promised the Duke I'd look after Wallis, and I'd like nothing better. But I can't get near her. Meanwhile, explain to me why her possessions are apparently disappearing into the blue!" Ridiculous says Maître Blum. Nothing is disappearing from the house in the Bois de Boulogne; everything belonging to the royal family either has been returned to them or will be. The jewels are inventoried in triplicate. Every precaution is taken. The few items the Duchess has sold have been disposals such as anybody might make, to purchase something more desirable.

Maître Blum, who keeps watch on this scene, is capable, devoted, inflexible, tough and cold. Alert, dressed with careful formality, she does not look her age. Her present husband, aged 87, was a general. She has represented Darryl Zanuck, Jack Warner, Walt Disney and Charlie Chaplin among others. She is not accustomed to losing, or to mincing words.

Almost everybody I approached in Paris appeared to have reported to Maître Blum. "There are," she said, "nothing but vultures crowding around the garbage cans." Like

Frances Donaldson, for instance, whom Maître Blum says it would take a 400-page book to refute. (She had said the same to Thames Television, but when challenged did not provide any errors.) And like the two American writers Charles Murphy and Joseph Bryan, who for years have been writing a book about the Windsors, questioning everybody concerned. And like me.

Maître Blum had met the Windsors at parties in 1937. In 1947, she began her professional dealings with them, mainly through her first husband, also a lawyer. Sole executor of the Duke's will, she believes that no aspect of the Windsors' lives is open to criticism.

Staying with Hitler in 1937? "But *everybody* stayed with Hitler."

Contact with enemy agents during the war? "But the documents are forged."

But the documents are published officially on behalf of the Foreign Office! "Foolishness. Deception."

The mindless, nonstop party going? "The Duke was very quick to understand matters of law. He was also interested in charities."

Since the Duchess is past knowing about the television series, is it wise to put statements about it into her mouth?

Maître Blum acknowledges that the Duchess is, and always has been, unaware of the series, and indeed is in no position to be distressed by it.

Besides, I say to Maître Blum, the series neither shows nor implies that the Duchess slept with the Duke before they were married. But, I add, shouldn't we recognize that she was a mature, twice-married woman by the time she met him? Had she played the virgin, and obliged him to quit his throne in order to go to bed with her, she would have been a monster – while the Duke's sexuality would also have been called into question. Grudgingly, Maître Blum agrees that "nothing would be altered if they had slept together." She continues to maintain, however, that they did not before they were married.

56   Not an inch is yielded otherwise. Members of the staff have been released only if no longer required. The Duchess is nursed as she ought to be. The finances are fine.

But, I ask, what about the letters? Maître Blum will neither confirm how many there are, nor say where. She has nothing to say about the supposed historian.

I press on. Why this secrecy? If the letters shed favorable light on the Duchess, it cannot be to her advantage to shroud them in mystery. Maître Blum explodes with more vivid imagery about vultures and garbage.

Charles Murphy, with TimeLife-Fortune for most of his career, is retired now and lives in Washington. For five years, on and off, he worked as a ghost writer on the memoirs of both the Duke and Duchess. Recently, in collaboration with Joseph Bryan, a writer who saw a good deal of the Windsors socially, he has been polishing a definitive biography of the Windsors. "I took the King's shilling," Murphy says, "and so as a politesse I decided to postpone publication until after the Duchess's death. The book is 97 percent finished; we're just tying up loose ends." The book is thought to be explosive, but for now both writers will say only that they "will show it all the way it was."

Neither has the letters, neither knows about them. Had the letters existed, Murphy feels sure, they would have been brought out while he was writing the Windsors' books. The Duke loathed the act of writing, Murphy says, and had no powers of expression.

The authorities are unanimous on one fundamental: The Duke loved the Duchess to the bitter end. He needed a woman to dominate him, with the abjectness which Freda Dudley Ward had early on found so disconcerting. "After marriage, she ran everything as it would be in a well-conducted nursery," Donaldson explains. "I think his motive was to get out of being King, to pass on the responsibilities. That's why he misled her into believing that they might reach safe ground. The great attraction was that she enabled him to give up the monarchy." But his great attraction for her was precisely that he was King. Their ambitions ran counter from the beginning: Each person could be satisfied only at the other's expense. Many witnesses relate how, throughout their marriage, the Duchess would openly spoil some occasion for him with the thrust "Remember you aren't King now." Disappointed, she was also locked into that disappointment. From the evidence, it seems that to leave him would have been to deny all meaning to what she had done, and what they had made each other do. In effect, this is what Maître Blum is trying to suffocate. It is she, not Thames Television, who wishes the world to credit a fable.

By coincidence, the television series was launched when Prince Charles had his birthday. Comparisons between the two Princes of Wales were inevitably drawn, particularly in the obvious respect that Prince Charles has also delayed getting married. A poll, commissioned from the Opinion Research Centre in October, had found that only 22 percent would object if Prince Charles were to marry a divorced woman. Eighty-six percent thought the monarchy "provides the best head of state," and 97 percent think the Queen "does a good job." To the huge majority, it can be safely asserted, the monarchy continues to reassure in a crumbling landscape. Even the handful of left-wing republican critics give the impression of being perversely in love with the Queen.

Still, like everything else in the country, the royal family cannot escape the remorseless trend of proletarianization, and it is here that the television series touched something very much more profound, which accounts for all the controversy.

Edward VIII, once King of England and Emperor of India by the Grace of God, was, we see clearly on our television screens, first and foremost a chap in plus fours and checked tweeds of a brassy yellow and blue, a chap for cocktail shakers and golf clubs. A perpetual adolescent schoolboy, a chinless wonder, a twit – who in the world does he resemble more than P. G. Wodehouse's Bertie Wooster? A Bertie is the great archetype of the British national character in the 20th Century. Bertie never did a hand's turn except use money he had not earned to play golf and run after a besotting girl. Just so, Edward VIII. And if the King of England cannot be bothered to do his job, why should anyone else? He was perhaps the first and certainly the most notable dropout. No *moral* struggle at all. And let someone else pay for it.

So rich and so free and so unconcerned, was he at least happy, doing his thing with the woman he loved, in that ideal welfare state of his, in that expanding dream of moneyed idleness to which we must aspire?

Well, no, as a matter of fact, not at all and that's the rub.

The New York Times Magazine
March 18, 1979

The Girl with the Most Famous Cello in the World

THREE FLOORS UP the backstairs of the Festival Hall, I wait outside the Green Room. A cello is being played on the other side of the door. A man with a tray of tea-cups goes past in stockinged feet. At last the door opens and Jacqueline du Pré comes out, a rush of long blonde hair over a blue mackintosh. Daniel Barenboim, the pianist and conductor, takes her by the arm to the morning's rehearsal.

People keep coming into the near-empty hall. Very much at her ease throughout her Haydn concerto, Jacqueline smiles at friends and mouths a greeting at Larry Foster, who in Los Angeles recently conducted her playing this piece. Her life at 22 is bound together by such camaraderie with other musicians of her age – Ashkenazy, Steven Bishop, John Williams, Zubin Mehta – to the exclusion of almost everything else. Of the more famous like Karajan or Bernstein she is likely to say that they are "wonderful." Once a conductor was rude to her – "it was awful." Professional admiration swaddles her and has done so since her first public concert at the Wigmore Hall six years ago. Women cello soloists are a rarity. When I mentioned this, she gave me the names of two other women cellists in the country but added that in America she had just played with an all-female orchestra.

After the rehearsal Daniel hugs her. Back in the Green Room she is joined by an elderly reporter from Wales, who in his interview settles down to the questions with which Jacqueline, now having crossed the threshold of international success, is growing familiar. She has no views about Welsh audiences, she tells him, nor about the Arts Council's musical policy, and thinks that nowadays young musicians of talent are not overlooked.

There is a slight foreign intonation in her voice and I ask if this is linked to her name. The accent, she says, has been picked up from some Argentines she is seeing a lot of and with whom she will be flying after the concert to Berlin for five days of rest. Her parents came originally from Jersey, although now they live at Gerrards Cross, Buckinghamshire, in an atmosphere of family stability: not that Jacqueline ever had time to waste on being bohemian. While she was growing up, her father was secretary of the Institute of Cost and Works Accountants. In a shed in his garden he has a collection of hundreds of geological specimens. Mrs Du Pré keeps her daughter's scrapbooks and showed me the latest cuttings from *Life* magazine. On the hall mantelpiece still stood Jacqueline's gilt-edged invitation to an official dinner for the Prime Minister and the visiting Mr Kosygin.

It is eleven at night when she arrives from Germany at the Midland Hotel in Manchester. Practice next morning in her room, rehearsal in the afternoon. At the Free Trade Hall, Sir John Barbirolli is late and Jacqueline sits in the stalls while, without him, the orchestra starts an overture. The tune is high-spirited. "I wonder what it is?" Jacqueline turns to me and, improvising, she accompanies the orchestra. Entering, Barbirolli apologises, but he had this Mahler rehearsal and one of the singers is having a baby, as they always do just before performances. "What about you Miss Du Pré?" he asks. She hands back the joke. "I'll be all right tonight but I'm not sure about tomorrow."

She plays the Elgar concerto with which she first made her name, and Barbirolli embraces her. On her way to the evening concert, she recalls that once in Manchester a strange young man had come three times to her dressing-room and proposed marriage on the strength of her performance.

After the final curtain-call and the presentation of a bouquet come the autograph-hunters – and back in the hotel, supper and long-distance telephoning.

The following morning the Shostakovitch concerto has to be practised for a concert at the end of the month but "I don't feel like it." She delays. "Do you know you are looking at the most famous cello in the world?" she asks. It is the Davidov cello named after a Russian prince who was head of the Moscow Conservatoire at the turn of the century. When she first went to Leningrad she did not have the cello with her, but Rostropovitch had arranged for 100 student cellists to play a hymn by Davidov as a tribute to her and this instrument. It had been taken out of Russia at the Revolution and had been sent to her through a New York dealer as a gift from an anonymous admirer. This was the second such elegant gesture to be made to her, for another unknown patron had given her a Stradivarius.

Her face becomes resolved and she plays the Shostakovitch. She does not respond to much modern music, a fact she brings up almost apologetically. "I hate all this, it's so ugly, and it takes a lot of sorting out finger-wise."

In the afternoon she fetches Daniel at the airport on his return from a concert in Venice. The Argentines she has been seeing prove to be the Barenboim family, and Daniel is her fiancé, a secret still. But soon he has to return to London: Jacqueline has to go on to perform in Sheffield, glimpsing her parents who were staying there with friends. She has just finished two major tours – her first in America and one with the BBC Symphony Orchestra to Prague, Warsaw and Moscow. Next week she leaves Britain with Yehudi Menuhin and the Bath Festival Orchestra to play at Expo '67 in Montreal and later at the Lincoln Centre in New York.

To keep some kind of equilibrium in this disarrayed journeying is hard, but Jacqueline is helped by her temperament. The only outward sign of her intensity is an occasional determined tilt which makes her seem like a figurehead on the prow of a ship. Time and again the question returns: how can someone so young and relatively sheltered play with such adult completeness?

Born in 1945 in Oxford where her father was working for Army intelligence, she grew up at Purley and went to Croydon High School for the formal education that came her way. Her turquoise eyes and her physique might look closer to Gymkhanas than anything else. Nevertheless at the age of five she had her first cello lesson, and her mother, herself a pianist and now a music teacher, wrote special music for her to play.

Mrs Du Pré knew what to do about Jacqueline's talent and sent her to children's classes at the London Cello School, now defunct. As a student she had met William Pleeth, a cellist who teaches at the Guildhall School of Music and also privately, and who, as a member of the Allegri Quartet, has a long concert past. As it happened, Mr Pleeth had already heard the rumour around this child, but from the beginning he recognised the talent under the guise of an ordinary nine-year-old.

In a year she was to win the Suggia Award (Madame Suggia was a cellist, wife of Casals) which enabled her to have a double lot of lessons. The award was open to anyone under 21; she was the youngest entrant. Barbirolli was a judge, as was Yehudi Menuhin when she won the Queen's Prize at the age of 15. Menuhin rang Mr Pleeth with the news and the compliment, "I knew she must be your pupil."

Mr Pleeth recalls giving her on a Wednesday the Elgar concerto and Piatti's *Caprices*, which are to the cellist what Scarlatti's exercises are to the pianist. At her Saturday lesson she played the Piatti impeccably from memory, and then one and a half movements of the Elgar. She was 13. But the essential was to subject facility and technique to the work of art itself and Mr Pleeth's contribution, uniquely self-effacing, was to allow his pupil's personality to develop in its own right, at its own pace. "There was this volcano in her," he says. She too thinks that in some ways these years of arduous adolescence were a torment, in spite of the vocation given to her by music. Her mother says: "She was always worried she wasn't good enough. You've no idea of the miseries she could go through."

A prodigy? "I was, but one doesn't remain one for ever. There are lots of prodigies, it's nothing rare." This matter-of-fact attitude seems to be an instinct of self-preservation. She characterised Casals, for instance, with whom she had taken master-classes in Zermatt. "He was surrounded by all the old ladies who just wanted to lie at his feet. He listened but he was dogmatic. He wanted everything to be played his way and I could see what he wanted and did it without being told, but I was a bolshie 15 year-old." Five months in Paris with Tortelier and another five with Rostropovitch – "Both of them are so dramatic." She said, "they are Cinerama. All these cellists take one aside and say that only they can play Bach." She added that she could not play Bach. The stays abroad were not unmixed experiences. In the Moscow hostel there were 400 students living communally but only 20 practice rooms. The competition was fierce as the students' poverty, and the trumpets began overhead at 6 A.M.

Yet as Mr Pleeth says: "The graph has been steadily going up" – from a dozen selected concerts a year at the age of 17 to full-blast exposure now. Her tour in America was a crescendo of rave publicity. Yet the moment is neither too soon nor too late, as it can be for so many artists. She and the public are ready for one another. Daniel, she said, may well be the musician of his generation. His father thinks that Jacqueline will make her mark in musical history.

Returning from the Manchester trip, she had gone down to Brighton because that weekend Daniel was performing at the new festival there. On Monday morning she was recording at the EMI stdios with the English Chamber Orchestra conducted by Daniel. Larry Foster again came to listen. So did a young Hungarian pianist, Balint Vaszonyi.

Some 15 people, we hurried out to a basement restaurant in St John's Wood for *Rostbraten* and *Palatschinken*, and a medley of Spanish, German, Hebrew. Itzhak Perlman, the brilliant young Israeli violinist, listened that afternoon to Jacqueline. He imitated her playing until she smiled back, but he found her playing "*Yofe, yofe*" – Hebrew for "beautiful."

Jacqueline will marry in September, when for the first time she can share five clear days with Daniel. She hopes to live in Israel, but their way of life must commit them to the whirl of airports, states, hotels and perhaps to piano-cello duos. Friends tease her that her sensitive projection of herself comes from her "Jewishness." She plans to convert to Judaism, but her knowledge so far is limited to such cries as *Oi, oi, Mamele*, and a visit to a synagogue with Daniel.

The glass-coach of fame is parading her. Mr Pleeth thinks that she cannot but get better, "like a circle going on and on, there is endlessness in her development." To have such a gift is also to be its prisoner. She quotes Rostropovitch as saying that to be a great artist one must suffer. "But that's Russian. One must know happiness too." Her future is joined to her inclinations; and besides, she is booked up all over the world for three years ahead.

The Daily Telegraph Magazine
June 16, 1967

WHAT DO CHILD PRODIGIES grow into? Adult prodigies – at least in the case of Sir Georg Solti. He seems always to have had about him an air of being phenomenal, gathering everything within reach into his music making.

Born in Budapest just before the First World War, he was one of those wonder-stars which ordinary Jewish families, by some quirk of the genes or of destiny itself, throw into the wide world. At the age of 12 he was a performing pianist, and then was educated privately, going on to the Franz Liszt Academy. For a brief while Bartok was his teacher, and Kodaly too. "Talent, yes, I made rapid progress, I had absolute pitch. Fortunately I didn't get ruined. I was a lazy boy. Wonderful talents get lost, but I loved football too."

Everyone thought he was mad when he announced that he would be giving up the piano to become a conductor. "It was a problem, but I had decided. You cannot force what you want to be. I just stopped practising at 18." And he had the job of *répétiteur* at the Budapest Opera, in other words the coach who takes the singers through to piano accompaniment. "That is the essential way for opera conductors, you cannot miss that apprenticeship."

As a Jew in Hungary, his career was blocked, and he was fortunate enough to leave on 15 August 1939; a fortnight more and the frontiers would have been closed for good. He had no idea how well-timed the exit was, he was merely taking up an offer in Switzerland to be Toscanini's assistant. Having refused to work with the Nazis, first at Bayreuth and later at Salzburg, Toscanini with Adolf Busch and Bruno

Walter had organised a festival at Lucerne in Switzerland.

"Toscanini had very little human connection, he had few friends." Solti recalls. "It was musical adoration on my side. He gave me one essential point, that you cannot take music seriously enough and learn enough. Of course he was like a spoilt child – it was his romantic expression – no orchestra would tolerate it today, but it wouldn't be needed. Musical standards are much higher now. Furtwängler was also extremely nice to me. I learnt through him to get away from Toscanini's rigidities. I am midway between them, standing on my own feet."

The path before a conductor is smoother today. "That was a hell of a life I went through. In Switzerland I had my visa extended by the week, by the month, then by the year. I had to play the piano again for a living."

Only after the war could he start his conducting career, at the late age of 34, succeeding Clemens Krauss at the reconstituted Munich Opera. Then he moved to Frankfurt, and in 1958 took over the Salzburg Festival production of *The Magic Flute*, his first real international hit.

By 1961 he was installed as musical director at Covent Garden in London, which set the seal on his fame, while he made it one of the world's very best opera houses.

Bruno Walter had persuaded him to accept the job in London. "He told me that I must do it, I was the generation link. He was right." The major ingredients were there, he hastens to add, in that the orchestra, the chorus, the techniques, were sound. "If I have merits, then it was to develop English singers. I changed only one thing, the emphasis on quality; we showed that it was possible. I'm very proud of that. My ten years at Covent Garden were very happy ones. But I had to move, or else stay as a piece of furniture."

Anyone less likely to become a piece of furniture is hard to visualise. He stands up straight and fit, as limber as an all-in wrestler. Vitality courses from him. Though his face is stern, expressions flit across it to give away his thoughts. Not a compliant man. He has always known his way ahead, and fundamental instincts like his are not to be thwarted. To look at his deep brown eyes is to guess that a player in his orchestra would do well not to arrive late for rehearsal.

His perfectionism is celebrated in the musical world. "I try to discipline myself. I love my work, and have contempt for everyone who doesn't work." There speaks the man who has lived through the breakdown of society in Europe, and who finds that "nothing is more hateful than an ism, any ism." Music is one of the defences of civilisation and right now, in his view, it needs every helping hand.

For him, a sabbatical year really means a couple of months with fewer performances than usual – for instance only these television recordings. He is at home in the studio as is his second wife, who used to be Valerie Pitts, a familiar face on BBC television. Today she has returned to her old haunts for a canteen lunch with Sir Georg and their two daughters, Gabriella and Claudia, aged five and two, both entranced by the studio monitor. When the day's recording is done, Sir Georg is anxious to rush home to catch them before bedtime; all the keener for coming to fatherhood late in the day.

The Soltis, like all families of first-rank musicians, have to lead a fragmented life. They have a London house, but must spend four or five months of the year in the Drake Hotel in Chicago, for since leaving Covent Garden Sir Georg has been director of the Chicago Symphony Orchestra. This involves about 50 symphonic concerts a year with them, probably about half his workload. "1976" he droops a little at the mouth, "will be very heavy." He also has standing engagements in Paris, having been, until lately, conductor of the Orchestre de Paris. In Vienna he has a month of recordings, and there are guest appearances here, there and everywhere. Since February he has been doing a regular "Solti series" of concerts with the London Philharmonic Orchestra.

68

"My life is always divided between two wishes, for I'm a polygame musician. I want to be conducting both opera and symphony. It used to be 80 per cent the former, now it's the other way round." Polygame? That is the kind of word which slips into Sir Georg's marvellously varied language, properly called Emigranto, a mongrel mixture which somehow the world's great artists share.

But in Italy there is a villa on the Tuscan coast, to which the Soltis retreat for summer water-skiing, reading books and scores, piano-playing. To paraphrase a famous line, he's just a guy who can't say No. But that is the vocation. He compares it to being in a monastery. Great gifts lay on their possessors the obligation to use them to the full, and beyond. He is conscious of taking his place in the history of musical performance. "Look, I'm 63, very soon I'm going to be a Grand Old Man. Who else is there? Only Karajan and me, that's all that's left."

Radio Times
April 29, 1976

THE ENGLISH NATIONAL OPERA has a policy of staging works which, for one reason or another, are not part of the standard repertoire. Rossini's *Moses* seemed to fit the bill. Originally performed in Naples in 1819 – as *Mosè in Egitto* – with an enthusiastic Stendhal at the first night – it was subsequently revised by Rossini for audiences in Paris, where it proved popular with a whole generation: Balzac and Berlioz both wrote in its praise.

Rossini himself spoke of the opera's "tragico-sacred action" but its contemporary Romantic idiom emerged in the role of Miriam, a young Jewess who creates havoc by falling in love with Pharoah's son Amenophis. The programme at the London Coliseum immediately revealed that authenticity and the original drama were not about to be respected. Here were photographs of clenched fists in Johannesburg and stocking-cap terrorists in Londonderry, tricked out with quotations from the likes of Menachem Begin and Zinzi Mandela. And sure enough, the curtain rises on Moses and the children of Israel in military-camouflage tatters. The Egyptians enter in Latin-American style double-breasted grey suits. *Moses* has been perverted into a text about national liberation movements and power-coming-from-the-barrel-of-a-gun.

Rossini – of all men to be politicised! Rossini, who can hardly wait to escape from the lamenting minor key into the vitalising major, in whose music is a spring of irrepressible delight in life, who was a wit and free spirit if ever there was one. He venerated Mozart, whose final chorus "Gloria Tutti" in *Figaro* is the properly idealised ending of opera, in which the complex ties between comedy and tragedy are understood and reconciled. "Gloria Tutti" might be Rossini's own perpetual and life-enhancing motto.

70   Once he noted of himself, in the margin of a score, "*Peu de science, un peu de cœur, tout est là!*" Not too much science, but a little heart. In the course of a celebrated encounter with Richard Wagner (as recorded by a French musicologist, Edmond Michotte) Rossini told his visitor, "The feeling that moved me most during my life was the love that I felt for my mother and my father, and which they repaid me at usurious rates. I am happy to tell you ..." Wagner was destined to suffer even more from corrupted producers, and when the talk turned on the topic Rossini gave advice on how to respond: Ill will is legion, he said, and it can be fought only with silence and inertia.

No doubt this attitude involved temperament, as well as good manners. Rossini had too much sense and humour to be combative. In another famous literary memoir, Stendhal has described how after the first performance of *The Barber of Seville*, Rossini mistook the noise of applause for heckling and hid under the bed in his lodgings. In April 1848 – at a time when his admirer Richard Wagner was (with Bakunin) in Dresden, participating in a revolution – Rossini happened to be accidentally caught in a political incident, insignificant in itself but nevertheless impressing its mark of horror on the rest of his life. A demonstration was taking place in his home town of Bologna, and when Rossini came out on the balcony of his house, some Sicilians below shouted at him: "Rich reactionary!" He departed for Florence at once returning later to Bologna with a police escort, and then only for the purpose of selling his house in order to settle in Paris. In 1866 he wrote to Pacini reflecting on his withdrawal from composing: "This art, which has for sole basis idealism and sentiment, cannot separate itself from the influence of the times in which we live; and idealism and sentiment have been exclusively diverted in these days *to steam, to rapine,* and *barricades ..."*

Now an opera of his has been presented as a barricade, and nothing else. This Moses at the Coliseum is as hairy as Castro, his arms almost all the time extended high above his head, accompanied by his nephew Eleazor as Ché Guevara, with a lugubrious blue beret and brief-case.

Nor is it enough to dress up the Egyptians as fascistoid capitalists. Pharoah has the look of a Hafiz Assad or a Gaddafi, complete with dark glasses and decorations. Red banners create an apparent Nuremberg rally everywhere around them. At each and every moment when Egyptians and the children of Israel are on stage together, barbarities are enacted as belted uniformed policemen brutalise the masses with crowd-control barriers and sinister weapons. Not a single opening is lost to jab a Sten-gun into someone's ribs, to rehearse physical abuse and even torture, as in a scene of gratuitous branding. In one particularly blatant piece of stage business, the Jews are shown preparing for liberation by secreting stolen arms. The beautiful second act duet of Amenophis and Sinaida (in blonde wig and shirt-and-tie, ostensibly a parody of Mrs Thatcher) has as backdrop a teleprinter flashing slogans about "Brethren of Egypt," amid vast bulletin-boards of newspaper clippings worthy of your local radical cell. More than once, the music is actually interrupted by simulated gunfire and other such crudities.

"You Jews, you are going to die," we hear in the final act, in which of course Miriam's ill-starred love is rather weaker than her nationalistic zeal.* Making their way to the Red

---

* The service performed by the libretto in English translation may be discerned from the opening stanza, in which *"Et permets que dans leur patrie, Les Hébreux rentrent triomphants!"* has been rendered as "To their land, to the promised country. Proud and free, let your people go."

Sea, the Jews are represented as a tragic column very evidently designed to evoke Auschwitz. This time they have an armoury of stolen weapons with them. The Egyptians are not then overcome by an act of God, but by an armed uprising of the people. The red ribbons which had been used to manacle the prisoners now serve, untied and unfurled, as a sea of revolutionary flags. The meaning of these ubiquitous red banners becomes clear as the Egyptian dead are left to lie under them. In a final outrage, Moses puts Pharoah and Sinaida and other Egyptian survivors before a People's Tribunal, and he gives the execution orders by banging his biblical staff upon the earth. If the Bible had not made God's *parti-pris* in the story all too familiar, there could have been staged the even more fashionable and absurd rhetoric of a radical-chic Arafat leading the Palestinians home in victory over Zionist imperialism.

To whom, I wonder, should the blame go for being first to distort the past for the sake of propaganda in the present? Shaw-Mayakovsky-Brecht? What is unhistorical or anachronistic might be overlooked as ideological aberration and aesthetic delusion on the part of a producer who thinks himself a very fine up-to-the-minute fellow. But false analogies serve to obscure and even to defame the truth. Ancient Egyptians have their faults, and so do Assad and Gaddafi; but they have very little in common with one another, and none of them is in any sense comparable to the Nazis. Theatrical suggestions on these lines vulgarise and trivialise what is already difficult enough to define accurately. To compare the European Jews of Auschwitz to the ancient tribes who crossed the Red Sea, or to any other people at any other time is to exploit the Holocaust as a symbol. It is to try to score debating points at the expense of these people, and thus empty their death of its reality. To treat the victims of Nazism as an easy and convenient illustration to something else, to any particular subject at hand is to display inhuman contempt for them.

Nor does the abuse stop there. A production like this denies the spectator the right to his own judgment; for with agit-prop arrogance it is instructing him that he is too stupid and unimaginative to hear echoes or reach conclusions of his own about what he is seeing, and therefore everything has to be explained in a hammer-blow manner which allows no argument. A threat is implied – go along with this, or else …

No doubt this reflects the militant cultural attitudes of a hitherto important public sponsor, the Greater London Council, now fading away upon the hour. A private business company by the name of Norwest Holst has also put up money for *Moses*. (Shareholders in the company might well be advised to get out at any price – since their capitalistic board is so obviously unaware that rope is being sold *à la* Lenin, upon which to hang them.)

Duly warned, the public should stay away from the London Coliseum until it is clear that opera will no longer be put to grotesquely tendentious purposes. Admirers of Rossini far outnumber politically obsessed directors and producers, and it would be fitting to use his "silence and inertia" in this way against the handful who wish him, and us, so ill.

Encounter
April 1986

I met Wilfred Thesiger in the High Atlas Mountains. I wish I could add that I had been walking through them "against the grain of the country," as Mr Thesiger did recently. In fact I was at the next table to his in a French restaurant in the Ourika Valley, where he was lunching with Field-Marshal Auchinleck. No need for introductions. Mr Thesiger is unmistakable, a tall broad-shouldered man standing on heavy feet, his head as fine and drawn as an eagle's, its most distinctive feature the ridged and bony nose "like an alpine slope," I wrote in my notebook. He looks the part, the Englishman of legendary achievement in his lifetime, having twice crossed the Empty Quarter of Arabia; the Last Explorer.

In Marrakech he was staying in a small hotel in the old city. One evening we had a drink in a café on the Boulevard Mohamed V, coffee because Mr Thesiger drinks little alcohol. Above us a television set was switched on and an Arab woman in evening dress began singing pop-songs. At first turning his back, Mr Thesiger soon moved right away to the far side of the bar. He had been touched on the raw, because to him that television programme represented an ugly victory of all he most dislikes. Once the Arabs had a culture of their own; now they were enthralled by this machinery which offers them only a parody of Western culture, this singer with her French clothes and her French tunes.

Time and again Mr Thesiger returns to this hatred of his for all machines, for inventions which nobody wanted and nobody can stop even with doomsday at hand. Down to small details, the scientists have made us all alike. He points to a chubby little man at the bar. "He looks ridiculous in that European suit, doesn't he? Standard mass-production because it's cheap. Even he might have a bit of dignity in a *djellabah*."

In 1936 he had come to Marrakech and he described the famous square, the Djemma El-Fna as it was then, with sorcerers and story-tellers, scribes and Berber dancers. "There were no Westerners then and it was something to see." Now he comes here every spring with his mother, an indomitable lady nearing 90. Together they will motor a few thousand miles in Morocco and, when his mother falls ill, Mr Thesiger looks after her.

To hear about his parents is in some part to understand Mr Thesiger. His father was consul at Lake Van ("he must have been keeping an eye on the Russians, part of what Kipling called *The Great Game*"), then in Belgrade, in Boma where he witnessed the Belgian atrocities in the Congo, and finally minister in Addis Ababa. Mr Thesiger's mother rode up there by mule, a three-week trek, already expecting her eldest child Wilfred (born 1910). The legation was a mud hut and there were no wheeled vehicles in the whole country.

Three more sons were born during the ten years she spent there. Uniforms of gold braid and cocked hats, but also a life of hardship. At the age of three, Mr Thesiger recalls, he saw his father shoot an oryx. "There were hyenas round the camp-fire and all that." As a small boy he was in Berbera when it was invested by the Mad Mullah and a few months later while in Aden he was taken into the frontline to watch our artillery pound the Turkish trenches.

His father died, and the ten-year-old Wilfred returned to live on the Radnorshire hills. At his preparatory school he was victimised by a master who beat him with a steel-shafted riding-whip. "Couldn't get my pyjamas off in the morning because of the blood." This was the kind of sadism which foreigners believe to be built into English life. Similarly at Eton, he was beaten regularly and he took to boxing, for which he was later to get an Oxford blue. But by some nostalgia of hindsight, Mr Thesiger has come to think he was happy at Eton and the school and its slang crops up in his talk, and indeed in his books.

Unpopular because strong and violent, he was also unlike others. During sermons in chapel, he writes in *Arabian Sands*, he would picture scenes of childhood. "I had watched the priests dancing at Timkat before the Ark of the Covenant to the muffled throbbing of their silver drums; I had watched the hierarchy of the Ethiopian Church, magnificent in their many-coloured vestments, blessing the waters. I had seen the armies going forth to fight in the Great Rebellion of 1916." The family photograph album has views of corpses hanging on trees, of a man lying next to his arm and leg, severed in punishment. Also a posed group of the Young Wilfred and his brother sitting at the feet of their uncle, Lord Chelmsford, Viceroy of India, on the steps of Government House, Delhi, behind them the close rows of provincial governors and soldiers. His family was spending three months' leave there, the highlight of which for Wilfred was a tiger shoot.

His favourite reading at the time was *Prester John* and *Jack of the Bushveldt*, but he began to collect travel books, some of which are now very valuable. Rowland Wards and the Natural History Museum were his haunts. High imperialism was certainly the background but Mr Thesiger selected from it only its adventure, what it offered in the way of diversity and personal achievement. At Eton he would go along to Spottiswoode's the bookshop to get the latest news of two of his heroes, Abdel-Krim of the Riff Wars and Sultan Pasha el-Atrash, leader of the Druze revolt, both fighting the colonial power.

Identifying with the Zulus, he still talks admiringly of Lobengula and Chaka, regretting that he was not himself pushing up into Rhodesia at the time. The first Lord Chelmsford, his grandfather, had commanded the British army during the Zulu war. When in Morocco he had spoken to me of his recent travels in the Karakorams and in Nuristan; he had said: "Coming up from Peshawar reminds you of Kipling." But he returns often to a key idea which he expressed in *Arabian Sands*, and which all those British officers and gentlemen behind him on the steps of Government House would reject out of hand. "While I was with the Arabs I wished only to live as they lived and now I have left them, I would gladly think nothing in their lives was altered by my coming."

In London for the few weeks he is here, he stays with his mother in a flat in Chelsea. As he opens the door, his height and austere appearance dominate the narrow entrance; he looks caged. A Moroccan dagger to deal with burglars hangs on the nail; his bowler hat lies on a table.

I find him reading a book by John Buchan which he has just bought. As an Oxford undergraduate he would visit John Buchan at Elsfield and there he might have met Lawrence of Arabia but never did. He has Lawrence's books, including the rare ones, in the large glass-fronted bookcase which dwarfs the drawing-room – Burton's *Arabian Nights*, a complete Kipling, a complete Conrad. He shifts rather uncomfortably in his armchair as if the thing were not designed for him, while beyond him I can see his portrait painted by his friend Anthony Devas, accentuating the clean lines of his face and the ice-grey eyes unchanged since youth.

His passport calls him a naturalist. "I'm not a writer, I have no compulsion to write, my books are merely the by-product of travels." He fetches me some of his learned papers read to the Royal Geographical Society which he has had bound in red morocco. Also an envelope which contains seven photostat pages listing his travels, a *curriculum vitæ* in the briefest form – 1949 May–June. Bahrain, Riyadh, Kuwait, Basra, Bushira, Shiraz, Isfahan, Chalus, Tabriz, Ruwunduz, Mosul, Urmia, Baghdad." Out of this envelope falls a passport photograph of a handsome Arab in traditional dress and *keffiyab* with Arab-style moustache and trimmed beard. It is of Mr Thesiger.

In 1930 he worked as a fireman on a steamer in the Mediterranean and the Black Sea. "When I went to the Acropolis there was only a shepherd and an old photographer with his head under a black cloth. Go there now and the tourist guides harass you." The past seemed happier to him, truer, a period when men lived in harmony with their surroundings – and this conviction has only been strengthened with the enormous weight of his own experience.

Still an undergraduate he went as a member of the Duke of Gloucester's mission to the Coronation of Haile Selassie. A photograph of this mission, all plumes and medals, is in his bedroom as also a photograph signed in Amharic of Haile Selassie "one of the really great men of Africa." On the steps of the legation (back home), Colonel Cheeseman, an earlier explorer, suggested that he go to Danakil country in Southern Ethiopia. Three European expeditions had previously tried to open up this territory but had been massacred. "Three in, none out," as Mr Thesiger now puts it. "The Danakils kill to prove their manhood and they've got this curious habit of collecting testicles." Intact, Mr Thesiger survived. It was one of his most dangerous exploits, extraordinary for so young a man and after it there could be no going back to a dull life. "I wanted colour and savagery, hardship and adventure." So in *Arabian Sands* Mr Thesiger explains his driving urge. Testing himself to the limits is essential to him. He feels that all men need challenge, and its absence is to him the central *malaise* of our society. He understands why Mods and Rockers need to declare war on each other, and adds that if he were 20 he would feel frustrated by the impossibility of finding an acceptable challenge.

Of course there are many different ways of being put to the test, and Mr Thesiger, shy and lonely and assertive, could probably never have fitted into any usual English slot. One still senses the unease when he tells a story against himself of misquoting a Latin tag at dinner in All Souls College, of which his uncle, the former Viceroy, had become Warden. Is he a masochist? He repudiates my question, remembering how in a review Simon Raven had accused him of wearing a hair shirt, loving austerity for its own sake. Anyhow, he asks, what is a hair shirt?

Having turned to primitive tribes, to the desert, he saw the last stages of a doomed shrinking world when he worked for the Sudan Civil Service. His District Commissioner, Guy Moore, had a strong influence on him, believing that the Sudanese tribesmen should not be shaped into second-hand Europeans but were better off humanly as themselves, even if that meant no knowledge of a car-engine or a radio. He crossed the Sahara by camel, to Tibesti. To be a soldier in the war continued these personal enterprises, first with the Eastern Arab Corps, then with 101 Mission and Gideon Force under Wingate when he won the DSO. Wingate he found egocentric and ruthless, which Wingate might well have thought about him.

Driving in the desert with SAS was to him boring, not because of the sabotage of the German lines but because a Land Rover is an enclosed box which does not permit those inside to know the country or its inhabitants.

Retrospectively these were tough and lengthy preparations for the peak of his life, the journeys to Arabia between 1945 and 1949.

Two English explorers, Bertram Thomas and H. St John Philby (father of Kim) had separately crossed the Empty Quarter of Arabia in 1930. Some 60 years before them Charles Doughty had reported his unique travels in *Arabia Deserta*, a book which he hoped would restore the purity of the English language. The tradition of the English affinity with the Bedouin has long been established, but after Lawrence it was vulgarised although as Mr Thesiger points out, without Lawrence the Arabian tribes would never have united but would have kept up their customary rivalry.

"All that is best in the Arabs has come to them from the desert." Mr Thesiger takes the full romantic line. In the desert Arab, "passionate yet austere," he found something against which to match himself at last. Unlike the other Englishmen in his position, he always felt himself their inferior in the virtues which matter in those wildernesses of sand and rock. One of his closest friends said to me that his relationship to the Bedouin was that of prefect to fag. Mr Thesiger's youngest brother Roderick, a partner in Colnaghi's the art dealers (Welsh Guards, Parachute Regiment, captured at Arnhem), pointed out to me that on the contrary Wilfred remained inflexibly himself, that he found the mental and not the physical strain of living with Bedouin almost unbearable; that when it was suggested to him that he become a Moslem, he had the nerve to answer: "God protect me from the Devil." Wilfred Thesiger explains that he could not afford to risk demeaning himself, feeling as he did among them "a crude barbarian."

Nevertheless he was Umbarak to the Bedouin, Wilfred being unpronounceable, distinguished only by his height and his habit of sitting astride a camel. In his mother's drawing room there is a framed photograph of him leading a camel, and he looks like any wild, sun-blackened tribesman. "It was for the companionship of the Bedu, their patience, courage and humour," he says. "Without that it would have been a pointless ordeal." And certainly he has paid tribute to his Bedouin companions, to bin Kabina and bin Ghabaisha in particular, men alive beyond the pages of *Arabian Sands* which they are unable to read even in a pirated Lebanese edition.

No other European has experienced Bedouin life so intimately. Ten years afterwards, "when I thought it had all gone past recall," Mr Thesiger was persuaded by an agent and a publisher to write his account of these journeys.

He retired to a bed-sit in Copenhagen and worked as tirelessly as he had once travelled. When he finished passages of manuscript, he would post them to friends for comment and correction. The result is a monument unmatched in recent literature. It comes out of a background which no longer exists. One realises that its strength comes from the Edwardian conventionality that governs, even represses, Mr Thesiger keeping his ego hidden, the conventionality of bowler hat and gold watch chain and simplified values.

When he talks about what is important to him, his eyes and mouth have a way of narrowing into more lines, and he jabs at you with his thick index finger. "It's essential I get down to fundamentals when I travel, away from the life I've been living, back to something hard, harsh and primitive."

After the test by fire, the test by water. Mr Thesiger went to live on and off for eight years among the Marshmen of Southern Iraq. Although formally unqualified, he had acquired enough medical skill to win acceptance among them, curing various ills but also sometimes circumcising up to a hundred boys a day or taking out a damaged eyeball. One day he received a letter from the late Gavin Maxwell, a stranger to him, not yet author of best-sellers. A teller of stories himself, it is to be expected that Mr Thesiger would attract another teller of stories. Gavin Maxwell was invited to accompany Mr Thesiger to his private paradise and wrote an account of it, *A Reed Shaken by the Wind*. The two men had an odd sort of love-hate relationship, which Mr Thesiger elaborates with some amusement. Gavin Maxwell was in the marshes for less than a month, but Mr Thesiger found him a parting present of an otter destined to fame.

Myths inevitably form. Another traveller, Eric Newby, at the end of his trip in Afghanistan, met Mr Thesiger in the mountains, "a great long-striding crag of a man." When Eric Newby and his friend blew up their air-beds because of the rocks on the ground, "God, you must be a couple of pansies," said Thesiger. One evening I was leaving Mr Thesiger's flat when he pulled a book off the shelves, *A Dinner of Herbs* by John Verney, painter, writer, baronet, and his friend since childhood. "I'm supposed to be Matthew Prendergast in it," says Mr Thesiger. I read: "Matthew is the sort of man who will happily walk barefoot for months across a waterless desert, subsisting on a handful of dates and occasional sip of camel's piss, but who, back in civilisation, cannot endure the most trivial discomforts."

The trouble is that there are no more deserts, no more room for the myths to flourish in. The doors are closing just behind Mr Thesiger. In Nuristan only ten years ago he had found an almost unexplored area complete with brigands, but recently it has been opened up and now the university expeditions are queuing in the valleys waiting to go. When Freya Stark fell ill in the Hadramaut, an aeroplane was sent for her, and Mr Thesiger points out that previously she'd have had to continue or die. "You don't get the *feel* of it any more."

To cross the desert on foot when an aeroplane is available is now a mere stunt, and the anger rises in his voice. Oil-drills are everywhere, and American bases and men in Stetson hats playing at being Hopalong Cassidy. Administration is a bad word in his vocabulary; so is visa. "Corner-boy" is the pejorative he reserves for the town Arabs, their tribal existence broken by the promise of money which is not enough to go round but whets their greed. In Arabia the Bedouin are attracted to the oil-fields, forsaking the old way of life for one which they cannot master: "It is not death but degradation which faces them." This exile haunts him. In 1966 and 1967 he was in the Yemen on the Royalist side. Shortly beforehand, the cartilages in his knees had been removed. "I'd walked 'em through. Done 40,000 miles on 'em and they weren't designed for that."

83

Caught in a valley by strafing Russian MiGs, he was unable to run away up the heights as the tribesmen had done and was lucky to get away with a small wound. Once while under fire and taking cover behind a rock, a Yemeni tribesman dodged up with a letter. It was from Lord Adrian, the Chancellor of Leicester University, and offered him an honorary degree. "The chance of standing up on a platform to receive it just then seemed 50–50." But he did receive it and was pleased at the recognition, just as on his return he wrote two articles for *The Times* putting the Imam's case, and went to see Sir Alec Douglas-Home. Mostly he cannot bring himself to take an interest in the new Arab politics. He had heard that the Marshmen hoped he would return. "In Iraq I'd just be bumped off now." He shrugs.

Awkwardly he accepts that his travels and books attract attention. In London he has a clubman's routine, lunching at the Travellers' or Brooks's, seeing a small number of his old friends among whom he nonetheless gives the impression of loneliness. Otherwise he is in the Northern Province of Kenya, among the Samburu and Turkana. "I just buy half a dozen camels and set off round Lake Rudolf." Although he has lived abroad so much, he cannot contemplate settling anywhere as an expatriate, while regretting most of the changes in England. "In my childhood the sparrow hawk was one of the commonest of birds in England and now it's almost extinct."

Not long ago he was standing on the platform of an underground station. When the train came in, a woman carrying her shopping bag, including oranges, jumped down to kill herself. Some people looked away from the sight but the civil servant type next to Mr Thesiger on the platform said between clenched teeth: "Dammit, I bet that makes me late." For Mr Thesiger the story is a complete comment on our urban existence.

Western technology is rolling flat all human differences, stamping them into a single industrial mould. There can be no more explorers now, only tourists, men temporarily released from working machinery. Cars, oil installations, nationalism – this is what the rest of the world has taken from us in the name of progress. To Mr Thesiger it is the litter under which lies buried the Garden of Eden. "All the time I get letters from young people telling me that they want to lead a life like mine and asking how. What can I tell them? They can't."

The Daily Telegraph Magazine
November 7, 1969

JEAN-FRANÇOIS REVEL is the latest in the famous and honorable line of Frenchmen who say things their compatriots would prefer not to hear. Albert Camus did so after the last world war and André Gide before it, Zola at the time of the Dreyfus trial and Voltaire earlier still. All were attacked by the Establishment of their day, sometimes by critics or opponents who ought to have known better, and all were generally admired in the end as upholders of truth and justice. Revel is a publicist and pamphleteer as fine as any of them.

Through a dozen books and a great deal of journalism he has become a foremost analyst, as well as a conductor, of French intellectual passions. Since 1966 he has been writing a column in the influential weekly magazine, *L'Express*, and this platform allows an estimated three million or more readers to appreciate his steady and witty onslaught against humbug in all its forms. He has rallied a large public around his opinions, particularly since he has committed himself to defending one of the simplest and most urgent propositions: that democracy is diminishing to the point of extinction, and this ought not to pass unchallenged. He comes to politics with the tried and trusted view that such matters are too important to be left to politicians, that now is the time for all good men to come to the aid of freedom and sanity and creativity.

In his 53 years, Revel has already lived through two spells without democracy – first Marshal Pétain's Vichy government, which enabled the occupying Germans to hold down France during the last war, and then what he calls the Caesarism of General Charles de Gaulle in the late '50s and '60s. Recently he has been anticipating a third phase, should the French general elections of next March be won by the Left, specifically by the seesaw alliance of the French Socialists, under their leader François Mitterrand, and the Communist Party. This electoral alliance, known as the Common Program, can count on a small but absolute majority of voters, according to the polls, though this has effectively been put in doubt by the series of public feuds between the two partners during recent months. The Left may really have split into its component halves, but having held together for so long, it may manage to reunite at the 11th hour.

As the reward for bringing the Socialists to power, the Communists had been demanding key ministries and such irrevocable measures as the nationalization of many major industries and all banking and credit. The Socialists might have accepted this on the grounds that ideological debate had to be postponed until victory was in the bag. But the third element in the grand coalition of the Left, the fractional Radical Party led by Robert Fabre – accounting for perhaps as little as 3 percent of the overall vote, but the very 3 percent which might swing the result – proved not so pliant. It declared itself unwilling to be the accomplice of communism. The Socialists were then obliged to say the same; their hand had been forced and the Program revealed to be far from Common. The French air now hums with recrimination. All bets on the election results are off.

Whatever the eventuality of the Common Program might prove to be, Revel excludes neither future disorders nor a Marxist police state and civil war, and in his view, already the one certain loser is democracy. "The parties of the Left have only been pre-empting positions and making claims against the day when things break up for good and each can then try to seem blameless by pointing a finger at the other's impossible demands," he explains. "It wasn't ideologically conceivable for the Socialists and the Communists to share a platform. It was a temporary stratagem for them both and, in the end, if they had persisted there could be only one outcome: The one would have to swallow the other alive."

Prosperity in France, Revel points out, has increased more since the war than in the previous century and a half. The rich have certainly become richer, which intensifies rooted class feelings, but within a generation the French as a whole have risen from being half as well-off as the English to being almost twice as well-off, according to the criteria of average wages and productivity. It is not the crisis of capitalism but its success which has made the average Frenchman feel he can comfortably ignore the fact that the Communists are not politicians like any others – Karl Marx would not be able to make heads or tails of it. And the illusion angers Revel. "Our floating voters on the Left imagine that it'll be different here, that there'll be nothing but a few social reforms, that the Communists would never dare do anything to us." In practice the French Communists, copying the classic maneuver in Eastern Europe after 1945, have been using the Socialists as a screen behind which to advance to a totalitarian state. No Socialists, no democrats, should allow themselves and their beliefs to be so exploited for even a moment, because they risk being taught a frightful lesson – this is the burden of Revel's charge today.

At first glance, Jean-François Revel seems an unlikely figure to be waging this war. Medium in build, he has long since lost the battle of the waistline, and he has the look of someone who enjoys life too much to want to spend it picking fights. He is mellow, at ease with himself. He talks as spiritedly as he writes, he pounces on amusements and ironies, and his laugh is a spontaneous chuckle which does justice to the humor in him. Like all the best serious people he can never quite rid himself of the notion that the doings of the species *Homo sapiens* are a bit of a joke. Since his youth he has been a bullfighting enthusiast; he likes to spend his Saturdays at the horse races, and the energy he puts into spotting winners has been a wonder to his friends; he goes skiing in the French Alps every February. He loves a bottle of good wine and the company of beautiful women. In the literary world of Paris, and among the rich and grand who run after writers and habitually flatter them, he is sought after. But he works hard, so goes home early. Though his first marriage ended in divorce, the two children from it have turned out well.

An all-rounder, in short, not a man in the blinkers of anti-communist obsession. But Revel's face is large and strong-featured and when he starts to argue with a sus- pected enemy, the righteous anger sets in very magisterial lines indeed. Then as men with thin hair often do, he passes a hand over his scalp; the undoubted killer instinct is sleek and dangerous. Many have found that, his charm notwith- standing, he is never to be taken lightly.

Revel lives in a Paris apartment with his second wife, Claude, who is the daughter of the novelist Nathalie Sarr- aute and reviews television for the daily newspaper *Le Monde.* They have a schoolboy son and also living with them is the son of her previous marriage to Tristan Tzara, the Romanian poet who was an apostle of Dadaism. Revel, Sar- raute, Tzara – three names below the bell at the entrance to their apartment suggest some literary quiz. They occupy two floors of the building. A rather delicate spiral staircase delivers Revel from the upper, domestic level down to the two rooms where he works. Both rooms are whitewashed, with a suggestion of monkishness as well as of a military headquarters. Books are everywhere, cramming the shelves, springing up from the floor in leaning towers. Here on the surface is a presentation copy signed by Philippe Soupault, the old poet, who recently came to Revel to ask forgiveness for having romped his life away in the meadows of Surrealism, Stalinism and Maoism. And another from the novelist Michel Tournier. I am given armfuls of new books to take away in a shoulder bag Revel once bought as a souvenir in India. An elegant young woman arrives to photograph him for a book jacket, and she too has her pick from the rejected review copies piled up by the door.

Every morning at half-past 5, Revel is down here in his dressing gown to listen to the BBC World Service. Then with cups of black coffee always at hand, he reads or writes at the wide, leather-covered desk in front of the window, with a view over the tops of plane-trees to the river. The apartment is in one of the oldest and least spoilt corners of Paris, the Île Saint-Louis, a small island in the Seine surrounded by bastions where the fishermen sit patiently and linked by bridges to either bank. On the tiny graveled square in front of the building where he lives, Revel says, a republican ball is still held every 14th of July to celebrate the fall of the Bastille. Before walking through the neighborhood on our way to lunch, Revel makes himself the respectable householder and paterfamilias by putting on a jacket and tie. He is greeted first by a French diplomat he once met in Ecuador, then by the patron of a local café with whom he exchanges notes about shrimping – Revel has a holiday cottage at Paimpol in Brittany. Altogether he is set up, one might suppose, for the kind of exclusivity the French have perfected.

Quite the contrary, Revel has been saved from anything like provincialism by his background, as well as by his tastes. Born in Marseilles, he was taken at the age of 6 months to Lourenço Marques, today Maputo, the capital of Mozambique, where his father Joseph Ricard had an import-export business ("Revel" was originally a literary pseudonym, but it has come to nudge aside the family name). Revel's first language was actually Portuguese, and he and his younger brother, now an army officer, were sent back to Marseilles only for their education in a private school run by the Jesuits. This made of Revel the classic French anticlerical, unable to resist a joke at the Church's expense, but it also grounded him in a tradition of rigorous reasoning.

Revel was 16 when France collapsed under the German blitzkrieg of 1940. "It was something unthinkable," he says. He would not be the kind of writer he is, though, if he did not add that "the comic aspects of the Vichy government" really brought home to him what had happened. Conventional militaristic France was something for which he could have no respect, and he once personified it as "a man with a minuscule head, medals all over his chest, with a constricted throat and congestion of the liver, his eyes bloodshot."

By 1945, he was active in a Resistance network under the command of Pierre Grappin, later dean of the University of Nanterre. Among his colleagues were Pierre Courtade, future editor of the Communist paper, *L'Humanité*; a Hungarian called Sekeres who became a minister under Matyas Rakosi, the Stalinist whose infamy precipitated the Hungarian uprising of 1956; and August Anglès, another future Nanterre professor who was to undergo the bitter experience of being called a Nazi by students during the riots of May 1968. As for the civil war in France which he speculates may be imminent, Revel had a foretaste in 1945, when he had to prevent the summary execution by the Resistance of collaborators, among them Charles Maurras, the writer whose virulent nationalism and anti-Semitism were exactly what he could never stomach.

Revel graduated from the Ecole Normale Supérieure in Paris, where he received his degree in philosophy. Pupils,

normaliens, who emerge from this institute of higher learning have an unmatched prestige as the cream of the country's intellectuals. They often become professors or academic
administrators, and they are liable to be cast in a political
mold, usually left wing. Revel fits the bill: He considers himself a man of the Left. Self-confident, with more than a
touch of didacticism, he has the *normalien* ease in the handling of ideas. He might well have spent his life in a university, writing about Montaigne and Descartes, two of his
intellectual ancestors, and turning out radical students
much like himself. (Almost as a sideline he has published a
three-volume history of philosophy.)

His first job after the war was to teach in a Moslem
school at Tlemcen, just on the Algerian side of the border
with Morocco. His experience there confirmed his opinion
that the French ought to withdraw from North Africa, and
such anticolonialism earned him a black mark with the
authorities. From 1950 to '52 he taught at the French Institute in Mexico City, adding Spanish to the languages he
speaks fluently, and travelling as much as he could in the
United States. Then he taught in Florence for four years – his
Italian is like a native's. So thorough a cosmopolitan could
never have settled down to become a French pedagogue.

"Histoire de Flore," his first book and only novel, written
in 1953, was odd and rather incomplete, impregnated with
spirituality in accordance with the theories of Gurdjieff, the
Russian émigré who once ran the utopian community outside Paris. This unique foray into mystification was soon
overtaken by a virtuoso account of his life in Florence, "Pour
l'Italie," which catapulted him to the quarrelsome fame he
has enjoyed ever since. He had found the Italians more mel-
ancholic than lively, adept at deceiving tourists and even
more adept at deceiving themselves, their male supremacy
ridiculous and the legs of the women hairy.

One career which got away, so to speak, was as an art critic. Several of his closest friends are museum curators or run galleries. As a young man he was influenced by the somewhat socially conscious art criticism of André Perminier in *Le Monde*. Revel's tastes now are for traditional art, but he keeps a fairly friendly eye on modernisms and has one of those encyclopedic memories able to recall which pictures hang where. Over the years he has edited a series of books about art and aesthetics introducing to the French such scholars as E. H. Gombrich, Edgar Wind, Erwin Panofsky and Anthony Blunt.

Early in his writing career, he also published two book length essays to the effect that philosophy was no longer a serious subject – if it ever had been. Philosophers baffled the public with their private language but, far from being scientists, they were merely theologians defending preconceived positions. If the facts did not accord with their faiths, so much the worse for the facts. Revel was gunning for assorted gurus, including Heidegger, Husserl, Jean-Paul Sartre, Teilhard de Chardin, Claude Lévi-Strauss the anthropologist, and Maurice Merleau-Ponty, the political theorist who had been much impressed by Stalinism. Looking back today at these blown over controversies, he says, "The point was that even then the Left couldn't accept me. Several of those I was criticizing were supposed to be on the Left, though I could never tell why. There was no answer to my criticisms. Instead it was felt that if I was on the Left myself, I ought not to provide arguments unhelpful to it, but keep quiet. In France it's a question of where you line up."

The wittiness of his style has always cut too deep to be forgiven or forgotten. Contemporary French writing he once dismissed as a whole with the remark, "except for statistics or raving, there is nothing to it." Or, another sample, he said that Saint-Exupéry, the writer and star-struck aviator whose books have topped bestseller lists in France since the war, had simply "replaced the human brain with an aircraft engine." Does he enjoy polemicizing for its own sake? He laughs. "Not in the first place. But then it somehow seemed to be expected of me. Editors invited me to do what I was good at, and it's gone on from there. I have all sorts of plans for literary essays and novels, but not enough time."

Like the child in the Hans Christian Andersen fable, Revel has never been able to stop himself from crying out when he sees an Emperor wearing no clothes. And the most naked of Emperors on whom his sights were fixed in the 60's was Charles de Gaulle. Mercilessly, he devoted an entire book to dissecting the General's purple prose, with its affectations such as capitalizing the title of General for himself but for no other general. Continuing to poke fun at his chauvinism, bigotry and totalitarian cast of mind, Revel was well away on a career from which there could be no turning back; virtually a one-man opposition, he had made himself a public personality.

As an ambitious politician, François Mitterrand hoped to turn to advantage these skirmishes with the General. There was a time when Revel wrote Mitterrand's speeches, and he was even persuaded to stand, unsuccessfully, as a Socialist candidate in the 1967 parliamentary elections. They know each other well, though they do not meet much nowadays because, as Revel expresses it, "I was not anti-Gaullist for 14 years in order to have imposed upon me a new gospel quite as retrograde and still more dangerous than Gaullism – the Common Program."

"Without Marx or Jesus", published in 1970, sold over a million copies all told and spread Revel's reputation far and wide outside France. It was a superb example of the "Emperor's clothes" technique of stating what ought to be obvious. During increasingly frequent visits to the United States, lecturing or attending seminars, he had been struck by the advance of technology and the ferment of ideas, out of which he felt something new and hopeful was evolving. "The revolution of the 20th Century will take place in the United States." These were the opening words and the thesis of the book. The shock and outcry in French intellectual circles, and elsewhere, raised the roof.

By "revolution," Revel did not mean the overthrow of capitalism, and this is what a good many critics, notably Mary McCarthy, held against him. She, for instance, joked that he risked being taken away "in a straitjacket," and she went on to argue, more seriously, that he liked the shock value of dissenting from orthodoxy. To her, his "revolution" was only a metaphor, "a play on words," and there was a good deal of truth in this. Revel's concept of revolution was indeed the kindly notion that institutions in America were so structured to cope with change that capitalism with a human face would ensue and everyone would live happily ever after. Though admitting to ills on the contemporary American scene, he sketched them rosily enough to arouse hope that they would go away, and this did expose him to well-founded criticism. But to put in a good word for American society – more to flatter it – is simply not done. As the Left saw it, Revel was a renegade, an "Atlanticist," a crypto-Anglo-Saxon, a tool of the Right – in any case a marked man.

Five years ago, Mitterrand committed the Socialists to the alliance with the Communist Party, and this, on top of the Left's critical reception of "Without Marx or Jesus," was Revel's moment of explosion. To him the Common Program has been nothing but a surrender to totalitarianism, to Soviet foreign policy, and he has resisted it all along the line. "Mitterrand wants power by any means," he says. "In him the Communists found their ideal instrument. I've told him that the Communists would turn on him the moment he had served their purpose, the way they always do. His answer was, 'Leave it to me. It'll be different in my case.' That was how de Gaulle used to talk."

"One of the problems in France," he explains in a favorite argument of his, "is that the two main groupings, the Left block and the old Gaullists, don't correspond to the electorate. As a result the country is polarized into two ideological but artificial camps." Defending the democratic center is a lonely business among French intellectuals. Revel is too deeply committed to greater social justice to feel at home with politicians like President Giscard d'Estaing. Revel does have his friends and supporters, like Raymond Aron, doyen of French political writers, Max Gallo and Olivier Todd of *L'Express*, Alain Besançon and François Fejto, who have made special studies of communist affairs. As an editorial adviser to Robert Laffont, the independent publisher, he is also in a position to promote books on current events which owe nothing to the Common Program. Mario Soares, the Portuguese Prime Minister, Zbigniew Brzezinski, Alberto Ronchey, one of the best known Italian journalists, and Carlos Rangel, the Venezuelan writer, are the kind of people he is in touch with and whose names crop up in his talk. Encouragement also comes from the so-called "new philosophers" such as André Glucksmann and Bernard-Henry Lévy, Maoists and Marxists themselves in May 1968, who have since reacted against totalitarianism. They admire Revel, see him regularly and, in a sense, form a movement behind him.

What puzzles Revel, what arouses every fiber in him – in short, what has been his main study – is why everybody does not hate totalitarianism as naturally as he does. Where do they spring from, these totalitarians of the Left and Right alike who time and again are prepared to subordinate each and every individual to the demands of the collective?

How is it conceivable to advocate suppression of democratic liberties with the examples of Nazi Germany and Soviet Russia fresh before the eyes? By way of an answer, Revel's "The Totalitarian Temptation" published in French early in 1976 and in English this year, argues that free men wish, at least with some part of their being, to be relieved of their freedom, and can be tempted into totalitarianism as into suicide, conscious that everybody will be sorry afterwards. People who themselves would never choose to live under communism, for instance, defend communists in Portugal against social democrats; they applaud regimes resting on force in Vietnam, Cambodia or Angola; they see monstrosities in the Chile of President Pinochet but none in the Chile of the late President Allende, who was not averse to bending the democratic rules, either.

This is the phenomenon of "unofficial Stalinism," the phrase Revel coined in "The Totalitarian Temptation" to describe the inexplicable groveling of all manner of supposed democrats before plain violence and tyranny. They share a catch-all outlook which Revel calls "pidgin Marxism" because it seeks to justify communism not so much on its own merits as by insisting upon the shortcomings (invented often as not) of capitalism. These pidgin Marxists and unofficial Stalinists are further down the totalitarian road than fellow travelers of a generation ago. If communism comes, Revel says, they will have accommodated to it far enough in advance to share in the spoils. If communism does not come, they will continue to glory in their opposition to their own society. Unofficial Stalinism has so greatly helped to mystify people with slogans about progress and liberation that they feel obliged to apologize for not being communists; they have been put on the defensive from the start, when they ought to be exposing the discrepancy between communist words and actions. The true reactionaries today, the book points out, are the communist leaders who impose sacred dogma upon anyone insufficiently strong to resist, as if they were medieval monarchs claiming divine right.

Finally, "The Totalitarian Temptation" stresses that Marxism by definition is not susceptible to change; in other words, that communist parties can never be anything but totalitarian agencies. Eurocommunism, it follows, is just the latest illusion of the fashionable left, for it does not express a willingness among communists to accept parliamentary rules, but is merely the tactic appropriate for the final seizure of power in France, Italy, Spain, Portugal or wherever. A Berlinguer in Italy or a Carillo in Spain may be sincere in holding off Moscow, but this can only be tested by trial-and-error, and the gamble is much too big for Revel.

Europe has often had such warnings addressed to it, but its inhabitants have usually felt too snug to be bothered to listen. No more. "The Totalitarian Temptation" immediately sold 100,000 copies in France, a quarter-million more in paperback, and the same again in Italy. Press clippings reach Revel by the boxload. He receives 50 letters a day, virtually all favorable. Meanwhile, the communist parties and unofficial "Stalinists" have ransacked the vocabulary of insults for him. Not since Solzhenitsyn's "Gulag Archipelago" has a book had such an impact in Europe. "It's timing that counts," says Revel. "Say something a year earlier than everyone else and you're original. Three years earlier, and you're a genius."

The Left has done its best to create around him an atmosphere of quarantine. So much so that Revel has just published a book called "La Nouvelle Censure" ("Censorship, New-Style"), rounding on his enemies and pulverizing them in a manner not often seen even in literary infighting. The scorn combines memorably with the mockery.

98 In Greece, for instance [Revel writes, but these translations are mine], my publisher no less, without consulting me, did me the honor of personally writing a preface in which he declared that my theory of Stalinism as a fixed and immutable paradigm was completely out of date now that communism was everywhere evolving toward some kind of luminous democratization and the Stalinist mentality had vanished. Sending me the finished book, he included a letter trying to justify what he had done, arguing, with some embarrassment, that Stalinists were still so thick on the ground in Greece that he had been obliged to write his introduction in order not to offend them. I had to have the book withdrawn until the publisher agreed to remove his commentary.

In Italy, it was my translator who, still without consulting me, took it upon himself to embellish the book with notes of his own, designed to "correct my errors" and put the reader on his guard against them. He was then at pains to refute and ridicule me in articles and interviews, claiming that I had not grasped the essence of the Eurocommunist metamorphosis. There again I wrote to the publishers to protest and suggested a debate on television. This seemed straight forward enough, as over the years Italian television had often invited me to talk on other topics and to comment on current events in France. "Quite impossible" came the reply, since the second of the two channels on Italian television was controlled by the Communists and the first by the Christian Democrats, who were themselves manipulated or intimidated by the Communists. "I was told, complain? Your book is selling fine." The idea that an author might write not only in order to be selling fine but to be correctly understood seems beyond the comprehension of our Eurocommunists.

French critics are particularly nailed. The editor of *Le Monde*, Jacques Fauvet, and several members of his staff appear to be waging a vendetta against Revel, which is awkward since his wife, Claude, works for the paper. The day "The Totalitarian Temptation" appeared, Fauvet put his signature to a brief dismissive note about it in his paper, misrepresenting the arguments and denigrating the author. Revel complained. After some delay, a personal letter arrived from Fauvet; it is printed in the book and pulled to pieces by Revel as "bric-a-brac without any weight, in no way constituting an answer.... He invokes as his excuse the pressures and rhythms of daily publishing, the assumption being that this authorizes him to write without any scruples – that opens up all sorts of possibilities – and so Jacques Fauvet hands on the torch of editorial responsibility ..."

Jean Daniel, editor of *Le Nouvel Observateur*, a weekly which is more overtly left-wing than the sententious *Le Monde*, similarly attacked Revel in his columns while writing him personal letters of apology, even approval, which are also duly quoted in full in the book. "Typical" is Revel's comment on such duplicity. "They mostly admit to themselves that I'm right, but find excuses for lying – things like 'This can't be said aloud,' 'This isn't the moment for telling the truth,' 'There's no call to play into the hands of the Right.' There's always some such prevarication."

Those who have defected to Marxism, most of them place-hunting on the Left, receive the shortest shrift. "The Socialists," Revel writes, "far from having cured the Communists of their principal moral vices, have contracted them: sectarianism, the sense of their infallibility, the incapacity to conceive that disagreement with them can be the result of honest analysis. So what type of democracy are they preparing? It is striking that French critics of 'The Totalitarian Temptation' display the ever-growing kinship between Socialist and Stalinist methods."

Among many examples of Socialists doing the Communists' dirty work, Revel concentrates on a television debate he had with René Andrieu, present editor of the Communist daily *L'Humanité*, and a Stalinist of impeccable lineage, and Jacques Delors, an economist and from 1968 to '72 a minister under President Georges Pompidou, but eagerly converted to socialism of late. Like almost everybody taking issue with Revel, Delors wrote privately to propitiate him before the television show, expressing the hope that they would be "far enough removed from political passions to get to the bottom of things." In fact, Delors stuck to a more orthodox Communist line than even Andrieu, "clearing the ground," in Revel's expression, "by hand grenade."

For the old Stalinist campaigner, this was his dream come true: To get the job done by a hired hand who is no "card-carrying member" has always been the end to beat all ends. Delors has been a quick learner of Leftist reasoning. Under the delighted eye, not to say the holy amazement, of the chief editor of *L'Humanité*, on whose face, even as the words were tumbling from his lips, this former adviser and minister of Georges Pompidou kept a fearful though adoring eye, checking that his labors really were softening up Communist reservations about him so that he could take a few giant strides toward a minister's portfolio in the future government of the united Left.

On one of my visits to his apartment, Revel told me how a French newscaster had just felt obliged to slip in an apology because two successive items on his broadcast had not been in the Soviet interest. "But 15 anti-American items would get the day off to a good start. And then I'm accused of primitive anti-communism! In the Cold War period, when there was no communist threat to speak of, the West behaved hysterically. Now the Russians have military parity, they engineer coup after coup and pour money into communist parties, and it's supposed to be not nice to point out what's happening, it's witch-hunting, it's McCarthyism. But if in the McCarthy days you'd said that within 20 years Africa and Southeast Asia would be under communist control, you'd have been certified insane."

To keep up to date as a commentator, Revel makes field trips every autumn, to India and Bangladesh in 1975, then around South America, and last year to southern Africa, including his childhood home of Mozambique (now reduced, he says, to a primitiveness and misery not known there within living memory). He went into Angola with guerrillas of UNITA, the liberation movement opposing the Marxist government and its Cuban mercenaries. Only once, in 1965, has he been behind the Iron Curtain: to Romania, and "that was quite enough."

Meanwhile, bulletins, reports, private letters, confidential circulars, learned journals and new books pour into the Île St Louis apartment to be studied with that *normalien* intensity. Revel reads the French, German, English, American, Italian, Spanish and Portuguese press as a matter of course. In his two whitewashed workrooms he is like a man posted on sentry duty, challenging the follies and wickednesses of the world. He often brings to mind George Orwell, who also made his pseudonym more current than his name, another man always on the tail of hard facts, warning that without democracy there can be neither equality nor progress nor justice, a pessimist in spite of himself but too recalcitrant finally to throw in the game. "After what I've written, I am obliged to stay here," is Revel's parting shot as we go our ways, "but if you're looking for someone to dig your garden next year, keep the job open for me."

The New York Times Magazine
December 11, 1977

BORN IN 1911 in Lithuania, at that time a Grand Duchy incorporated into Russia, Czesław Miłosz began life as a subject of the Tsar. Minor nobility, the family was Catholic in faith, Polish in nationality. Szetejnie, their manor in Lithuania, was built in the eighteenth century and expanded later. The adult Czesław claimed to have been bored by unvaried neighbors whose conversation was restricted to coats of arms, estates and family trees, but a number of his poems have a lingering nostalgia for Szetejnie and the forests and river of its rural setting.

Miłosz: A Biography shows how an individual in such a place at such a time has had to march in step with history.* At the outbreak of World War I, Czesław's father, a squire by inclination and an engineer by profession, was conscripted into the Russian army. One consequence of the chaotic transformation of Tsarist Russia into the Soviet Union was that Lithuania gained its independence. The family moved into the beautiful and historic city of Vilnius (Wilno in Polish) with its university and its Jesuits, Jewish scholars, and Radziwill Princes in their palace. According to someone who grew up with him, Czesław had an extraordinary sense of destiny. Hardly more than twenty years old, and still a student, he sent his poems to Jaroslaw Iwaszkiewicz, a poet in a Poland that has always taken poetry seriously. Early in the lifelong correspondence that followed between them,

---

* *Miłosz: A Biography*, by Andrzej Franaszek; Harvard University Press, 526 pages, $35.

Czesław gives himself away with a confession that he feels "stuck up to my neck in the atmosphere of dead Wilno," and went on to plead "the need for my poor little deadened soul to be fired up."

In October 1934, an impatient Czesław duly left for Paris. An uncle, Oscar Miłosz, had made a successful life for himself there. Aesthete, poet and playwright, he wrote in French and knew luminaries like Oscar Wilde and Maurice Maeterlinck. He also had a premonition of the caterpillar treads of tanks crossing the Mazovian plain, and he died just as this became reality. Copying his example, Czesław came close to reinventing himself as a French intellectual, a Catholic humanist and philosopher on the lines of Jacques Maritain. From December 1935 until the outbreak of war, he settled instead in Warsaw. There he met Janka, described as beautiful, intelligent, domineering and terrified of Czesław's volcanic energy, moreover married to some other man. The couple were to spend nearly half a century together, in this biography's rather strained phrasing for their relationship. Returning to Poland, he was not to know that he was choosing to be a victim rather than an exile.

Andrzej Franaszek is a professor of Polish literature in Krákow. He admires Miłosz without reserve. At the beginning and the ending of his new biography, he repeats with unconditional approval the opinion of Joseph Brodsky, himself a fine poet, that Miłosz was in their day the greatest living poet. In this view, Miłosz's poetry goes beyond the material to the spiritual, the universal. An enormous number of pages in this biography carry verses or whole poems, and Franaszek is at his academic best relating these lines to whatever Miłosz was doing or thinking while composing them. In addition to using secondary sources, he has also quarried unpublished material from relevant archives, mostly Polish. It has to be said that he refers to scores of Polish intellectuals as though everything about them is common knowledge when their work, and usually even their names, are familiar only to specialists like himself. Now and again, his admiration of Miłosz as a poet generates prose of purple mistiness. For instance, another regular correspondent was Stanislaw Vincenz, an extreme highbrow, whose influence is said to have made Miłosz "experience the world by touching it with foot and hand, tasting things, humbly taking in its limitless forms, and so prised him away from human madness and Satan's murmured whispers." Franaszek concedes that much of the time Miłosz spoke of himself as disappointed and depressed, but whether this was Werther-like *Weltschmerz*, frustrated ambition, or plain affectation remains an open question. Half a deadpan paragraph treats as more or less normal the moment when Miłosz swallowed a quantity of vodka, loaded a revolver with a single bullet, and played Russian roulette. Graham Greene, a not-so-dissimilar character, also gave way to this particular form of nihilism – or is it vanity? But all in all, and nevertheless, this is a formidable book.

In the years before the war, Miłosz was a Communist fellow traveler like many another known by anti-Communists as a *poputchik*, an insulting term for someone doing Soviet bidding unasked, whatever it might be. In another strained euphemism, Miłosz "found himself swayed at times by the collective emotion of the moment." According to Marxist ideology, history, and therefore progress, is determined by something known as dialectical materialism; and again like many another fellow traveler, Miłosz seems to have tried hard to extract intelligible meaning from this abstraction. Enlightened dictatorship was meanwhile supposed to lead people, even against their will, to a wonderful tomorrow. Holding this ideal at bay was Polish nationalism, Vilnius's regular anti-Semitic rioting and unwanted class distinctions, altogether a lot of "nonsense," Miłosz's favorite word of dismissal.

Hitler's invasion of Poland, Miłosz later admitted, "freed us from the self-reassuring lies, illusions, subterfuges." As a result of the German blitzkrieg, though, he was forced into the first of several mortally dangerous escapes. Flight from Warsaw on the one available road took him away into Romania and the Soviet Union. Crossing a border on one occasion, he had to eat his Lithuanian passport because its dates did not match those on other documents; on another occasion a Gestapo officer slapped his face. In *Native Realm*, his autobiography, he describes the dramatic moment in June 1940 when he was sitting in a café in Vilnius and heard the sudden heavy scrape of metal on the pavement. He then "watched large dusty tanks with their little turrets from which Soviet officers waved amicably." The Germans were in Warsaw, the Soviets in Vilnius; the trap had closed and there was no way out.

Positions had to be taken in the face of evident and continuous Nazi atrocities. Polish intellectuals, almost to a man, resisted the Germans, and many paid for it with their lives. Miłosz drew the line at participating in sabotage and propaganda, partly because he felt that such activities were playing irresponsibly with other people's lives, and partly because his sense of destiny was so strong. A Catholic priest who knew Miłosz in the war has recorded him arguing with great conviction that his duty was to write, not to fight: "The possible loss of his life would be of no use, but his writing was very important to the country." Afterwards, among critics who accused him of pacifism and lack of nationalism, was Zbigniew Herbert, a one-time volunteer in the Polish Home Army and at least his equal as a poet.

One day, Miłosz happened to see a couple with a pram walking near his house when the Gestapo arrived, arrested the man and shot dead the accompanying Jewish woman as she ran down the street crying "No! No! No!" Or again, it was a beautiful quiet night in 1943 when the Warsaw ghetto rose in revolt, and standing on the balcony of their house he and Janka had goosebumps hearing the screams of thousands of Jews being murdered. In August the following year, the two of them were walking to a tram stop just as machine-gun fire suddenly marked the start of the Warsaw Uprising, one of the bravest but most costly epics of the war. Unable to return home as the fighting became more and more intense, they hid in various buildings as best they could. The Germans then caught and interned them in a collecting center from which they were certain to be deported. Czesław smuggled out an appeal for help and recalls in *Native Realm* that "a majestic nun" rescued them by pretending to be an aunt. "I had never met her before and I never met her again. Nor did I ever know her name."

The Sovietization of Poland was bound to be fraught with moral choices that would lead either to reward or to punishment, possibly a concentration camp and death. As early as January 1945, Miłosz joined the Writers' Union, the instrument of the Communist Party designed to direct and control public opinion. Franaszek makes the classic apologia that "it was crucial for Miłosz to maintain an active position in the literary field." He further applied for a job in the Polish Ministry of Foreign Affairs, already committed to spreading Party ideology. Franaszek apologizes for that too, on the grounds that this was the gateway to defection: "It seems highly likely that Miłosz's eagerness to obtain a diplomatic post was prompted by a desire to have the opportunity of staying in the West." Once he was in the West, Miłosz himself was to observe, "All I wanted was to get out, and see what would happen next," accepting that this amounted to making "a pact with the devil." To another Polish writer,

Melchior Wankowicz, who questioned motives and morality, he was candid: "You ask whether I believed or not. Not in Stalinism. But, of course, I believed. . . . I am definitely and irrevocably against this new faith. It is a great threat to humanity because dialectical materialism is a lie."

108

Serving from 1946 to 1949 in the Polish Consulate in New York and then the Embassy in Washington, Miłosz was able to associate with notable Americans such as Dwight Macdonald and other contributors to *Partisan Review*, James Burnham, Robert Lowell, and Thornton Wilder, all of whom would have wanted to discuss his freedom and his constraints as an official from a Communist country. The onset of the Cold War put an end to prevarication. The Nomenklatura in Warsaw suspected that he would defect, confiscated his passport, and then transferred him to the Paris Embassy. Janka was frightened that France was not safe, the Soviets might do anything and she refused to leave the United States. Outraged that a man of his standing would collaborate with the Communists, Polish émigrés in the United States made sure to denounce Miłosz. Picking up on that, the American authorities refused him re-entry into the country. Bureaucrats had effectively separated Miłosz and Janka. Another trap had caught him.

Years later, one of his friends, Natalia Modzelewska, published a reminiscence of Miłosz by himself in Paris at this time: "He became mentally unstable, and suffered from bouts of depression, which gradually got worse. I met him every day, because he telephoned me every day and from his voice it was easy to discern that he was close to a nervous breakdown." His learned friend Stanislaw Vincenz had an even more extreme memory of meeting in a café in the Latin Quarter where Miłosz used to come thinking he would commit suicide that very day.

Miłosz defected to the West in 1951, the same year that

Guy Burgess and Donald Maclean defected to Moscow. In the opinion of the general public, a more or less unknown Polish poet and two pillars of the British establishment embodied the overriding question of that early Cold War period: In the light of Communism as practiced by the commissars and the Red Army, why did some people refuse to have anything to do with it, while others believed in it, no matter what the evidence? The encounter between totalitarianism and human nature had to be explored. The CIA thought fit to finance the Congress of Cultural Freedom, in effect a government agency whose vital purpose was to invite politicians, historians, and commentators to discuss at conferences or in the media what exactly was the appeal of Communism, and how democracy would get the better of it.

Usually writing out of personal experience of the totalitarian phenomenon, Raymond Aron, Hannah Arendt, Victor Serge, Gustav Herling, Primo Levi, and Arthur Koestler have left a literature special to the twentieth century. Czesław Miłosz is also of that elite company. Published in 1954, *The Captive Mind* is partly a memoir and partly an inquiry into behavior conditioned by Communism. The Party has the power to do as it likes, and every individual must make of that whatever he can. To protect identity, Miłosz gives lightly fictionalized sketches of friends and colleagues who have accommodated all the whys and wherefores of Communism. Rationalization of morality becomes a matter of course. Communist ideology found the way to present bad character traits such as ambition, greed, lust for power, as positive, and hypocrisy was therefore a virtue.

Of course, this brilliant book destroyed the perception among émigrés that Miłosz was a Red who should be kept out and down at all costs; he obtained his visa for the United States at last and accepted a job teaching Polish literature at Berkeley. In 1980 he was awarded the Nobel Prize, but there was still no happy ending to a difficult life: Janka was to die of motor neurone disease. By the time I met him at a conference in Budapest in 1989 as the Soviet bloc was falling apart, he had become a Grand Old Man, handsome, upright, and well dressed, just as he might have looked if he'd spent his life in Szetejnie when the Tsar was on the throne. The egregious Susan Sontag and a gaggle of British lefties did not like it that I spoke against socialism. One of them said in true *poputchik* style that the Soviet Union may have had Stalin, but Britain had Mrs. Thatcher. Miłosz crossed the room and said to me loudly enough for others to hear, "I have nothing but contempt for these people."

The last thing Miłosz wrote was a request to Pope John Paul II: "In the last few years I wrote poems in which I consciously adhered to Catholic orthodoxy, but I am not sure whether I was successful in achieving that. I therefore ask for your words confirming my pursuit of our common goal." The Pope replied, "I am happy to confirm your words about our 'pursuing a common goal.'" It may serve as Miłosz's message to posterity. Having returned to Kraków, he died there in 2004, by then an American citizen.

The New Criterion
September 2017

Two volumes of essays, *The Chatham House Version* and *Arabic Political Memoirs*, have proved that on the topic of the Middle East, there is one man at least who does not seek simply to reassure his friends. Great interests are at stake in the area, and naturally myth has been pressed into the service of those interests. To put myth to the scrutiny of truth is to realise its vulgarity, and also how original and lonely Professor Elie Kedourie is. His impact smashes the idée reçue of contemporary Arab evolution which is fanciful – to use a Kedourie key-word – and which he has distilled in this way:

Fifty or a hundred years ago an author who felt drawn to middle-eastern subjects had a tremendous variety from which to choose: Barbary corsairs, belly dancers, fanatical Mussulmans, sultans, pashas, Moors, Muezzins, harems. Now in a decidedly poor exchange, it has to be the Arabs.

By Arabs, of course, we do not mean the lively and interesting denizens of Cairo, Beirut, Damascus or Baghdad. We mean rather the collective entity which writers of books manufacture and in which they manage to smother the charm and variety of this ancient and sophisticated society. This collective entity is a category of European romantic historiography, and judged by its results, it is not a felicitous invention; for as they are described by their inventors the Arabs are a decidedly pitiable and unattractive lot; they erupt from the Arabian desert; they topple two empires while making grandiloquent speeches in their rich and sonorous language; but all too soon the rot sets in, materialism and greed erode their spirit, and their caliphs change from lean puritans into fat voluptuaries. After that, it is all up with them: they are engulfed and enslaved by the Turks, hood-winked by the British, colonized by the French, humili-ated by the Jews, until at last they rise up again to struggle valiantly against Imperialism and Zionism under the banner of Nationalism and Socialism.

Note the confident rhythm of the language, how it car-ries its ironies with an almost dangerous patience; pointed, in the manner of a lightning conductor, straight to the storm; and obviously indifferent to popularity. Professor Kedourie will be heard for what he is saying, and not because he is the one to be saying it. About himself, he drops only chance remarks in the essays, that he grew up in Baghdad, went to the Alliance Israelite school there, and so benefitted from the rigours of a French-based education. His several accounts of the spoliation of Iraq have a compressed pas-sion which may result from experience, but he is not stand-ing upon a soap-box of personal suffering. Unlike refugees and émigrés the world over who posit from the particular to the general, he looks to the archives first, for the records of governments against which the actions of citizens are to be measured.

Perhaps only a pessimist would do such a thing, perhaps only a pessimist has the stomach for the facts, when the fan-cies are so much easier to deal in. Professor Kedourie does not fall into the mundane style of journalistic abasement before some "problem" which has its "solution," after which the Upwards and Onwards of mankind will be resumed until the nations shall bask in light perpetual. He believes that human beings make mistakes, repeatedly, that out of the best intentions as often as not spring calamities, and that since description of complex events is so hard, moral judgments on them are not likely to be well-founded, or even valuable. I mean to say!

It is a truism now to observe that the Ottoman Empire was deprived of the joys of the 18th-century enlightenment. Confronted by European powers able and willing to express their dynamism by means of commerce and war, the Ottoman Empire held to custom. No Ottoman Hume or Watts or Voltaire analysed what had gone wrong, nor what was to be done about it. Therefore Ottomans bad, Europeans good. The trick was to make the poor people themselves believe that in so far as this proposition was true, it was the whole truth.

It is the common fashion today to denounce the imperialism of western powers in Asia and Africa. Charges of economic exploitation are made, and the tyranny and arrogance of the Europeans are arraigned. Yet it is a simple and obvious fact that these areas which are said to suffer from imperialism today have known nothing but alien rule throughout most of their history and that, until the coming of the Western powers, their experience of government was the insolence and greed of unchecked arbitrary rule. It is not on these grounds therefore that the appearance of the West in Asia and Africa is to be deplored. A curse the West has indeed brought to the East, but – and here lies the tragedy – not intentionally; indeed the curse was considered – and still is by many – a precious boon, the most precious that the West could confer on the East in expiation of its supposed sins; and the curse itself is as potent in its maleficence in the West as it is in the East. A rash, a malady, an infection spreading from western Europe through the Balkans, the Ottoman

114

Empire, India, the Far East and Africa, eating up the fabric of settled society to leave it weakened and defenceless before ignorant and unscrupulous adventurers, for further horror and atrocity: such are the terms to describe what the West has done to the rest of the world, not wilfully, not knowingly, but mostly out of excellent intentions and by example of its prestige and prosperity.

These volumes of diverse essays may be considered doctor's reports upon this fifty- or hundred-year-old malady, which has proved irresistible from its first unlikely symptoms; the Ambassadors and envoys plenipotentiary, the cocked-hat party, who came urging upon sultan, khedive, and bey the need for reforms, without which assistance would have to be declined, regretfully. In a trice the talk was of constitutional government, public opinion, the intellectual classes, self-determination: all of which presumed the self-evident values on which the majesty of the West rested, and which in the East might one day take as transplants, but for the time being had as much real-life substance there as a magic carpet. In the Arab Middle East to this day, only Lebanon has what can be called a constitution. Parliaments elsewhere, if they exist, are and always have been arranged to express the power of the rulers, not the wishes of the ruled.

Here among the ruled, as Professor Kedourie says, "a robust and uncomplicated approach to power has always existed." Tyranny they had expected, and had learnt, sadly but wisely, how to temper it by a variety of well-proved methods. A happy man, to their way of thinking, was one with a beautiful wife, a comfortable house, a secure job, and who did not know government, and was not known by it. The spread of Western notions was incompatible with such luxuriously private ends. In these essays are some absorbing biographical sketches of the small number of men quickest off the mark in adopting and then spreading Western notions, renegades from Islam and Christianity, the go-betweens of chancelleries, men driven off their heads by the Future and its possibilities, but whose practical significance lay in the openings they offered the great powers in the widening competition of their interests. Missionaries, notably at the American University of Beirut, must take their share of the initial blame.

"Three with a new song's measure may trample an empire down." So it proved. The Young Turks had little support, and in describing the onset of their revolution Professor Kedourie shows in a wide-sweeping *tour d'horizon* how baffled and suspicious the Arab provinces were when Abd al-Hamid, supposedly the Damned, fell into the hands of Westernisers – who in the event were to lead their fellow-citizens into the catastrophe of 1918.

Had the conquering British and French taken over where the Ottomans stopped, confusion would still have arisen; but the relation of ruler to ruled might have remained comparable, and the fabric of settled society not been utterly shredded. But accustomed to their own power politics elsewhere, the British and the French primarily sought advantage over one another, although the general interest of all concerned would have dictated a common policy. Professor Kedourie's energies have gone into establishing what exactly was happening behind the scenes in the time between the Sykes-Picot Agreement (1916) and the capture of Damascus (1918). In his view the people who were double-crossed in this high play of World War I politics were neither the Sharifians nor the Zionists, but the French, and that would only be normal, nothing for the romantic historiographers (who do seem dumbfounded into silence on the matter, especially now that *The Times Literary Supplement* is no longer a public alleyway for nameless muggers).

The inability of the British and the French to imagine that the Arabs might have standards of their own to be judged by and were not simply lingering at a historical fancy-dress ball, is the Original Sin from which so many monsters were spawned. But had not a whole lot of new countries for them just been specially run up? How to proceed with them was a genuine dilemma, with no easy way out, though it had been met before not too badly (in India, for instance). Now numbers of the ruled were encouraged to believe that to have been satisfied with a beautiful wife and a comfortable house was a proof of backwardness, which they must set about rectifying. The hour of the chancellery go-betweens was at hand. Anyone who could turn his tongue to the approved political lingo of the West was sure of a career. Sa'ad Zaghlul, the Kings of Iraq, and lesser nationalists too, are examples to Professor Kedourie of agitators who have brilliantly turned the tables on the West by words alone. They represented neither force nor tradition, nor the public, not even when grievances were articulated through them. They were "little officers."

There was also always the waiting mob. All that had to be done was to repeat certain slogans loudly enough, those slogans which the Western powers were expecting to hear because they had gone to the trouble of educating and phil-osophising around them. Constitutions were therefore improvised, self-determination encouraged, nationalism blessed, for were these not the rewards of catching up with modernity at last? The curse was at hand. The Armenians or the Assyrians might be put to the sword, the Kurds dis-persed, ancient Jewish communities and the Palestinians alike ruined, settled society altogether dispossessed – but was it not possible for "foolish academics and excitable journalists" to claim that in spite of these temporary mani-festations all was for the best in the best of all possible worlds, as laid down by the believers in the sovereign rights of majorities whoever and wherever they are, and further guaranteed by fatuous diplomats sodden with emotion, the host of Arabian star-gazers in the train of T. E. Lawrence? It was and is.

The conquest of one country by another is a neutral fact of history to Professor Kedourie, to do with the nature of man, and therefore futile as a basis of reproach. To knock the Turks out of the ring was all very well, there was nothing else for it, but it imposed the duty of dealing with a settled fabric of society as it had been found. After years of committees and conferences and White Papers, after a succession of institutions devised by famous generals and pro-consuls, the ordinary citizen of the Middle East found himself abandoned by the great powers who had brought him up to date in their own image, without any of the accustomed fabric at all, at the mercy of wars and *coups d'état* and internal terror as never before. When today there are calls for a state in the Middle East in which Moslems, Jews and Christians may live together, one has to ask whether in their imperfect way the Turks did not provide such a state?

To have pursued their own interests would have been one way for the British to proceed, and there would have been nothing new or illegitimate about that. To have pretended that British interests were pursued for the sake of bringing Civilisation, or Independence, or Happiness to the natives was ignorant, confused, sentimental:

> the outcome not so much of intellectual debility, as of that failure of nerve, that weakening of the will to rule, which became manifest among the British ruling classes in the aftermath of the first World War, and which was to make the dissolution of the British Empire so ugly, and vicious, to subjects and rulers alike.

118

The heirs of Hume, Watts and Voltaire ought to have realised that their consciences were of less moment than the fate of faraway peoples for whom they were responsible. What sort of principles are they when other people die of them? It was quite impossible for the faraway subjects (Professor Kedourie is actually speaking here of the Jews of Iraq, but as representatives of a wider range of victims) to discern "the prodigious spectacle that appeared, of deliquescent Liberals and *Tancred* Tories banding together in London to utilise the might and authority of a victorious empire in order to bring about in the Middle East, consciously and willingly, such conditions as had hitherto been seen only with the decay of authority and the decline of empire."

And banding together as they did, our deliquescent intellectuals and statesmen, men of principle without doubt, were able to work the older syllogism into a newer form, just as suitable and jolly: Ottomans bad, Europeans as bad, all rulers bad, ruled good, therefore Arabs good. Those who have put their shoulder to this endeavour inspire Professor Kedourie. The title essay of *The Chatham House Version* in which he goes over the work of Arnold Toynbee, the most venerable of romantic historiographers, with a whole school in tow, and discovers in it "the shrill and clamant voice of English radicalism, thrilling with self-accusatory and joyful lamentation," may claim to be the most powerful and damaging polemic to have appeared in recent years. Professor Kedourie also moves quickly to the bedside of expiring autobiographies, for instance Albert Memmi's *Portrait of a Jew* and Lord Caradon's *A Start in Freedom*. Nobody has done more than he to bring out the feelings of Western guilt and shame and inadequacy which have been twisted inside out to emblazon the banners of Arab Nationalism and Socialism. Nobody has done more to show what it is like to be on the receiving end of these feelings. There is a classic to be written about guilt as a colonising and de-colonising motive, and these essays are indispensable studies for it.

As for the Arab-Israeli conflict, which some think the dominant issue of the region, it should be obvious that Professor Kedourie will see it as quite secondary, a by-product of the greater upheaval occasioned by the West. To him, the Zionists suffer from many of the same afflictions as the Arabs. At the hour of their supreme trial at the hands of a nationalist ideology, Zionists were able only to draw in under their own version of a nationalist ideology.

Professor Kedourie is fastidious to the end, but those who dislike such a temperament and call it morbid, or clinically dispiriting, are still left blocked by his scholarship. The city may be saved for the one just man in it, though that consolation is fragile and literary. Meanwhile we know that human beings in both East and West cannot bear very much reality.

Encounter
February 1976

THE DECLINE AND FALL OF THE BRITISH EMPIRE is a title suggesting that its author, Piers Brendon, sees himself a worthy successor to Edward Gibbon. And, indeed, Gibbon is often invoked in these pages as though he were a guiding spirit. A man of the Enlightenment, Gibbon attributed right and wrong in accord with the preconceptions of his day. But he had the imagination, the empathy, to appreciate that people in the past had other beliefs and standards and so did things differently. For the historian, description is one element in coming to terms with the past, and passing judgment is another, and the ability to keep them distinct is what makes Gibbon great.

Piers Brendon is instead an anti-historian, that is to say one who describes the past not in order to capture how it really was but only for the sake of passing moral judgments about it. For him, the past is to be judged solely in the light of the present, as though the outlook in today's moral and intellectual arena is not just the product of the times but rather some sort of final word. The anachronism is deliberate, for the whole purpose of this book is to give substance to the single, very simple, and eminently fashionable preconception that the British Empire was always and everywhere a criminal enterprise. Those who ran it were scoundrels, profiteers, or boobies, whose talk about spreading civilization was nothing but hypocritical cover for murdering innocent natives, for racism and spoliation. "Lust for loot," in Brendon's phrase, was the real and abiding motivation of all such.

Sketching pen-portraits of the Empire's proconsuls, governors, and soldiers, Brendon maintains a steady level of scorn for their activities, rising to mockery for their persons, sometimes in singular details concerning their domestic lives and tastes, the shape of their moustaches, and even their foreskins. However much these men may have been praised in the past for their contribution to the nation, not one earns Brendon's unqualified approval or escapes his sneering. Clive of India suffered from "nervous attacks" but still "garnered several hundred thousand pounds." Arthur Wellesley, later Duke of Wellington was "a man of majestic littleness." Governor-General of Canada, Lord Durham advocated reform "while treating all humanity as his inferior." Lord Palmerston, one of the most successful of Foreign Secretaries, was "incurably frivolous." Ahead of the Blackshirts by almost a century, Thomas Carlyle was nevertheless "anticipating the language of fascism." Prime Minister Salisbury was "A thick-skinned, short-sighted, cross-grained reactionary, known as the 'Buffalo.'" (Even minor personalities have their nicknames slung round their necks – thus Sir Bartle Frere is "Sir Bottle Beer," Walter Monckton is "the Oilcan," Sir Hugh Foot is "Pussy-foot" as though the cut and thrust of long-ago politics furnished lasting judgements of character.) Viceroy Lytton was "a minor poet and a major popinjay." Viceroy Curzon was said "to have the habits of minor royalty without its habitual incapacity." And so on and on and on.

Those who stood in the way of the Empire are in contrast admirable, no matter how many lives were lost as a result of their opposition. Tipu Sultan (the "Tiger of Mysore" who was killed by the British in India in 1799) was "intelligent, cultured and witty." The Maoris were "formidable warriors," as well as "adept at commerce." Zaghlul Pasha, organizer of the first nationalist riots in Egypt, was "Ruthless, charming, eloquent, and vain" while the al-Azhar mosque at the center of the agitation he aroused was "radiant" and "revered." In Iraq, King Faisal, scheming against the British who had set him on his throne, was "slim, bearded, and aquiline," bearing himself with "regal dignity." In India, Gandhi's "god-like moral stature, which transfigured his wispy frame, gave him unique authority." Although engaging in warfare that set back his country for decades, Gamal Abdul Nasser "behaved like the embodiment of national will." In Kenya, Jomo Kenyatta "preached patriotism and moral uplift," and Robert Mugabe was "the Lenin of Africa." And so on and on as ever.

The British habitually over-reacted to resistance and protest, according to Brendon, as evidenced for instance by their brutality after the Indian Mutiny, all the more barbarous because the setting was one of picturesque beauty and riches:

> The storming of the city ... was a bloodbath.... A prolonged and ferocious battle followed through the narrow streets, walled gardens, white mansions, domed mosques and cypress groves. The British advance faltered as soldiers got drunk on pillaged alcohol.... The carnage shocked even a hardened young subaltern like Frederick Roberts.... Lieutenant William Hodson compounded the horror by murdering three of Bahadur Shah's sons, who had surrendered with their father.... The city was sacked with the same ruthlessness and a vast amount of hidden treasure was unearthed. As usual, Queen Victoria (who deplored the unchristian spirit of vengeance) acquired some prize articles.

In the equally beautiful and placid Ceylon, no less typically, the brutal British overthrew the ancient Kandyan kingdom. They exiled its monarch to the subcontinent, looting his throne, sceptre, sword, footstool and other royal regalia. They turned his Audience Hall first into a church and later into a court.   123 They imposed their own system of rule. They suppressed resistance ferociously, provoking a national abhorrence for the conquerors.

Or again, General Sir Gerald Templer was "dynamic and dogmatic ... also surprisingly lucid" as he set about using "Dyak head-hunters and Fijians descended from cannibals" to build "a police state" with "totalitarian restrictions" for the purpose of suppressing Communism in Malaya. Following this example, another general responded to the Mau Mau in Kenya by masterminding "a regime of searches, curfews, contagions, restrictions, shortages and forced labour," which on one page prompts Brendon to evoke the Soviet gulag and on the next page Auschwitz. And so on, and still on, until the Empire met the wretched end it deserved.

Imperialism is a complex phenomenon, one bearing on the entire human race throughout recorded history. Two parties are involved, necessarily one stronger and the other weaker. Over the centuries the countries of Europe had become too equal for imperialism among themselves, territorial disputes notwithstanding. Among the causes of British strength were trade, exploration, Protestantism, and the industrial revolution, but these could never have amounted to empire-building without the weakness of others. Muslim and Hindu rivalry in India, despotism in Asia, and tribalism in Africa ensured that whole areas of the globe were stagnant, incapable either of progress or defense, but exposed to outsiders with the vitality to conquer and colonize them. If history has a law, it appears to be that the strong will always dominate the weak until such time as the weak learn how to become strong themselves. As it happens, countries that were never within a European empire – Afghanistan, Yemen, Ethiopia – have experienced the greatest difficulties in overcoming poverty and backwardness.

In common with every empire, including those in the Asia and Africa of earlier centuries, the British certainly waged some destructive wars, and were capable of the stupid or self-serving acts that so excite Brendon, and especially in the treatment of Ireland. What he leaves out altogether is the other side of the picture. The British suppressed slavery and piracy and a good deal of tribal and customary barbarity as well. Hitherto unknown in those parts of the world, political processes began through the formation of parties and movements and elections. Legislative and executive councils were first steps in representative government. Judges, civil servants, and District Commissioners by the thousand were responsible for civil and legal administration free from bribery and corruption. The phrase "law and order" at last crops up some 500 pages into the book, but Pax Britannica was a reality, the achievement of the men Brendon so easily jeers at.

Brendon either ignores public works, or deprecates them. For instance, he believes that the railways were laid in India not for the general benefit but in order to transport artillery, and that telegraph lines were only a means of control. But besides railways and communications, the British built harbors and ports, hospitals, schools, technical colleges, and universities. Veterinary science was a novelty. Hundreds of printing presses spread free speech, also a novelty. Why is there no mention of those who devoted their careers to improving what they found abroad, men like Greene Pasha who eliminated cholera in Egypt or Willcocks Pasha who built the Nile dams? Sir William Jones was one of the greatest Orientalists of all time, the founder of Sanskrit scholarship, enrolling Indians in his studies through the Asiatic Society of Bengal – Brendon confines discussion of him and his work to a slanderous aside purporting to show racism towards Indians. James Prinsep drained malarial swamps and also researched the origins of Buddhism. Unrecorded by Brendon, there were thousands of such benefactors, men of the quality of Henry Thomas Colebrooke, A. H. Layard or Henry Rawlinson. Taken together, they were responsible for recovering in one country after another identities and cultures that had disintegrated and almost disappeared, and as a result people all over the empire became aware of their past and could take pride in it.

In the end, recovery of identity and culture was bound to finish as nationalism. People proud of their past would no longer tolerate foreign rule; the British had always known that their presence could not be extended indefinitely. Nationalism was the agent that mobilized the weak, and converted them into the strong. In addition, the two world wars had shrunk the moral and the military standing of the British. Ambitious nationalists saw their chance to take power. Well over twenty independent countries emerged, and the record is mixed, sometimes tragic, because a majority of them came under one-man rulers or military regimes. Resentment and anger, if that existed, has long since been generally tempered with regret for lost stability.

Someone who analyzed the process of imperial withdrawal as though speaking on behalf of the voiceless masses was Elie Kedourie. Born and growing up in Baghdad, he had taken for granted the protection afforded by the British. Once the British had left, however, Iraqi officers soon seized power and Kedourie was forced into exile to save himself. Responsibility for this lay primarily with the Iraqi regime, but indirectly with the British who had not prepared a better

alternative. Whether out of guilt or some sense of abasement and defeat, British intellectuals have proved unwilling
to criticize any aspect of the new Third World, instead almost
uniformly blaming Britain for whatever miseries nationalist rulers were inflicting on those within their reach. The
historian Arnold Toynbee, then widely considered a sage,
was an outstanding representative of the type. This is how
Kedourie described Toynbee's contribution to the formation of public opinion:

> Listening to the far-fetched analogies, the obscure refer-
> ences, the succession of latinate, polysyllabic words, and
> one involved period following another, we begin to dis-
> cern the shrill and clamant voice of English radicalism,
> thrilling with self-accusatory and joyful lamentation.
> Nostra culpa, nostra maxima culpa: we have invaded, we
> have conquered, we have dominated, we have exploited.

Brendon writes more straightforwardly than Toynbee,
but he plays comparable linguistic tricks. A selection of
unfamiliar and unexplained words in his narrative includes
*shroffs, lorchas, joey, fumarole, huma, moshag, ackee, xebecs,
cenchona, karosses, pombe, dura.* Furthermore he borrows
terms from many of the languages of the empire, with their
translation in brackets. What is served by the information
that shrimp paste in Burmese is *ngapi*? Or that *kotoko* means
porcupine in Ashanti? Or that a flaxen cloak in Maori is
kakahu? These and dozens more examples can only have
been dug up from the literature, and borrowed to intimidate
by giving an impression of omniscience on a par with Toynbee's obscure references and latinate polysyllables.

The source of the thrilling and self-accusatory lamentation that both these writers have in common remains a mys-

tery, one that is central to the time. In reality, the virtues and vices of the British Empire have to be compared to those of the Romans, the Mongols, the Arabs, the Spaniards in South America, the Mughals, the Ottoman Empire, the Germans in Africa or the African tribal rulers among themselves, Russia in its tsarist expansion and then its Soviet incarnation, even the French in Annam and Algeria. Britain does not come out worst. The depiction of special and one-dimensional British villainy rests upon suppression of truth as well as suggestion of falsehood. But why the masochism, why this perverse confusion of description and judgment?

One possible answer is that the likes of Toynbee and Brendon are snobs, believing themselves to be morally superior to those they are writing about. They are laying claim to a finer and more up-to-date sensibility that permits them to condemn and ridicule the crude and benighted figures of another age. Another possible answer is that they have staked out a comfort zone. The Empire was certain to dissolve sooner rather than later, and since the loss is within living memory, and still raw, the British should console themselves with the thought that it was not worth having in the first place – as schoolboys like to say, good riddance to bad rubbish. Alternatively, there may be an uncomfortable perception that the strong and the weak of former times have unexpectedly exchanged positions, and it would be as well now to profess a guilty conscience for past strength and apologize to all those with whom the British came into contact in the days of their eminence. And perhaps there is a yet further underlying perception that without the protective periphery of the empire the metropolis itself is now collapsing and in their turn the British are experiencing the disintegration of their identity and culture, and must accustom themselves to it. This would necessitate a total misrepresentation of their past, indeed the replacement of their history with a complete anti-history, and Brendon is just the right man for that.

The New Criterion
November 2008

'THE WRITER IS a glamour figure ... he is the last free man."
V. S. Naipaul pursues his own judgement, which has no loyalty except to himself. "I had no belief; I disliked religious
ritual; and I had a sense of the ridiculous." To be free is to
see others as they are, and that means to be able to laugh.
Nothing guarantees freedom so much as a sense of the ridiculous. Mr Naipaul has been reproached that as a West
Indian writer he does not deal with the conflict of races
which is the West Indian experience.

> Mahadeo distrusted and feared Mr Cuffy. He was old, he
> was black, he lived alone, he preached, and he read the
> Bible ... One Saturday morning he had gone into Mr
> Cuffy's yard to watch Mr Cuffy whitewashing the walls
> of his house. On a sudden Mr Cuffy had turned and vigor-
> ously worked the whitewash brush over Mahadeo's face.

A frightened face being whitewashed delimits the conflicts of races – fear is the other side of the sense of the ridiculous. "I had never wanted to stay in Trinidad. When I was
in the fourth form I wrote a vow on the endpaper of my Kennedy's *Revised Latin Primer* to leave within five years. I left
after six, and for many years afterwards in England, falling
asleep in bedsitters with the electric fire on, I had been wak-
ened by the nightmare that I was back in Trinidad." Such
fear has no freedom in it, and can only be allayed by comedy.
A joke will disarm the fearful unknown, reduce it to some-

thing more humble and serviceable, like calling the Fates the Kindly Ones.

The humour of Mr Naipaul's early novels is also the humour of Evelyn Waugh's early novels. Foibles are rehearsed by the author with the knowledge of standing gratefully outside them. The author will note that the whitewash is being worked vigorously, on a sudden impulse. To be objective is to be cruel – the laugh is built into the point of view, it creates the writer's glamour by its distance. *The Mystic Masseur* and *The Suffrage of Elvira* are as precise and uninhibited as anything of Evelyn Waugh's, and they have the same ring of truth to a particular personality, one which knows how simple people are gulled. We read in *Miguel Street* of a man with "no big ambitions to make him unhappy." Ambitions provoke comedy and fear alike, because they cannot be realised and therefore are first ludicrous, then dangerous.

Men's ambitions, if not aroused, are manageable. As the title *A House for Mr Biswas* suggests, all Mr Biswas wanted was a roof over his head. Mr Stone, of *Mr Stone and the Knights Companion*, wanted to smooth the groove in which he was content to run. Mr Biswas dies, Mr Stone retires, "he had no doubt that in time calm would come to him again." Ambition is decently contained. Not so in the real Caribbean and India which Mr Naipaul visited for *The Middle Passage* and *An Area of Darkness*, two of the most individual of recent travel books. Both journeys end in thankful flight, with Mr Naipaul snatched away by the wings of an aeroplane. He had seen ambition rampant, race conflicts and nationalisms, power half-understood, corruptions in the name of causes. "Hate oppression; fear the oppressed," he writes in *The Mimic Men*. The oppressed have now become oppressors, but more deviously, more anonymously than their old imperial masters. The masses close in, their ambitions tightening on to selfish aims; the world is no longer concerned, as another phrase in *The Mimic Men* has it, with "the discovery of little intimate things."

Mr Naipaul has become a novelist of loss. "Diminishing" is a favourite word of his, "narrow" is another. "Labourers of the olden time! Not yet the people!!'" reflects the narrator of *The Mimic Men*. The people is everywhere, engulfing, digesting the variety of experience into a mass pulp. The wholeness of a single man, of a family, has become the wholeness of all, and therefore has ceased to exist. Frenzy (another favourite Naipaul word) has replaced it, as the narrator says, when estimating his own political failure: "Our power was air. We had no trade unions behind us, no organised capital. We had no force of nationalism even, only the negative frenzy of a deep violation which could lead to further frenzy alone, the vision of the world going up in flames."

The Mimic Men is about the way that freedom has shrunk to become the possession of the lone fastidious writer; it is a literary despair of politics. From an English suburban hotel the narrator in exile looks back on his forty years. His childhood has been spent on the West Indian island of Isabella. His father had suddenly taken to the hills where he became a holy man with a protest following drawn from the unemployed, and he was responsible – astonishing moment – for the sacrifice in an Aryan ritual of a racehorse belonging to a rich Creole family. Scholarships brought the narrator to London, to "my London fear" and to an English wife. The return to Isabella meant success, fortune and place, and without the wife, a job as a colonial politician among men whom the narrator sees "without talent or achievement save the reputed one of controlling certain sections of the population, unproductive, uncreative men who pushed themselves into prominence by an excess of that bitterness which every untalented clerk secretes." Fear is everywhere in that ambition: "They were easily frightened, these colleagues of ours. They feared the countryside, they feared the dark, they grew to fear the very people on whose suffrage they depended. People who have achieved the trappings of power for no reason they can see are afraid of losing those trappings. They are insecure because they see too many like themselves." The wings of an aeroplane will rescue the narrator too, returning him to the safe disgrace of London. Ambition has been seen for what it is. The career of the colonial politician is short, and "my present urge is to secure the final emptiness."

But the colonial politician is also subject for satire. "It is that his situation satirises itself, turns satire inside out, takes satire to a point where it touches pathos if not tragedy." It is here that Mr Naipaul seems to add his special pleading to the voice of the narrator, exactly as Evelyn Waugh once did. He has built in minute and beautifully evoked detail the emergence of his colonial politician, has given exact weight and shape to the events which will run through and catch up the story's development. We have this highly self-aware, articulate narrator who has reached an office prominent enough for him to be sent to London to negotiate the nationalization of private estates. That he merely gives up at the obstacles seems to support a thesis that "we mimic men of the New World" are pretending to be real while in fact copies of a vanished model. Whatever was feasible for them in their colonial society, "a tiny dot on the world's map," has been destroyed; ambitions and achievements have been unsuitably grafted on to them. Satire and fear is all that is left to be recorded. "There is no such thing as history nowadays ... and on the subject of empire there is only the pamphleteering of churls," says the narrator. Yet by the end of his personal account he is thinking that perhaps after all he might spend the next ten years working on a history of the British Empire – a book which Mr Naipaul is uniquely fitted to write. The politician proves to have been his own creator, the man of letters, all along.

The final judgement on the narrator is that he has been a disturber. In his Hindu-cum-protest movement his father too had been a "passing disturber of the peace." And what else might have sustained him? Is there more than the "religious stillness" which father and son have so differently attained, another goal besides the vows to leave written in the books of youth, besides the security of "final emptiness"? "I have visions," says the narrator, "of Central Asian horsemen, among whom I am one, riding below a sky threatening snow to the very end of the world." This is the poetry of loss, fastened by metaphor as only a first-rate writer can do. It is to place a strain on language and sensibility which Mr Naipaul, unlike most of his contemporaries, can easily and impressively bear. It is also a way of looking at things, of bringing ambition to rest in the imagination, of living in freedom when there is no God except pain, no belief beyond laughter.

The London Magazine
May 1967

THE BROAD RIVER of the Left is made up by little streams of pacifists and defeatists, Hollywood exhibitionists, 15-minute celebrities, well-meaning but deluded clergy and hippies, the French and the Germans who resent any and all action on the part of the United States, anti-globalization freaks and others discontented by temperament, all calling for peace but actually promoting tyranny. Prominent in this crowd is the thriller writer John Le Carré.

A recent article of his with the title "The United States of America Has Gone Mad" has echoed round the world. Article isn't quite the right word for this rant. It is a pure specimen of left-wing anti-Americanism, in its way a collector's item to treasure, offering insight into Le Carré and the fantasies he cherishes and promotes – fantasies tragic-comic in their distance from reality but which undoubtedly comprise the world-picture of the Left. There is a "Bush junta" and it is immersed in conspiracy, having planned a war for a long time. Far from being a blow to them and the entire nation, September 11 was a wonderful opportunity to distract attention away from their conspiracy and the shameless protection of their own vested interests. Confronting Saddam Hussein, "Bush and his junta" are leading everyone to perdition in an action worse than anything in living memory, worse than McCarthyism and the Bay of Pigs, "in the long term potentially more disastrous than the Vietnam War."

Inconsistences and sub-Marxist clichés confuse this apocalyptic stew. On the one hand, there's "America's need to demonstrate its military power to all of us," and on the other hand Bush "has an arm-lock on God" who appointed America to save the world and further appointed Israel to be "the nexus of America's Middle Eastern policy." (It's so helpful to give a little Jewish tinge to conspiracy.) It is also all about money and oil. "If Saddam didn't have the oil," Le Carré throws out, "he could torture his citizens to his heart's content." (Which is exactly what he is doing anyhow.) And the next sentence reads, "Other leaders do it every day – think Saudi Arabia, think Pakistan, think Turkey, think Syria, think Egypt." Some of these countries have oil, some don't, and that's got nothing to do with torture, except for the neat implication that the United States is really responsible for the torturing that others do. Le Carré is kind enough to allow that Americans are "thoroughly decent and humane" – they support the overthrow of Saddam only because they have been browbeaten and "kept in a state of ignorance and fear." Not gone mad, then, but victims of a massive public-relations trick.

In regular interviews, John Le Carré likes to describe how since childhood he has been unhappy. His mother deserted him when he was still small, his father was a conman in and out of prison, and this upbringing still has the power to hurt. In his youth in the Sixties he had worked for MI5, the British security service, and MI6, the espionage service. He made a reputation writing thrillers about the rival intelligence services operating during the Cold War and very successful they proved to be, depicting the world as a place of darkness and betrayal in which nobody and nothing can be trusted. These thrillers convey (with considerable literary skill) an atmosphere of distress, a general sense that nothing ever comes right – you don't have to be much of a psychologist to see this as a projection of the limited inner self. In the days when the Cold War was still at its height, the perceptive historian Walter Laqueur was the first to point out that Le Carré was not merely writing thrillers with a special setting, but positing moral equivalence between the Soviet Union and the West. Both sides were as bad as the other in his view, and there were neither heroes nor villains, only stale and untrustworthy careerists. More than a caricature, this was a lie, but it was titillating coming from someone who presented himself as an insider with the key to the hidden mechanisms of international politics.

The end of the Cold War, critics used to speculate, threatened to leave Le Carré without a subject. Not so. After its long incubation, contempt for the West and all its works immediately became his primary expression. The rather hapless struggle against Communism has long since clarified itself in his writing into a more urgent struggle against the United States, the West and capitalism in general. He despised President Reagan, and still takes every occasion to lash out at the Thatcher era, which he compares to the stagnation, greed and lack of culture existing in Brezhnev's Soviet Union. In fact, Gorbachev's failure to reinvigorate Communism brought no joy to this one-time intelligence officer. The West may have won, he declared, "but the sweets of victory elude us." Instead of showing generosity, the West left the Chechens and other colonized Third Worlders to their fate. All the talk of freedom and democracy involved illusion or hypocrisy. If ever Castro were to fall, he said in one typical rhetorical flourish, the American administration would "wander about like a lost child in the wood, calling for Uncle Fidel." In the manner of drug addicts, the United States and Britain were unable to free themselves from "war nostalgia," and "prayed for some great new conflict to come along that would make us safe again" (though how war meant safety he did not attempt to explain).

For the last 20 years, Le Carré's writing has been steadily and angrily simplifying and reducing moral considerations, raising up right-wing bogies against whom to take sides, and in the process preaching more of the hellfire sermons beloved of those who are sitting pretty and know it. Here is how in 1993 he characterized Americans and their ambitions: "They are the global architects, the world-order men, the political charm-sellers and geo-political alchemists who in the Cold War years managed, collectively and individually, to persuade themselves – and us, too, now and then – that with a secret tuck here, and a secret pull there, and an assassination somewhere else, and a destabilised economy or two, or three, they could not only save democracy from its defects but create a secret stability amid the chaos." And yet – incoherence again – at the same time he was saying, "I don't think there's any way on earth that the United States can escape the responsibility of repeated and risky foreign interventions in the coming decade."

That makes for the perfect villain; a powerful and secretive agent whose role and even duty it is to interfere, but whose purposes and plans are doomed to turn out badly for everyone. So Le Carré raves against capitalism and Wall Street and corporate America and the pharmaceutical industry, or Big Pharma as he calls it. In hindsight, the Cold War looks different to him, for it provided "the perfect excuse for Western governments to plunder and exploit the Third World in the name of freedom, to rig its elections, bribe its politicians, appoint its tyrants, and by every sophisticated means of persuasion and interference, stunt the emergence of young democracies in the name of democracy." Needless to say, the actual record is nothing of the kind.

September 11 prompted Le Carré to publish an article encouragingly entitled, "We Have Already Lost." The real enemy, it turns out, is ourselves ... The Bin Laden armies "will gather numbers rather than wither away" while we flounder in institutionalized racism, white male dominance, and obscene private wealth (which of course has no connection with literary royalties). There is no moral right on our side and nothing to be done except beat our breast and await more casualties.

Le Carré and the pacifists and defeatists mustering with him represent nothing much more than graffiti scribbled on a solid wall of society. Their self-righteousness is a thing of the mind, conditioned by egoism, impervious to reality. It is possible that in a few weeks Iraqis will be cheering their liberators. It is possible that Saddam's regime will implode like Gorbachev's, that tyranny will be overthrown, and freedom and even democracy will prove to be well-founded. It is not madness to hope for this outcome, but common humanity.

National Review
February 10, 2003

FOR A NUMBER OF years now, Graham Greene has been living in the south of France, at Antibes. One day there in 1976, at a moment when he was writing *The Human Factor*, the novel with an apologetic view of a Philby-type defector to the Soviet Union, a telegram arrived. Out of the blue, here was an invitation to visit Panama, sent on behalf of its dictator, General Omar Torrijos. "Fear can be easily experienced, but fun is hard to come by in old age." With that rather appealing remark, Greene was off.

One jaunt led to another; four in all by 1981, and a fifth two years after that. These experiences have resulted in a memoir, *Getting to Know the General*,* much more self-revealing than his two previous volumes of autobiography, which are remote and formal to the point of claustrophobia. It has obviously been a pleasure and relief to emerge from the literary closet for the sake of political commitment: to place, without qualification, his talent and reputation at the service of a campaign against the United States and its purposes in the contested arena of Central America. Animus against the United States is the sole key to his observations and judgements. Using the privileges and freedoms of residing in Antibes, Greene is praising and promoting those who would destroy such privileges and freedoms elsewhere. In that sense, *Getting to Know the General* is a period piece, a strangely delayed but instructive example of the genre so

---

* *Getting to Know the General*, by Graham Greene; Bodley Head, 223 pages, £8.95.

characteristic of the Thirties, when fellow-travellers constructed totalitarian paradises upon travesties of their democratic societies.

140 Greene professes to have no idea why he had been invited to Panama. This is disingenuous, to be kind about it. Torrijos was not offering something for nothing, he had a specific aim. In 1968, as a young officer in the National Guard, the country's only armed unit at the time, Torrijos had seized power and exiled the opposition. To protect himself, he had then recruited a paramilitary force known as the Wild Pigs and ruled as an erratic but on the whole benevolent autocrat. His single serious political objective was to have a revised Canal Treaty with America, whereby as much as possible of the Canal Zone would be returned to Panama, with as many dollars as Washington could be induced to pay. Three previous American Presidents had agreed in principle to revisions, and after his election in 1976 Carter was as anxious as Torrijos to draw protracted negotiations to a close. In his memoirs, *Keeping Faith*, Carter explains how he liked and trusted Torrijos, and fought a recalcitrant Congress over a fair deal for Panama.

What lay behind the telegram to Greene was the need for a sympathetic presentation in opinion-making circles of the Panamanian case while negotiations were reaching a climax. The choice of Greene for such a presentation was inspired. Though obviously his own master, his record of anti-American agitation throughout the Cold War was already second to none among writers outside the Communist orbit. Over Vietnam, Cuba, Chile, developments in Eastern Europe, he could be relied on to publish something to undermine whatever position the United States might have; he had resigned from the American Academy of Arts and Letters; he had signed petitions and written persistently to the press; he liked to vaunt his friendship with Castro and Allende, his tea-time chat with Ho Chi Minh; directly or indirectly, he had often expressed a preference for life within the Soviet bloc to life outside it. In his novels, those with positive or attractive roles had long been Marxists, while Americans had become stereotypes, either of greed or of a misplaced and damaging innocence.

At a first meeting with Greene, his host the General was in dressing-gown and underpants, with bare feet. In the course of conversation the General produced the one and only memorable sentence which Greene records, one which also gave away the game:

"Intellectuals are like fine glass, crystal glass, which can be cracked by a sound. Panama is made of rock and earth."

How in practice he set about producing the sound to crack this particular intellectual is the real interest of this book.

First of all, Greene had to be provided with the standards of comfort to which he was accustomed in Antibes. Understandably for someone of his age, Greene was fretful on this score, and refers on almost every page to travel arrangements (always first-class, though Concorde was a sad disappointment), to hotel accommodation (the rooms were usually either too grand or too beastly), and to preoccupations with food and drink. "We had a not very good dinner.... When we reached Santiago, we had a very bad meal.... I ordered a gin, but whatever the bottle contained it wasn't gin.... we lunched very badly in the mess of the Wild Pigs ... a restaurant called Sarti's – an elegant one by Panama standards ..." Gastronomes in Panama will find here something of a standard reference work, with its recommendation, three times repeated, of dinner at the Marisco owned by a Basque, its praises for the Colón, and its warnings, also repeated three times, against the rum punches of the Holiday Inn.

To supervise Greene, the General allocated his own personal bodyguard, Chuchu Martinez. There was a humour about this, for Chuchu was a Marxist professor who in middle age had enrolled in the Wild Pigs; altogether a leading character, potentially, in what has become the typical Greene novel. Soon Chuchu was helping to produce the perfect sound for Greene, teaching him the Wild Pigs' song about pushing the Americans into the water, "where the sharks can eat *mucho Yanqui*." Military planes and helicopters whizzed him between plantation, mine, collective, and island resort. So quickly and thoroughly was Greene recruited to the Panama cause that he thought fit to confide to Torrijos his doubts about the trust-worthiness of Colonel Flores, chief of staff of the National Guard. To Greene's surprise, Colonel Flores afterwards appeared to look at him askance. With impressions "clustering like bees round a queen," a lurid novel about the General and Chuchu did indeed start to find shape under the title *On the Way Back* – and behind the novel, naturally, this book.

The conducted tour culminated in the miserable slums where Panamanians none the less were managing to endure gaily, and the adjoining Canal Zone in which the Americans lived amid their glum banks and churches, talking of God and Country. At a political meeting of theirs, the main speakers were a man with legs "bandaged in tight brown trousers," which rubbed "perhaps to make music like a grasshopper," and a blue-haired old lady "like a Universal Aunt." Sarcasm was the only response to such freaks and their setting: "There seemed to be innumerable golf courses and you felt the jungle had been thrown back by a battalion of lawn-mowers."

1977, according to the General, was to be the year in which his patience and American excuses would finally run out. That point was well taken in the article which Greene published in *The New York Review of Books*, as early as 17 February 1977. He addressed himself to the iniquities of the

American perception of Panama. "Panama is not an insignificant banana republic with politicians and presidents up for sale, nor is General Torrijos in any way a typical military dictator." Unless America ceded the whole case, war might well follow. It was intended as praise rather than contradiction to assert that Torrijos was establishing a popular democracy while dreaming as a soldier of the simple confrontation of violence with the United States. If this was the price of the freebie, as invited trips like Greene's are called in the trade, then it was paid eagerly.

The propaganda effect, if any, of this presentation of the Panama case was overtaken by events. 1977 actually proved the year of signing the revised Treaty. Torrijos held another timely card up his sleeve for Greene to play. Issuing Greene with a diplomatic passport, he enrolled him as an honorary member of the Panamanian delegation to Washington, to witness the Treaty's final ceremonies. It was Greene's luck that so many of his favourite hate-figures were also present, Generals Pinochet, Videla, Stroessner, Banzer of Bolivia, all with eyes too close, no neck, or other physical oddities for the novelist to pick upon. Carters and Kissingers and Rockefellers completed the ridiculous scene, along with the apparently colonialist Archbishop MacGrath (in spite of his name, a native Panamanian, though Greene does not say so). How long-sighted was Torrijos in his promotion of such satirical copy? Did his humour extend to the thought that those who were celebrating happily that there had been no simple confrontation of violence in Panama would one day be jeered for it by his honorary delegate and publicist, as though by a jester with a bladder?

In the anti-climax after the Treaty, Torrijos realised that Washington might take its friends for granted but hastens to propitiate those who make nuisances of themselves. Too intelligent for crude anti-Americanism, he sought leverage through calculated sponsorship of the revolutions then impending in Nicaragua and El Salvador. Several high-level Sandinista guerrilla *Comandantes* and their beautiful girl-friends were given shelter in Panama, and Greene was soon introduced to them in expense-account restaurants. One of these revolutionaries even arrived in Antibes to raise money for arms. "Alas! I was of little use to him" – Greene may be revealing more of his cast of mind here than of his assets as a world best-seller – "I could only send off a small cheque of my own to Panama City in the hope that it would buy a few bullets, one of which might put paid to Somoza."

Of course Greene put paid to nobody and nothing, but once again, at no real cost to Panama or Torrijos, he could be given the chance to contribute effectively in print to the anti-American cause. Between 1978 and 1980, Chuchu flew him in military planes to see George Price, Prime Minister of a newly independent Belize ("there had been nothing really to report – except my liking for Price and my dislike of his Conservative enemies with their wild accusations, their violent opposition to independence and their fake Union Jack loyalty"); to the Sandinista junta in Managua; and finally to Castro in Cuba.

The usual concerns continued to surface:

> Shrimp salad, the only edible form of food we were able to find in Belize ... we sat down wet through to a meal quite as bad as any in Belize ... the Continental Hotel was full of visitors for the occasion and we were driven to a very comfortable house beyond the periphery with two charming and pretty maids to look after us ....

Good food and drink granted, Greene was able to relax in the chic circles of the international Marxist Left. He writes of the Sandinista leader Tomas Borge, "now a good friend to me."

> At Managua I found some familiar faces on the tarmac
> to welcome me. Father Cardenal, the Minister of Culture,
> was there and Daniel Ortega's beautiful wife, Rosario,
> whom I had last seen in San José.... In the evening we
> went for our rendezvous to the house where my friend
> Garcia Marquez was installed. Castro had been dining at
> the Spanish Embassy with Gabo [the nickname of the
> writer Garcia Marquez]. I had not seen Castro since we
> passed some hours of the night together in 1966, and he
> had given me a painting by my friend Porto Carrero.

Such credentials were established that Greene was able to intervene with his Sandinista friends on behalf of a South African Ambassador whom they had kidnapped, but the man died in captivity.

Voice and style are those of the dowager tatlerising about dear days at court, with every grandee a friend. The élite has changed, the snobbery is the same. Many a detail slides towards spoof. Twice Greene assures us that Chilean wine on the table was bottled under Allende, not Pinochet, and therefore may be enjoyed. The Marisco's Basque owner is a refugee from Franco, so the luxury there is all right. What is nasty about Los Ranchos in Managua is that the other diners are in ties and waistcoats, for which reason they must be enemies, and in any case spoil the meal. When Greene discovers Chuchu loading clandestine weapons for El Salvador into the boot of his car, he exclaims, "I was overjoyed at this glimpse of Professor José de Jesus Martinez, poet and mathematician, at his proper job." It might be Baroness Orczy and the Scarlet Pimpernel.

Tomas Borge, fashioning a unitary Marxist state at gun-point, is tidied up with the phrase, "There must often be an impatience with patience." Salvador Cayetano, who ordered the murder of the South African Ambassador, then almost certainly arranged for another Comrade *Comandante* to be assassinated, and finally shot himself, remains "a mystery." The Archbishop of Managua, as critical now of the Sandini-stas as once he had been of Somoza, is acting out of wounded vanity. Eden Pastora, who broke with his former Sandinista associates, may be "tragic" but he also is "dangerous." Greene admits to speaking little or no Spanish, he interviewed no Miskito Indians, but still knows that these people have been removed to camps for their own good. An American nun told him so, and he has been quoting her ever after-wards, not only here but in letters to the press.

Admirers of complex novels about loyalty and betrayal, for instance *The Power and the Glory*, will wonder at these sentimental simplicities. If there are arguments against American policy and in favour of Marxist revolution in Cen-tral America, Greene does not make them. *Getting to Know the General* has no firmer foundation than a Nancy Mitford sort of feeling that because Americans have non-U trousers and hair-dos, everything they stand for is an abomination. Those who oppose vulgar America are by definition beyond criticism; what they say requires no corroboration, what they do requires only support.

Towards the book's close, the thought strikes Greene that he might have been useful to someone else's purposes. It is no worry:

I have never hesitated to be "used" in a cause I believed in, even if my choice might be only a lesser evil. We can never foresee the future with any accuracy.

That last sentence seeks to dissolve the distinction between right and wrong, but Greene's choice here was never between a greater and a lesser evil. The options also existed of not accepting the freebies in the first place, and then of refusing to write tendentiously. Greene has a retort to that too: "If one takes a side, one takes a side, come what may." Political commitment at that level may serve a Boy Scout or a fellow-traveller, but not a writer of experience and independent means and standing.

General Torrijos died when his plane crashed in 1981. Chuchu, stout Party man, believes that the CIA was responsible, and Greene duly pushes himself into line. In his last conversation with his hero the General, Greene had aired "a favourite theory of mine that one day the KGB would be in control and it would prove more easy to deal with pragmatists than ideologists." Never mind that the KGB has been in control, never more openly than in the person of Andropov – would Greene be able to recognise the difference between a pragmatist and an ideologist, between the privilege of carrying in one's pocket a subsidised ticket to a safe home and the reality of imposed tyranny?

How little it takes to manipulate opinion, to crack an intellectual – and all from one telegram. The General was quite right.

Encounter
February 1985

GABRIEL GARCIA MARQUEZ lived and died in Mexico City, and there he has received a sendoff that could have served for a head of state. A funeral cortège brought the urn with his ashes to a plinth in the Bellas Artes Palace. Eulogies were then given by Enrique Peña Nieto and Juan Manuel Santos, presidents respectively of Mexico and Colombia, the country where Garcia Marquez was born. Juan Manuel Santos had special thanks to offer: "Eternal glory to the man who has given us glory." Thousands of people filed past the urn to pay their respects. Three days of national mourning have been decreed in both countries, with flags at half mast. In living memory no writer anywhere in the wide world has been so honored.

National presidents are prone to claim glory, and Colombia is certainly in need of it. Assorted Marxist guerrillas and terrorists have been struggling with paramilitary groups and drug cartels for the best part of half a century. Cocaine is the country's chief product and source of income. Fear for his personal safety impelled Garcia Marquez to move to Mexico. His contribution to glory is the literary gimmick of "magic realism." Familiarly nicknamed "Gabo," he was awarded the 1982 Nobel Prize and praised as the pioneer of a cultural renaissance in Latin America.

Literature serves the purpose of showing that actions have consequences, and causes have effects. Great writers one and all have something to say about this inescapable fact of the human condition. Magic realism is the reverse, resting on the supposition that there are consequences without any need for action, and effects that have no causes. In one of Garcia Marquez's novels, a woman goes out of doors to hang her laundry out to dry, only to ascend physically to heaven. In another novel, the fully dressed corpse of a general is brought in on a silver tray, cooked with "a garnish of cauliflower and laurel leaves" and ready to be served to the guests at a banquet by a host who says, "Eat hearty, gentlemen."

Suspension of the normal operation of cause and effect leaves reality at the mercy of whimsy. Here are some random illustrations of the sort of prose that follows from this approach. "Children and adults sucked with delight on the delicious little green roosters of insomnia, the exquisite pink fish of insomnia, and the tender yellow ponies of insomnia, so that dawn on Monday found the whole town awake." "Octopuses swam among the trees," and "In December, when the Caribbean turned to glass …" A man has "an indefinite age somewhere between 107 and 232 years." (Why not 233?) A woman has been changed into a scorpion for having disobeyed her parents. The absence of specifics renders such sentences not merely unlikely but so abstruse that they could be interchangeable anywhere in any text. The most extreme of his novels consists of competing interior monologues in this vein: "I accept for this short time your noble hospitality while the justice of the people brings the usurper to account, the eternal formula of puerile solemnity which a while later he would hear from the usurper, and then from the usurper's usurper as if the God-damned fools didn't know that in this business of men if you fall you fall, and he put all of them up for a few months in the presidential palace, made them play dominoes until he had fleeced them down to their last cent …" and so on for another two pages without a period. Writing comes down to word-spattering. Garcia Marquez stands in the same relation to literature as Jackson Pollock to painting.

There is something more harmful still. Magic realism posits that powerful irrational forces are at work and people can do nothing about them. Events cannot be foreseen, behavior is unpredictable, and definitions of good and bad, right and wrong, are variable. That woman hanging out her laundry could not save herself, and those guests were obliged to be cannibals. When there is a plague of insomnia, or the Caribbean turns to glass, people can only feel sorry for themselves. Garcia Marquez's magic realism caught on because it plays into the self-pity brought on by political failure. Dictatorship has been the historic experience of Latin Americans. The unseating of every dictator has been a bloody episode of violence ending usually in the triumph of another dictator who leaves helpless people to make what they can of him.

Garcia Marquez wrote a dramatized account of the last days of Simón Bolivar, the prototype dictator, and generals and colonels and patriarchs figure throughout his fiction. Members of his family belonged to conventional political parties, but like many Latin-American intellectuals he turned to Communism. This was to meet violence with violence, and had Communism succeeded, it would have been only another version of dictatorship. In the years of the Cold War, Garcia Marquez was a classic fellow traveler, approving the Soviet Union loudly or disapproving quietly. He was a frequent visitor to the Soviet Union and the People's Democracies in Eastern Europe. Evolving into an ornament of the international Left, he hobnobbed with the like-minded Mikhail Gorbachev, General Torrijos of Panama, Graham Greene (who envied his Nobel Prize), and the Sandinistas in Nicaragua. His Russian translator maintains that Garcia Marquez and Fidel Castro were friends long before the Cuban revolution, and that Castro gave him financial support. Garcia Marquez used to argue that Cuba was not a

Soviet satellite but achieving its own brand of socialism in the face of a hostile and aggressive United States. A regular visitor to Castro, he claimed that the two of them talked about literature as one intellectual to another. If you can believe that, as the Duke of Wellington said in another context, you can believe anything. Castro killed, imprisoned, and drove into exile a far greater number of victims than did Augusto Pinochet in Chile, but at one point Garcia Marquez was proclaiming that he would not publish another book until Pinochet was overthrown. Here was magic realism in action: Dictatorship is good for some, bad for others.

Magic realism has a clear political purpose in Garcia Marquez's *The Autumn of the Patriarch*. The United States is depicted in that novel as a huge impersonal and irrational force. American ambassadors do nothing but assert, "Either the marines land or we take the sea." They mean it literally: "They took away the Caribbean in April, Ambassador Ewing's nautical engineers carried it off in numbered pieces to plant it far from the hurricanes in the blood-red dawns of Arizona, they took it away with everything it had inside." America is simply brute power, and for those helpless before it the only conceivable response is self-pity. Even American presidents internalize the naked anti-Americanism. Bill Clinton finds Garcia Marquez "the most important writer of fiction in any language." For President Obama, "the world has lost one of its greatest visionary writers – and one of my favorites from the time I was young." The eulogies in Mexico, the crowds attending the funeral cortège and the tens of millions who buy his books testify heartfelt satisfaction that one of their own, a man with talents recognized everywhere, is telling them that self-pity is natural and justified. That's the source of glory.

It doesn't have to be like that. A mysterious incident occurred back in 1976, when Mario Vargas Llosa punched

Garcia Marquez in the street and gave him a black eye. Nobody knows what the two Latin-American future Nobel Prize winners were quarrelling about: it may well have been some private issue, but they are genuine opposites. Vargas Llosa ran for president in Peru; he didn't win the election, but made it plain that actions have consequences and that there are peaceful political ways to be rid of dictators and be free from self-pity. Magic realism is never going to get the job done.

National Review
May 1, 2014

ERIC HOBSBAWM is no doubt intelligent and industrious, and he might well have made a notable contribution as a historian. Unfortunately, lifelong devotion to Communism destroyed him as a thinker or interpreter of events. Such original work as he did concerned bandits and outlaws. But even here there is bias, for he rescued them from obscurity not for their own sake but as precursors of Communist revolution. His longer and later books are constructed around the abstractions of the bourgeoisie and the proletariat and the supposedly pre-ordained class struggle between them, capital and capitalism, empire and imperialism – in short the Marxist organizing principles which reduce human beings and their varied lives to concepts handy to serve a thesis worked up in advance and in the library. This material, needless to say, was derived from secondary sources.

The purpose of all Hobsbawm's writing, indeed of his life, has been to certify the inevitable triumph of Communism. In the face of whatever might actually have been happening in the Soviet Union and its satellites, he devised reasons to justify or excuse the Communist Party right to its end – long after Russians themselves had realized that Communism had ruined morally and materially everybody and everything within its reach. He loves to describe himself as a professional historian, but someone who has steadily corrupted knowledge into propaganda, and scorns the concept of objective truth, is nothing of the kind, neither a historian nor professional.

It becomes quite a good joke that Communism collapsed

under him, proving in the living world that the beliefs and ideas in his head were empty illusions, and all the Marxist and Soviet rhetoric just claptrap. This Hobsbawm cannot understand, never mind accept. His best-known book, *Age of Extremes*, published as recently as 1994, still attempts to whitewash Communism as "a formidable innovation" in social engineering, glossing with fundamental dishonesty over such integral features as enforced famine through collectivization and the Hitler-Stalin Pact, and omitting all mention of the massacre at Katyn, the terrifying secret police apparatus of Beria, and the Gulag. At the same time, Hobsbawm depicts the United States "unfortunately" as a greater danger than the Soviet Union. Presenting him with a prestigious prize for this farrago, the left-wing historian Sir Keith Thomas said, "For pure intelligence applied to history, Eric Hobsbawm has no equal." Another left-winger, the journalist Neal Ascherson, held that "No historian now writing in English can match his overwhelming command of fact and source." So much for Robert Conquest, Sir Kenneth Dover, Sir Hugh Lloyd-Jones, Bernard Lewis, and other genuine scholars.

A mystery peculiar to the twentieth century is that intellectuals were eager to endorse the terror and mass-murder which characterized Soviet rule, at one and the same time abdicating humane feelings and all sense of responsibility to others, and of course perverting the pursuit of truth. The man who sets dogs on concentration camp victims or fires his revolver into the back of their necks is evidently a brute; the intellectual who devises justifications for the brutality is harder to deal with, and far more sinister in the long run. Apologizing for the Soviet Union, such intellectuals licensed and ratified unprecedented crime and tyranny, to degrade and confuse all standards of humanity and morality. Hobsbawm is an outstanding example of the type. The overriding question is: how was someone with his capacity able to deceive himself so completely about reality and take his stand alongside the commissar signing death warrants?

Not long ago, on a popular television show, Hobsbawm explained that the fact of Soviet mass-murdering made no difference to his Communist commitment. In astonishment, his interviewer asked, "What that comes down to is saying that had the radiant tomorrow actually been created, the loss of fifteen, twenty million people might have been justified?" Without hesitation Hobsbawm replied, "Yes." His autobiography, *Interesting Times: A Twentieth Century Life*, conveys the same point, only rather more deviously.* On the very last page, it is true, he is "prepared to concede, with regret, that Lenin's Comintern was not such a good idea," though for no very obvious reason (except as a cheap shot) he concludes the sentence by cramming in the comment that Herzl's Zionism was also not a good idea. Note that slippery use of "Comintern" as a substitute for Communism itself. The concession, such as it is, is anyhow vitiated by an earlier passage when he attacks America and its allies, bizarrely spelled out as India, Israel, and Italy and referred to as rich and the heirs of fascism. In this passage he predicts, "The world may regret that, faced with Rosa Luxemburg's alternative of socialism and barbarism, it decided against socialism." (Which leaves Americans as barbarians.) By my count, these are the only two expressions of regret in this long book. In contrast, the October revolution remains "the central point of reference in the political universe," and "the dream of the October revolution" is still vivid inside him. He cannot bring himself to refer to Leningrad as St Petersburg. Learning nothing, he has forgotten nothing.

155

---

* *Interesting Times: A Twentieth-Century Life*, by Eric Hobsbawm; Penguin, 464 pages, $20.

The key to this limited personality no doubt lies in his background and childhood. His father was an English citizen though of Central European Jewish origins, and his mother was Viennese. The hazards of his father's career meant that Hobsbawm was born in Egypt, in 1917, though very soon afterwards the family settled in Vienna. In the aftermath of the First War, the time and the place were unpropitious; his father found it hard to make a living as a businessman in Vienna; his mother helped out by doing some writing, including a novel. Both parents died prematurely, and Hobsbawm was brought up by an aunt and uncle in Berlin between 1931 and 1935. At school in that city, he says, he did not suffer any sort of taunting either as a displaced English teenager or as a Jew, but these years induced "the sense of living in some sort of final crisis" and this made him a Communist. When it suits him, of course, he uses his experience of Germany under Hitler to shelter under the convenient label of anti-fascist or socialist.

One of Stalin's major mistakes was to order the German Communists to side with the Nazis against the "social fascists" or Social Democrats, thus consummating Hitler's rise to power. Hobsbawm approved, but he can hardly have understood the implication at the time. A most likely factor determining his Communism, it seems to me, is the remoteness he feels for normal emotions. His parents and their sad lives leave him unmoved. His aunts and uncles are described here with a chilling one-dimensional detachment free from any gratitude for what they did. He also had one sister, younger than he, of whom he says baldly, "She did not share my interests or my life, increasingly dominated by politics." Elsewhere in the book, this sister is written off as "a demonstratively conventional Anglican country matron and Conservative Party activist." He is able to say of himself that his "intellectualism and lack of interest in the world of people" gave him protection. The confession does nothing to mitigate the coldness and inhumanity of such a character.

A scholarship to King's College, Cambridge, refashioned Hobsbawm's life after 1935. An English subject, he was not a refugee, but he was certainly an outsider, and one, moreover, who had the luck to fall into a milieu welcoming to outsiders. King's is one of the most historic English colleges, and one of the richest. Kingsmen have long been a byword for self-satisfaction, quick to attack the privileges they make sure that they are themselves enjoying. In the college was a semi-secret society known as the Apostles, which in the Thirties evolved from embracing a Bloomsbury aestheticism to Communism. Blunt and Burgess and Maclean – as well as other traitors and Soviet agents – had been Apostles slightly ahead of Hobsbawm. It was from this vantage-point that Hobsbawm applauded the Hitler-Stalin Pact of 1939, another of Stalin's major mistakes.

As an active and declared Communist, Hobsbawm remained unpromoted in the ranks throughout the war, and was kept stationed in the country. Hardly surprising, though it still rankles with him. He also suggests that his Communism delayed academic preferment, but in fact a telephone call to a colleague at King's was enough to gain him a fellowship there. After that, he became a professor at Birkbeck College, London, another fortress of the left. It was also always plain sailing for him to obtain his visa to the United States, where eventually he taught regularly. The Cold War saw him become a spokesman for Communism, and a visitor to the Soviet Union and its satellites. In this memoir he continues to glide over Stalin and the criminality of Stalinism. Communists allegedly did not recognize the extent of the Soviet camps. Why ever not? Everybody else did. The United States, he holds, was responsible for waging the Cold War, winning what he considers an undeserved victory.

An unfathomable contradiction emerges: the Soviet Union was a super-power inspiring a sixth of the globe yet helplessly weak in the face of the supposedly blind and selfish United States.

For Hobsbawm, Khrushchev's denunciation of Stalin at the Twentieth Party Congress in 1956 was a horror. Khrushchev wantonly sullied the October revolution and its dream. (The implication is that if he had only kept his mouth shut Stalinist criminality could have endured indefinitely.) An immediate consequence was the Hungarian uprising that same year, put down by the Soviets with the usual mixture of duplicity and brute force. Most of Hobsbawm's friends left the Communist Party. He himself made a point of staying, maintaining out of pride the refusal to admit that he might be in the wrong. He has the tiresome habit of quoting at length from his own writings, but he carefully makes sure not to quote the letter he published on 9 November 1956 in the Communist *Daily Worker* defending the Soviet onslaught on Hungary. "While approving, with a heavy heart, of what is now happening in Hungary, we should therefore also say frankly that we think the USSR should withdraw its troops from the country as soon as this is possible." Which is more deceitful, the spirit of this letter, or omission of any reference to it?

In the course of his life, the only people Hobsbawm seems ever to have known were Communist intellectuals like himself, a good many of them privileged people with private incomes. For many years he had a cottage in Wales on the estate of Clough Williams-Ellis, a rich landowner and baroque architect whose wife Amabel, born into the Strachey family of Bloomsbury fame, was a salon Communist. In a comic mirror-image of the more usual social snobbery, Hobsbawm lets drop, "I refused all contact with the suburban petty-bourgeoisie, which I naturally regarded with contempt." That "naturally" is worth a moment's pause.

Of course some of the people he did know tell a story too, a story of political hysteria and frenzy. He was a friend of Jürgen Kuczynski, an East German Marxist, and his sister Ruth, a Soviet agent who was the contact for Klaus Fuchs, who gave the Soviets the drawings for the atom bomb. He was also the friend of Alexander Rado, who ran a Soviet spy network in Switzerland, and finished up in Hungary. And of the Communist theoretician Louis Althusser, who murdered his wife, and E. P. Thompson and Raymond Williams, both Communist writers. (With the latter in 1940 he wrote a defense of the Soviet invasion of Finland.) A female comrade called Freddie was trapped by bomb damage during the London blitz. Thinking she was about to die, she cried out to the helpers, "Long live the Party, long live Stalin."

Hobsbawm was a contemporary at King's of James Klugmann, already then a Communist, and later a member of the British party's Politburo. His full story remains to be told, but what is known already is a striking illustration of the political hysteria surrounding these people, and the harm that this could do. Special Operations Executive was the wartime unit responsible for partisan warfare behind the German lines, and therefore a special target for Soviet infiltration. Security was lax, and Klugmann was able to worm his way into a senior position in the SOE bureaucracy. As the intercepts in the archives now reveal, as a good Stalinist he falsified the reports from agents in the field in Yugoslavia to SOE headquarters, in order to attribute monarchist acts of resistance to Tito's Communists. This influenced Churchill to switch support from the monarchists to Tito, an essential step facilitating the Communist take-over of Yugoslavia. At the time of the break with Yugoslavia, Moscow forced Klugmann to write a book denouncing Tito whom he had done so much to empower. This book is a collector's item in the rich library of Communist absurdity, along with the defense by Hobsbawm and Williams of the Soviet invasion of Finland. Hobsbawm's final judgement on Klugmann is: "He knew what was right but shied away from saying it in public." That "shied away" is also worth a moment's pause. What else did Hobsbawm ever do but shy away from what was right? The Communist Party and its claim to unconditional obedience governed him. "We did what it ordered us to do," he writes. Besides, "The Party got things done." The justification is still more childish because he makes sure not to specify or to analyze, and certainly not to criticize, what exactly were these things that the Party got done.

Reduction of human beings and their doings to cerebral figments is the sign of a cold, not to say nasty, character. And Hobsbawm further does himself no favors with his frequent sneering, for instance referring to Orwell not by his literary name but as "an upper-class Englishman called Eric Blair" or applying to American jails the phrase "*univers concentrationnaire*" (originally coined by David Rousset to cover both Nazi and Soviet camps). He multiplies euphemistic observations such as that the odious dictatorship of East Germany was a "firmly structured community" and deserving credit because it held show trials which did not end in executions. He has a passage attacking as "literally senseless" the familiar western Cold War slogan "Better dead than red." Needless to say, this is an inversion of the words, a pure fabrication. Pacifists and Soviet apologists coined the slogan "Better red than dead" in order to persuade the West not to defend itself with nuclear weapons.

Hobsbawm's autobiography brings out the further complicating factor of his Jewishness. His mother apparently told him never to do anything that might suggest he was ashamed of being a Jew. But the relationship between Communism and Jewishness does not allow for anything so simple and straightforward. The theoretical internationalism of the former is in conflict with both the nationalism and the religious separatism of the latter. Some Jews turned to Communism as a release from an identity they did not wish to have for all sorts of reasons, some high and some ignoble. Others became Zionists, who were often deviant Marxists to begin with. Hobsbawm shows the consistent Communist animus against Zionism and Israel, losing no chance to sneer on that score about "the small, militarist, culturally disappointing and politically aggressive nation-state which asks for my solidarity on racial grounds." He boasts of a visit to Bir Zeit University on the West Bank to display solidarity with the Palestinians. Why Palestinian nationalism is valid, and Jewish nationalism invalid, is something else Hobsbawm fails to analyze and explain. Quite crudely, he approves of nationalism in countries which proclaim themselves Communist and anti-American, like Cuba or Vietnam, while rejecting nationalism in countries which are not Communist and are pro-American, like Israel. Whatever he may profess about his mother's recommendation, this makes him in practice thoroughly ashamed of being Jewish.

The welcome given to Jewish intellectuals who denounce their identity is far greater than the welcome for those who assert it in whatever form. Hobsbawm's success is huge. Portentously but for once truthfully, he declares that he is at the center of the establishment. It says much about present-day Britain that the Blair government awarded him the Companion of Honour, a prestigious decoration, and it says much about Hobsbawm that he accepted it. According to Who's Who, he holds something like twenty honorary degrees, many from distinguished institutions such as the University of Chicago, Bard College, Columbia University. He is also the recipient of many other honors including membership in the American Academy of Arts and Sciences.

162   A companion piece to the dishonest *Age of Extremes*, his memoir has precipitated further cloud-bursts of hyperbole. A history magazine published by the BBC calls him a "key witness" to the twentieth century. Newsnight is a flagship BBC television program on current events, and its anchor man, Jeremy Paxman, makes it his trademark to be abrasive. A suddenly oleaginous Paxman called Hobsbawm to his face the greatest historian of the twentieth century. In *The London Review of Books*, Perry Anderson (once editor of *New Left Review*) elaborated in thousands of words on the large-ness of Hobsbawm's mind, and the "complex distinction of the life." Not content with that, in the subsequent issue of the *London Review*, Anderson followed up at many times the length with a turgidly Marxoid essay on his hero, criticizing him only for occasional lapses from Party correctness, and – rather surprisingly – for self-importance. (His reward is to be called "remarkably able" in Hobsbawm's book.) Even a conservative reviewer, Niall Ferguson, who found fault with Hobsbawm's Communism, nonetheless thought it undeni-able that he is "one of the great historians of his generation."

What can be going on? Part of the indulgence shown to Hobsbawm no doubt stems from admirable British civility, and the desire to accommodate even the most unaccommo-dating Jewish intellectual. And part of it is hagiography, the Left on their knees chanting prayers for one another. But more generally here is a hangover from the Thirties when apologia for Communism swept aside rationality and com-mon humanity. Proof against all evidence, proof against political reality, a fictitious representation of Communism as a benign force retains its hold somewhere in the imagina-tion even of quite intelligent people. The Soviet Union collapsed with hardly a sigh, like gas going out of a balloon, because it was all a lie. Hobsbawm and his supporters will never admit their share in the central intellectual and moral failure of the times. They lost out in the real historical process but they hope to win the historiography by turning Communism into some spectral romantic myth shimmering tantalizingly above the surface of things, out of range of truth, and therefore fit to be started up all over again. All it takes is what it always took – an unscrupulous character, lack of interest in the world of people, and well-crafted lying to the credulous.

The New Criterion
January 2003

THE SAHARA, that great and life-defying desert, contains within it some of mankind's earliest works of art. The scale is enormous: in effect, a kind of semi-accessible open-air museum of pre-history stretches right across Saharan Africa. Here and there mountain ranges rise like islands above the sandy wastes: and in them, from Mauretania and Niger all the way to Libya and Egypt, are rock engravings and cave paintings.

The most extensive and varied of them are on the Tassili Plateau, in the lower part of the Hoggar, the mountains which run from the southeastern corner of Algeria to Libya. Many hundreds of sites or settlements have paintings which amount to one of the richest collections of its kind in the world. The earliest date back 10,000 years, and their survival is an extraordinary witness to our prehistoric forebears and the lives they led. Paleolithic artists showed only animals, but in the Tassili paintings there are people, families, domestic scenes.

Comparable European cave paintings, such as those of bison at Altamira and Lascaux are older – from about 13,000 BC – but not so numerous. In France and Spain together there are perhaps no more than 100 sites with prehistoric paintings.

There are similarities between cave paintings in Europe and Africa, but they probably signify only that a pre-pastoral or pastoral existence was much the same for everybody everywhere. No evidence so far connects the paintings in Europe with those in Africa. The origins of the early inhabitants of Tassili are still debated, but they are held to have come from the southern Mediterranean, and to have been white.

First signs of Saharan Neolithic settlements were observed by archaeologists in Algeria a century ago. As the French army gradually conquered and pacified southern Algeria, its officers came across more and more rock-engravings. In 1933 Lieutenant Brenans of the Foreign Legion rode on a camel patrol through Wadi Djerat, where he was the first to notice the Hoggar engravings (the Wadi cuts down from Hoggar across the northern end of Tassili).

Sporadic attempts to explore Tassili followed. Then in 1954 Henri Lhote, a French Saharan specialist, at last mounted a full expedition. In the course of 16 months Lhote and his assistants found, and painstakingly copied, several thousand Tassili paintings, which they then brought to the world's attention. As Lhote said, "Here we have a discovery of extreme importance." Now in his eighties, he lives in Paris, and through the Musée de l'Homme still does everything to draw attention to his finds.

No doubt many more paintings and rock engravings in Tassili and Hoggar remain to be discovered, as the Sahara at last becomes part of the fully explored world. Meanwhile no more archaeological work is being done, although Ray Inskeep, a curator at the Pitt-Rivers Museum of the Department of Ethnology and Prehistory at Oxford, calls the site "one of the most important collections of prehistoric art in the world." Nancy Sandars, author of the definitive *Prehistoric Art in Europe*, agrees that "for their social and artistic significance the Tassili paintings ought to be much better known than they are." One reason is the difficulty of the terrain; another is the lack of funds – and there is, perhaps, a lack of professional interest in Algeria as well.

At first glance the barrenness of Tassili today makes it

seem improbable that there was a pastoral community there at all. In fact, during the last Ice Age the Sahara was temperate and well-watered. But as the ice in the north began to recede, and with it the earth's moisture, dramatic alterations of climate were set in motion in this part of Africa. If there were any Mesolithic settlements here, as might have been expected from 50,000 BC onwards, no traces are left. But towards 10,000 BC a pastoral people thrived in a country which must have looked quite like the Far West of America.

This fertile countryside deteriorated at impressive speed. Soil, eroding fast, was increasingly swept away by incessant mountain winds – and, perhaps, also by over-grazing. By 1,000 BC the desolation was complete, and the population had to seek pastures elsewhere, merging into black Africa.

The oasis of Djanet, at the foot of the Tassili Plateau, was the base for Lhote's expedition, and it is still the only feasible starting point for a visit to the paintings. A small oasis-hopping aircraft lands daily at an improbable strip in the middle of nowhere, with a tiny hut marked "*Aéroport de Djanet.*" A three-ton truck bounces crazily in a swirling sandstorm all on its own along the few desert kilometres into town.

The 3,000 inhabitants of the oasis are Touaregs, the so-called "people of the veil," because their men uniquely wear the *shesh*, a stylish turban-like covering for the whole head except the eyes. Historically the Touaregs controlled the desert, warding off encroachments from the north and south alike – a barrier between the Arabs and black Africa. They also resisted the French, who captured Djanet only in 1909, turning it into Fort Charlet. On a hill overlooking the oasis is the collapsed fort built for the Foreign Legion; on another hill stands the even older ruin of the Turkish governor's citadel.

"Doves sing in the palm trees," wrote Robert Hérisson, medical officer on the original French expedition entering Djanet. "The gardens, enclosed behind thorn hedges, have vegetables and fruits, tomatoes, melons, grapes, onion. We buy ripe fruit in season. Life seems to us sweet and easy after our privations." Not a word needs changing from this description for a traveller arriving today.

Djanet has good spring water. Fifty thousand palm trees encircle the low houses of mud-brick and whitewash, with a mosque in their midst and some more solid government buildings, including the local electricity generator. In the market or the merchants' stores along the one sandy street necessities may be bought: tins, fresh bread in the form of *baguettes*, cloth. But there are no luxuries, such as a postcard or a newspaper. Two smiths still hammer out locks rather than tourist souvenirs. The Hotel Zeriba is an assembly of palm-frond huts and has plumbing of a sort.

A modern hotel is planned, and a new runway capable of receiving Boeings is to be built. A government chief inspector had arrived to check on progress. "In two or three years Djanet will have become an international stopping place," he said. "You'll see, it's all been decided."

Do the Touaregs want this? "Of course." So soon Djanet and the Tassili paintings will be – or more probably, maybe – incorporated into the archaeological tourist-circuit, along with Minoan Crete, Petra, or the Valley of the Kings.

At present multiple permits have to be acquired or inspected in Djanet, and guides allotted. Ours was Ali, a man of 50, who has known Tassili since boyhood. Donkeys are needed to carry up the food and water and baggage for the trip. *Inshallah*, piously meaning "if Allah wills," is an expression soon echoing through the arrangements. We are to spend a week on the plateau, long enough for the main sites. Three-day tours are more frequent; or even the one-day clamber up to some paintings at Jabbaren, on another ridge of mountains.

168

At dawn we set off up the Tafilalet pass, leading steeply from each level and defile to the next higher one. The going underfoot is rough, rocky and unsteady. It is sprained-ankle country. There are occasional tamarisks and acacias, oleanders and thorns on the way, not to mention the bones of camels and donkeys that failed to make the passes. A party of four Germans is coming down, rather cowed by the experience, complaining of the cold at nights. The day is over before the top of the plateau opens out ahead, and with it an overwhelming landscape.

What had once been green prairies or pampas have become stony plains, vast amphitheatres which are hard and black, as the ceaselessly eroding stone has oxidised. Enclosing every view are shattered mountains, huge ranges, cliffs, crags: all of sandstone, apricot-coloured, purple, pinkish, a menacing brown, according to sunlight or shadow. On all sides fantastic impressions have been created – of fallen castles, blighted skyscrapers, with here and there an arch, a gateway, even petrified streets at a spot called Sefar, "capital" of Tassili, since many of the finest paintings happen to be there. Ali's robes are a unique splash of blue, of unrivalled brightness in so much stone and rock.

There is a disturbing feeling of natural catastrophe and ruin about the place, with only the brave signs upon the rock to prove that man once passed here.

In the evening, with the heat vanishing fast and the bitter night of the Sahara coming on, we make camp for the first time at Wadi Tamrit, which falls away down below us into an immense canyon, cutting through the plateau and leading down to Djanet. For the rest of the week we stop at other sites with Touareg names, each of them memorable for absolute solitude at night.

The Tassili paintings have been done not in grottoes, as at Lascaux or Altamira, but upon natural underhangs of rock face. Some have been weathered away – unfortunately helped to do so by a habit of splashing water over them to bring out the colours. This is now forbidden. Nothing has been done since Lhote's day to conserve the paintings, so that perhaps it is surprising that they have stood the test of discovery so well. Some of the paintings crowd one upon the other, in what are like open passages, while others are isolated. Perhaps 20 miles a day have to be covered in eight or nine hours. Without a guide in this labyrinth of stone it would be impossible to come across the right rock faces – impossible too, to find a way out.

On the evidence of radio-carbon tests the earliest paintings are commonly agreed to be around 8,000 BC. According to Gale Sieveking of the British Museum, one of the foremost authorities in this country on rock paintings, it is likely that the first Saharan agriculturalists were here on Tassili. Those who lived on the plateau were also those who painted the caves. The earliest settlers were pre-pastoral, the later agriculturalists. Lhote divided the paintings into stylised groups, of which the very earliest was "the round headed period," but Sieveking has reservations about such fanciful labels and merely comments, "That's as may be." However, "round headed period" is a literal description of the mysterious early figures, often life-size, in white or occasionally brown, faceless and even featureless, sometimes horned or masked.

One recurrent motif shows a circle with lines streaming below it, apparently a cloud with rain, or perhaps a life-symbol, for beside it are kneeling women, their hands movingly stretched out towards it in supplication. To the Touaregs these are Kel-es-Souf, or Spirit People. Ali is not altogether at ease with them.

Overlapping with these figures, but lasting until about 4,000 BC are those of the "hunter period," with quite different, more realistic paintings in red ochre, with white sometimes added. Some of the hunters, bows or spears in hand, racing and leaping after their prey, are as vital as any on a Greek vase. Mouflons and gazelles are their favourite subjects, presumably because they were the most plentiful game – today they are the only animals left on the plateau. But the entire wild life of the period has been depicted: herds of giraffe, ostriches often comically on the run, elephants, rhinoceroses, porcupines, monkeys. Most amazing, in the light of the present, are carefully drawn fish and crocodiles. One particular painting may be of a boat with two fishermen.

Domesticity enters into the paintings with the "herdsman period" between 4,000 BC and 1,200 BC, also in red ochre, with white and black. The population had evidently settled as agriculturalists. Men and women and children – whole families – are shown either inside or outside their round huts, with bowls and tools, wearing leather cloaks, armbands and leggings. Some are tattooed, or perhaps decorated with beads. In one picture a mother can clearly be seen dragging her reluctant child.

But the glory of these schemes are the cattle which the people are tending – long-horn or short-horn, standing, turning their heads, lying down, stampeding, life size or only a few inches high. Accuracy and attention to details reveal how closely the artists observed their subjects – the quality of work is exceptional by any standards. Some of the cattle have horns curling forward and downward almost into the ground, which must have obliged them to graze backwards. Herodotus, writing in the fifth century BC, described a Libyan people, the Garamantes, as the possessors of such oddly horned cattle, but this was always treated as one of his tall stories.

The horse reached Tassili around 1,200 BC, probably from Egypt, and appears in a final series of paintings. Pasture by then must have been failing, and wild animals would already have been forced to migrate. A few "horse period" paintings depict chariots, with one axle or two, but these present insoluble difficulties. The ground must always have been unsuitable for chariots. Iron was discovered late, and no trace of it has yet been found on Tassili. What, then, was used for the hubs and rims of wheels? Wood would have worn down too quickly. Crude paintings of camels also exist, but the camel was introduced from Asia only late in historic times, possibly with the Touaregs.

"Why the rock paintings are there at all is pure guesswork," says Ray Inskeep, an academic specialist, "and so is 99 percent of the meaning." Whether the paintings concerned rites, religious ceremonies, magic, wars, rulers, will in all likelihood remain a matter of interpretation. One large painting might represent a battle between warring tribes, for example, but it could equally well be a dance. To add to the confusion, paintings from every period have been super-imposed on each other. Artists obviously made no distinction between old and new, between what they had inherited and what they added. At all times the outstretched hand, that most ancient of signatures, has been imprinted on the rock face. And another puzzle: some paintings clearly show negro types. If they were nomads out of black Africa, why and how did they continue with a tradition of rock paintings not their own?

Outside the paintings there is little supportive evidence for any one theory rather than another. On many flat surfaces are the symmetrical bowl-like shapes worn deep into the rock by women once grinding corn, as well as smaller holes, often in patterned squares, which suggest a game.

Everywhere over the ground lie pot shards, decorated with dots or diagonals. Some of them are crude, others carefully wrought. In the course of eight days we picked up three arrow heads. Grinders, milling stones and even pieces of stone bracelets point to the apparent numbers of people once living there. Ostrich eggs were one of their staple foods, to judge from the quantity of petrified ostrich eggshell.

Between the main settlement sites are several Neolithic tombs, circular with heaped stones; but neither Lhote nor other archaeologists have excavated anything from them. Were these tombs merely symbolic? Were corpses cremated? Human remains appear not to have survived on Tassili – though animal bones are plentiful, some of them charred by fire (Ali points with grim satisfaction to the more recent graves of visitors who fell off the rocks or had heart attacks from climbing at this altitude).

Back at Wadi Tamrit, preparing to descend from the plateau and down the canyon to Djanet, we suddenly encounter a party of smugglers, at least 100 strong – from Mali, Niger, Senegal, Ghana – on their way to Libya, many of them barefoot on a trek of at least 1,000 miles which will last three months. They carry bundles on their heads or yoked around their necks, and have suitcases in both hands. Eventually they will return from Libya laden down with cartons of Japanese transistor radios and video recorders.

Caravans – more orthodox than this one, to be sure – are immemorially old in the Sahara, probably as old as the Stone Age people seen in the surrounding paintings. And historically there is still one last direct link from that lost Tassili past of rich vegetation and animal life – a grove of cypresses standing at the top of Wadi Tamrit. These ancestral trees have an immense girth, and roots hundreds of feet long. The largest of them are estimated to be 6,000 years old, older than any other living thing on earth and certainly known in their youth to the Tassili huntsmen and herdsmen. Their seeds no longer germinate. Beyond them the prospect of natural ruin widens: the signs of man may outlast even trees like these, but not in the end the spreading wilderness and desert.

The Telegraph Sunday Magazine
November 18, 1983

RIGHT ACROSS THE SAHARA run immemorial caravan-routes. Heavy-duty trucks have beaten a wide track, or *piste*, marked the whole way by rusting cars and the carcasses of sheep that were unable to withstand the conditions in which they were transported. Every few hundred kilometers is an oasis, its houses built against the sun in baked mud, then daubed in dark rich ochre. In the sweltering and sandy market squares of these places – El Golea, Insalah, Adrar, Timimoun, Tamanrasset – rally parties of Land Rovers, and Mercedes Unimogs, Peugeots and Toyotas.

A generation of Europeans, for the most part Germans and Swiss and French, are enjoying themselves as grease monkeys and rolling stones, as often as not on daddy's money. The men are bearded and the girls half-naked, in contrast to the Chaamba or Touareg of the Sahara who go veiled, and whose women stay as invisible as possible. Each passing vehicle, with its jerricans of fuel and water, supplies of food and whisky, tents and cameras, represents tens of thousands of dollars. The inhabitants of the Sahara, with no productive work to do, and virtually nothing to sell, gather around the new caravans. They have to squeeze a subsistence out of them.

Donne moi un Cadeau is the general demand. Children go barefoot and they wear little more than a ragged shift. They beg first for pens, then for a sweater or shirt. Their elders complain of headaches and plead for aspirin. The headaches are symptoms of hunger. Baffled by these encounters, the Europeans drive on southward through Algeria, across the empty quarter of the Tanezrouft, to the Algerian-Mali border at Bordj Mokhtar. The formalities at the frontier-crossing last hours.

Mali, one of the world's poorest countries, is emerging hesitantly from the Soviet model of socialism, which until lately was held to be an integral aspect of independence. But socialism proved unable either to maintain past achievement or to prepare for future improvement. As the Europeans travel into the country, they must stop at villages along the way. Permissions are paid for, prohibitions imposed – it is forbidden to visit the ruined city of Es-Souk, where in the 16th century Arab missionaries converted the local Songhai to Islam, for example, because the *piste* passes within a dozen kilometers of the state penitentiary at Kidal. Policing of the kind has to do with laying hands on enough to eat. The *chef de brigade* and his men who serve the coffee all ask for presents, and indeed, depend upon receiving them.

Gao is the terminal of the ancient caravan-route. After the final few hundred kilometers of broken terrain, palms at last break the horizon. Thin rows of maize or patches of melons color the floor of the desert, and suddenly the river Niger gleams ahead in an unexpected blue-green ribbon of water, a mile or more in width. Gao was once a city as prosperous and historic as Timbuktu, its rival entrepôt up-river. Here was the capital of the Mandingo king, Mansa Musa, one of the greatest of mediaeval African rulers. As in Timbuktu, so in Gao he built a mosque to be a center of learning and piety. Songhai rulers succeeded the Mandingos and the most powerful of these, Askia Muhammad, conquered an empire extending to modern Chad and Nigeria. The Askia dynasty was overthrown in 1591, when in an astonishing feat of arms, a Moorish army complete with artillery crossed the entire Sahara. By the time Europeans began to explore the Niger in the early 19th Century, tribal warfare had reduced the whole region to misery.

The present population of Gao is said to be at least 30,000, with estimates that two or three times as many may have moved in from the drought-stricken Sahel. From dawn onward, the market preoccupies virtually everybody. The daily risk is that deprivation will slide into starvation. Stalls of one sort and another spread across the town-center. Smiths are forging nails for the *pirogues* or for canoes on the river. Leather workers hammer at skins and make sandals. Here is a store for rice from Togo; another for salt blocks from Morocco.

The children somehow sort out among themselves which of the various Europeans they are going to attach themselves to. The children move in packs and are experts on the proceedings at the police station, where forms have to be filled out, declarations signed, passport photos stamped. In return for more and more fees, other offices with different officials grant different permits for tourism, for photography, for a canoe expedition across the Niger, for *droit de passage*, whatever that may be. Arguments flare up in these offices, the attendant children look grave and advise what to pay or to withhold. They recognize present-giving in all its forms.

The Europeans gather in the Hotel Atlantide, and they exchange stories about present-giving. Cholera is raging in the Sahel, and an Italian says he had the job of delivering vaccines to a hospital north of here, which he did, only to find that there were no needles for the hypodermic syringe. Italian money originally built the hospital; equipment and medicines were then donated by America. The Germans endowed it with a generator, but it required petrol and there was none. Without electricity, the equipment has sanded over, and is useless; the medicines have spoiled. Outside the hotel trucks from France have arrived, part of a program rhetorically dubbed "Camions de l'Espoir." Some brand-new and vitamin packed nutritive biscuit is inside, by the ton, says one of the drivers, but the consistency is such that nobody can swallow the stuff.

These are not natural disasters like drought, but man-made. Must generosity serve to reinforce failure and corruption? Uncertain whom to blame, dispirited, resentful of paying fees and fines to officialdom, the Europeans take to spending their time in the bar of the Hotel Atlantide. Within sight, one among the horde of children lies permanently in the dust of the square. Naked, he hauls himself along by the elbows, with his legs withered under him: presumably a victim of polio. In the heat of the day, a smart white Land Rover with UNICEF markings draws up. The passengers hurriedly scramble, one almost stepping on the crippled boy. It could be that such visitors no longer notice one more emergency among so many. As practiced out here, present-giving evolves from the expression of human solidarity into a moral degradation for giver and taker.

The New Republic
April 1, 1985

LEN AND FRED, both about 20, start on their duty-free vodka as we board the package tour aircraft at Gatwick. Neither has flown before. They are scared. Soon Len is also drunk.

"Ladies and gentlemen," the captain breaks in over the inter-com, "due to go-slows in air traffic control in France and Spain, we shall be delayed here for approximately three hours."

It is too much for Len who leaps up shouting and hits the steward. Fred, his mate, grapples and down the aisle they roll. "'ere we go," say voices behind me. A sigh escapes the entire package tour. Enter the police, and next Len is outside on the tarmac taking a swing at the fatherly sergeant. Not Benidorm but the cells for him.

At Alicante, after a long day, Fred has to identify Len's suitcase. A special trolley is moving out to the loading bay with woolly toy donkeys, three or four foot high, in pinks and oranges and purples, maybe a few hundred of them. A few hundred of us cram into buses, feeling in a mood of evening hangover. The tour representative – our rep in a company sweater – has a pep talk for us about Spanish brandy, Cointreau, Bacardi, Campari, sangria which "they top up with nail varnish," bar prices, and very capably he slips in the gen about possible local excursions and entertainments. Looking at us, he sees commissions.

A coastline of wild concrete is upon us. Prefabricated, splashily coloured, spiky and higgledy-piggledy, mini-Miami, The Pueblo, Tropicana, Reymar, Rosamar, Los Dalmatas, Los Pelicanos, where the famous overbooking battles of a few years ago were staged – the fortress blocks wear their names 15 or more floors up, like huge neon dog-collars. In every lift there is Musak. In every cellar there is a disco. The land-scape thrums. At nightfall women start to dance together by the edge of the swimming pools, while the ten year old girls try bopping along. The touts cluster, not quite able to believe their luck. Their keep and 200 pesetas a day when all they have to do is herd the kids into some joint. Round the clock, they go on handing out the leaflets which blow through Benidorm in and out of season. Drink as much as you like all night, the leaflets say, free drinks. Over in Bam-bino's with its terrace a chorus of *Viva Espana* erupts every 15 minutes. Happiness there is an alto saxophone. And like bursts of gunfire come the echoes of the town where the lads are out and about – "England" (clap, clap, clap), "England" (clap, clap, clap).

"There will be a Welcome Information Get-Together in the Bar Lounge at 10 P.M. Looking Forward to Meeting You All. My name is Hazel." No good at 10 A.M., for then Beni-dorm lies blotto. The light is too blue. The day is for sleep-ing off; on the beach maybe, for the midday tan, but the sun soon scorches and blisters. Anglo-Saxon skin peels like little rolled pancakes, and bikini-wearers weep for remedies in the chemists' shops. The hotel canteens are self-service, nice and aluminium, the wipe-down tables ready with HP and there is no need to wear a shirt. Bring your own Alka-Seltzer.

No carpets in any corridors. "The fixtures and fittings don't last a minute here," the tight-lipped manager explains, "chairs and even beds have got to be proof against the foot-ball fans; they throw them out of the windows, see, when they come back from drinking. We've given up with all lights except ceiling bulbs." The Bar Lounge is gory with red leatherette, Formica, PVC, a fruit machine. In rooms like that all over Benidorm 400 reps are repeating the sure-fire sales pitch of free drinks in order to fill the coaches and earn their commissions. It is what the public comes here for, say the reps, they want to be smashed for their fortnight. What else can you expect in a place like this? It is so cheap that everyone, but everyone, can afford to come. Only 25 pesetas for a bottle of wine. You Get What You Pay For – that is Benidorm.

So we pay for a barbecue. Six hundred strong we are, in 12 coach loads. Five nights a week this is *the* feature. The place is up a narrow road in the hills where neighbours will not be bothered. "Good evening, my name's Alfonso." We smirk at him. "You can do better than that." "GOOD EVE-NING" we roar. Alfonso, the guide, cocks his head. "Now when you leave tonight you'll be feeling a little happy, yes, so please ask me for a plastic bag. Your driver is off to the Grenada straight after and he won't have time to clean up."

Musicians in sombreros greet us in a courtyard. A sausage on a skewer is thrust into each hand and with it a paper cup of topped-up sangria. Where's the crumpet? The lads show bravado for about 15 minutes before the sangria hits them. Don Pepe, the highly satisfied manager of the barbecue, thinks that three cups are as much as anyone can take. The lads are woozy at a net cost to him of about six pence a head. In the hangar of a dining-room we are seated according to tours, Jetair, Ultramar, Horizon Midlands, Cosmos, Thomsons, Saga, Vingresor, Tjaereborg, Lakers, Melia, Sun Comfort. Such respectable people really. Dor (for Doreen) her hair like a Saluki's; Sue; Harry and his wife; life-and-soul Fred; a fireman from Uxbridge with his family; and the crowd from Gloucester.

The jugs are plastic, the plates unbreakable. A porron, that puzzling Spanish drinking jug, is passed round and sportingly we squirt wine all over our faces. A photographer snaps the spectacle, just for a quid. For another quid or two, a T-Shirt and a special poster can be had. And free drinks, free drinks. In no time, the Swedes are standing on their tables, arms linked, swaying, even the grannies among them. They never quite lose that perplexed look of having forgotten something terribly important, like their names.

Then the Germans. *Eins Zwei Hopsa, Bye Bye Fräulein.* Show 'em, the Gloucester mob and Harry begin: "England" clap, clap, clap. The whistle blows on them, so to speak, with the dance music. Dor and Sue and Jakki and all push off into the dark beyond the courtyards for the waiting Spaniards. The cypresses swaying on the hillside come gigglingly alive. The lads stick to the bar. At midnight, when *Valencia* is the signature tune which closes the proceedings with its na-na-na-na-NA lilt, girls emerge shaking down their frocks. "We know where you've been," cries out a voice from the back of the coach, and "Wouldn't you have liked to be there?" comes the immediate answer.

Good old Fred – his mate Len still in the nick – does take-offs of TV stars and he leads the singsong home to the hotels. *She'll be coming round the mountain ... roll out the barrel ... my old man's a dustman ... don't dilly dally on the way ...* What was that about plastic bags? Alfonso copes manfully. Did we have a good time? "Yes" roar those who can.

The Spaniards play a game here: one point for an English girl, two for a Swedish girl, three for a German, four for a French, 15 for a nun. Over a summer the winners score around the 200 mark, mostly in English singles. The sons of peasants pour in from hundreds of miles around. "I don't know what gets into these girls," a sad rep says. "They think nobody is looking. They'd never do it back home. The boy-friends are too smashed for anything, of course, and that's partly responsible. The Spaniards feel free to move in. They get maddened by the sight of English women and girls dancing together."

182

Derrick and Edith's Original British bar. Edna and Charlie's, from Aberdeen. Marr's Bar. The English Pub UK Rules. The Duke of Wellington, the Robin Hood. British-owned and proud to be showing the football results on TV at 3.30 every Saturday, clap, clap, clap. Some mock pubs have leaded windows and fox-hunting prints. Drink Hook Norton Beers. Sing Along With Eduardo at the piano. Eduardo is actually from Halifax and he dug unemployment, man, but this is better by far. Piano Music On The Bottles, Cockney and Scots Flamenco. Toast and Marmalade and Tea Like Mother Made It.

This is not tourism, it is war. Four Scots boys died last year because they believed they could jump from one skyscraper balcony to another. "When we hear them yelling that they belong to Glasgie we alert the police," says a hotel manageress with a disco to run in the basement. "As a matter of fact we have to call the police in every single night, but Glasgow means arrests, bail, the consul, deportation – the lot."

The Finns have a speciality too, which is throwing bottles from skyscrapers' roofs to break against the sides of the hotel pools and fill the bottom with shards of glass for the kiddies' feet. There is a Norwegian colonel, a Benidorm card in a solar topee, laying ambushes for one-pointers but too bottled to be able to utter more than "uuuggh" at them. One night a proper street fight breaks out and, in *Clockwork Orange* style, I lean out of my bedroom window and watch a group of tiny figures piling in. They then scoot under the umbrella pines. Next morning the kerb has a gloss of dried blood.

Bobby's has a floor-show. So does the Granada, where the desirable Conchita – or some such – is really from Coventry, for all her castanets and Spanish petticoats. There is also a baby bull-ring run by a real Spaniard called Paco. Fifteen coach-loads for this. Free drinks, sangria in paper cups again. The lads can try their luck with calves about the size of a St Bernard. Paco picks English girls, too, and one of them, black-haired and very pretty, does a good turn and is elected lady bull-fighter of the afternoon. Paco gives her a reward for the stunt; a T-shirt which she is invited to put on in the middle of the ring. Having no underclothes, she hesitates about stripping to do so. "Take it orff," yell two ladies who prove to be her mother and auntie. She does, and stands smiling in the September Morn pose, warmly browned all over. Paco jostles her to raise her arms into the T-shirt. The Spaniards present stampede in the expectation of the easiest one point ever seen.

"Smashing." The Gloucester lot really enjoyed that. Everybody has had a good laugh. Benidorm beats Malta every time, and Blackpool is nowhere. "Do you know, we have clean linen in our hotel every night." They are happy. They love everything about the holiday. Dissatisfied faces are hard to find. Nobody has to speak a word of Spanish; nobody will realise what the contemptuous Spaniards are saying about them. Spain stays a closed book. No venturing away into the nasty and foreign interior. Beach and hotel are the be-all-and-end-all of creature comforts. No sight of Spanish food either. All that oil. Beans on toast and eggs with chips are ever so lovely, and nobody understands that the waiters have a message when they rush the plates along as though they could not be rid of such stuff quickly enough. That must be good service. Yes, grateful regulars will return year after year.

Half a million beds exist within this sweep of coast alone. Benidorm, dormitory. The package tours have been penned into a promoter's strip of honky-tonk 500 yards wide, for the sake of the cash flow. "I could write a 1,000-page book," says an English boy who has worked here, "just on the history of the Cornish pasty in Benidorm."

It is a corner of England ripped off in a foreign field. We

183

Get What We Pay For because nothing but this was offered. Clever old Franco who had it all worked out at the exact never-had-it-so-good point. The place looks already prepared for wonderful ruins a century or two from now. In the mind's eye a Moorish horseman is again trotting alone on bare white sand.

There is a coach to go back to the airport, of course, with the reps speculating how many unmarried mothers the welfare state will be welcoming. Len never made it; his suitcase is lost property now. It is our turn to be coming on strong with woolly donkeys, lovely souvenirs. For every head, the final touch of a red straw sombrero, and a last-minute song for the road, too. *Viva Espana*, let's have it, it's duty-free. Come on, everybody. *Viva Espana*.

The Telegraph Sunday Magazine
January 1, 1978

A Redundant General
and a "Temporary" President

ON THE MORNING I arrived in Athens to meet General Grivas, two Jordanians exploded a bomb in the El Al office off the main square. A small child was killed. Here was a suitable reminder of the realities of terrorism. Ten years have passed since Grivas, under the *nom de guerre* Dighenis, was himself a terrorist, the leader of the underground organisation EOKA, with a British offer of £100,000 on his head.

The aim of EOKA, and of Grivas in particular, had been *Enosis*, or the union of Cyprus with Greece. The word still lives in blue paint on the whitewashed walls of Cyprus. Whether Cypriots really want it, or indeed ever believed they would get it, is something else. Where Grivas once used violent means to bring about *Enosis*, Archbishop Makarios, the Ethnarch and therefore spokesman of the Greek Cypriots, was diplomacy itself, denouncing EOKA terrorism but taking advantage of it. To deport such a man, such a symbol, to the Seychelles Islands was an admission that he was too complex to deal with. The move was as conspicuous as the failure of troops to capture Grivas on an island about the size of two English counties.

When at last agreements at London and Zurich in 1960 ended the EOKA struggle, Archbishop Makarios was seen to gather the whole harvest in his hands: he was suddenly head of an independent sovereign state. And Grivas, no less suddenly, was put on an aeroplane to Athens. A Greek diplomat who accompanied him told me that during this flight

Grivas, dressed still in khaki sweater and field-boots, was too bemused to speak.

The new constitution arranged between Archbishop Makarios, the Turkish representatives and the British, proved unworkable – or was laid aside by Archbishop Makarios at the end of 1963. Riots followed. Independence had brought fighting between the island's Greek and Turkish communities, a death roll of many hundreds, and a United Nations force, today 4,000 strong, to hold the ring.

Grivas returned to Cyprus in June 1964 as clandestinely as he had once arrived to start EOKA. In a broadcast from Nicosia he characteristically announced his presence: "March forward, Greeks!" He had been appointed by the Greek Prime Minister, Papandreou, as commander of the Cyprus National Guard and also of the Greek regular soldiers who had been illegally infiltrated into Cyprus, 8,000 of them, perhaps even more. For three years Grivas disciplined the Cypriot conscripts into something of a military body and he dug fortifications against possible Turkish invasion.

An attack led by Grivas in November 1967 against two Turkish villages, Kophinou and Ayios Theodorou, precipitated precisely such an invasion. More than 20 Turks were killed by Grivas's men, and subsequent mobilisation was serious enough to cost the mainland Turkish government some 100 million dollars. Invasion was called off at the very last hour only because of Greek concessions, notably the instant recall of Grivas and his soldiers. Since this downfall, Grivas has lived in seclusion in the village of Porto Hieli, writing hard. He has been ill. He never goes into society, although he sees his in-laws, the 11 brothers and sisters of Madame Grivas. He has no children. And unwittingly, Porto Hieli, conveniently close to Athens, has become a tourist resort around him.

I meet General Grivas in a large office block in the centre

of Athens, chosen by him because there he will pass unnoticed. In the street a fat policeman is on duty. On the third floor I go into an outer office, then into a boxlike inner room, and there Grivas is sitting on a sofa, his hands firm on his knees. He is small but compact, the coat of his grey suit always buttoned. His face is nut-brown and his moustache jaunty, its ends bristling up in the unmistakably heroic Balkan style.

With us are his lawyer Mr Papadopoulos (no relation of the colonel of that name) and the lawyer's nephew Mr Pappas, a statistician, once an LSE student who has come to interpret. Grivas, it appears, is taking weekly English lessons, but he speaks French, in a gravelly accent, and we can do without Mr Pappas. In the Twenties Grivas attended the Ecole Militaire in Paris and the artillery school at Chalons-sur-Marne. His instructor was Marshal Juin whose views, he says approvingly, were always unorthodox.

What about this bomb in the El Al office, I begin. Attacks on civilian targets are cowardly, Grivas answers, the culprits must be properly punished. He adds that he gave orders to EOKA to attack only military installations.

"I have lived as a Cypriot, I have felt as a Greek." At the end of the last century he was born in Trikkomo, a village on the coast south of Famagusta. "Love of Greece" – the phrase will crop up regularly and fondly: it is no slogan. His childhood was happy, but stern and lonely. Several times he is to tell me that his character was stamped for good by the firm truths he learnt in the village school and the village church. Zeal and fanaticism had been moulded by the time he went on to the well-known Pan-Cyprian Gymnasium in Nicosia, and in 1916 to what he called the "spartan" army cadet college in Athens. Until then he had held a red-covered British passport as issued to subjects of Crown Colonies.

The English themselves encouraged the nationalist idea

in Cyprus – he quotes a long-ago sentence of Churchill's on the subject. But then, he says, in what proves a favourite theme of his, British policy towards the Greeks has always defeated its own aims. As far back as he could recall, the Greek villages in Cyprus wanted *Enosis*: the English governors said nothing.

As for policy during the Second World War, the British promoted dissention in Greece by backing left-wing Communist partisans instead of loyalist and nationalist groups like the one he himself organised and led, and which was known by the Greek letter *Chi* or "X." It was Grivas's first underground venture, and to him the picture is clear. He wished to attack the Germans, then to cut their retreat along the only roads available to them. The Allies not only hindered him but promoted the Communists whose aim was not resistance but power for themselves once the war was over.

In October 1944 Grivas and the Communists shot it out. He was surrounded in his house in the Thesion, below the Acropolis, and had to escape along roof-tops. Of all his dangerous experiences, this flight alone seems to contain humiliation. It needed revenge. But "X" was disbanded and Grivas was retired for the first time. He went into politics, campaigning for a party of national rejuvenation, which received so few votes that nothing came of it.

The Communists accused him of collaboration with the Germans, I remind him. He smiles slowly, the harsh look fades from his dark eyes. They have always accused everyone, he answers, and of things they did themselves. It was a Communist who first gave away his Dighenis identity to the British in Cyprus, during a broadcast from Moscow. They can take power only through the mistakes of their opponents, and they have therefore to produce these mistakes. "When I was in Cyprus from 1952 to 1959 the Communists were a very few per cent. Look at them now, embraced by

Makarios, five of them in the Chamber and making propaganda in schools and churches. By 1967, say 70 per cent of Cypriots thought of Russia as a friend. I did everything for the army to be in my hands, but Makarios had press and police and church." For Archbishop Makarios, the politician who cut away the ground under his feet, Grivas has a whole vocabulary of anger revealing what an unyielding enemy he must have been. "You can suspect Makarios of anything. In Greek we have a word *charlatanismos*."

When Grivas begins to argue he hits the wooden arm of the sofa with his hand held open, hard as a guillotine blade. All compromises and half-and-half measures are hateful because they create misunderstandings – and chop, chop, drops that right hand of his. Those exhortations to the Greeks to march forward become more vivid. But Mr Papadopoulos tries to calm him down, picking up a big gold fob-watch which has been lying on his desk, and fussing about being late for lunch. Grivas puts on an old-fashioned grey felt hat and we walk down to the street. As a precaution, acquired in underground days, he never takes a lift. The fat policeman is still there. So is Grivas's black Dodge, on loan from the Greek army, along with Grigoriou the driver, in a suede jacket. As he leaves, Grivas tells me: "What I say is the truth, I'm a sincere man. I've always been a lone wolf."

On the following morning Grivas arrives punctually with a bundle of papers to substantiate what he has told me about his underground activities. Here, too, are letters from Americans asking for information for their studies of EOKA. Terrorism in Cyprus was first proposed by Grivas in 1951, but Archbishop Makarios was against it, saying that not 50 men would support it. At the head of successive Greek governments Marshal Papagos and Karamanlis did not help much either. The first EOKA arms had mostly been stacked away by "X" after the war. His cleverest method of smuggling them into Cyprus, Grivas reveals, was to send them through the parcel post. "Once I began war with the English, I realised that I might be killed. It was a matter of my strength and will. The ransom on my head . . . eh, I assure you. I had no worry on that score because I believed that the men I trusted were above money questions."

Looking back, what did EOKA achieve? He is reflective. It is impossible to know what Archbishop Makarios really thought or decided. He approved or condemned EOKA according to the day-to-day situation "I've nothing to say to him. I've said what I had to." The two men met face to face only once or twice. "Now I'm not in contact with Cyprus. The moment my objective, *Enosis*, was paralysed, I ceased to play any part in the struggle between factions. The goal of 1954 to 1959 has been abandoned." There are other little organisations in Cyprus now, political or nationalistic, the noisiest of them known as the National Front. These latter-day EOKA-style groups distribute leaflets, throw bombs and hatch plots, thinks Grivas, because the people have been denied the *Enosis* they cherish.

"I told Makarios I asked nothing from Cyprus for myself," he goes on. "Even if invited to be the head of state I would have to ponder whether to accept. I take decisions for the national interest, not for a party or myself. Here they are different. Ask our politicians about their principles and they begin scribbling in little magazines."

I remind him that in 1959 as well as in 1945, he presented himself as a candidate for election. He shrugs. "After my return from Cyprus as EOKA leader, they all wanted me to be in opposition. You haven't the right to rest on your laurels, they said. Politicians are all the same." Dictators are no solution, they have to be born not bred. The only way out is to educate the people. He had his opportunity and did not take it? "Yes, they used me, they all dropped me. It's not even politics. Say what you like, nobody listens." And the English, he counters, what did they get out of all their efforts in Cyprus?

Mr Papadopoulos has ceased interrupting and soothing. But he welcomes in a messenger who brings a paper. *The Fourth of August*, a weekly put out by a right-wing faction of former Metaxas supporters including Colonel Ladas, who is secretary-general at the Ministry of the Interior and one of the strong-arm men in the ruling junta. This issue blares out: "What Happened in 1967?" It links together the colonels' take-over in April that year, the Cyprus crisis in November, and the King's abortive coup ten days later. Some of the speculation is absurd and Grivas chuckles as he glances through the long article.

At the time of the November attack on the two villages of Kophinou and Ayios Theodorou, it was rumoured that the Greek Minister of Defence, General Spandidakis, had cabled the assault orders to Grivas, and had thus set off the chain reaction so disastrous to the Greek Government. The rumour was strengthened by General Spandidakis's downfall shortly after Grivas's. Grivas did indeed receive such an order to attack from the Minister of Defence. The charge therefore in this paper *The Fourth of August*, that "in the Cyprus question a scapegoat was found in the pure and credulous patriot, Grivas," is for all its language, true. (When I tried to buy a copy of the paper, I found that it was not legally for sale, and had to be slipped to me eventually out of the back of a kiosk.)

Once the bitterness is released into the open, Grivas seems to relax and talk with less inhibitions – to Mr Papadopoulos's alarm. His duty – that is what he comes back to – the simple ideas of honour, conscience, Hellenism, *philotimo* or self-respect which is so valued by Greeks. His dark eyes show not suspicion, one comes to think, but bewilderment that such obvious notions as these are not immediately accepted by everyone as once they were. It must be because of all the villains in the background, the placemen and self-seekers, the complacent old and the idle young, who are no longer taught to be patriotic.

His is a voice surviving from the age of Garibaldi or Bismarck, a voice of self-evident nationalism. About the present junta, whose outlook he probably shares while deploring their handling of Cyprus, he is silent.

Again it is time for lunch, Grivas's one meal of the day. For breakfast he has fruit-juice. Nothing else. "Why should I eat? To be strong at my age is no use." His shoes are shiny as a guardsman's. On the way out I tell him that he reminds me of my grandfather, a colonel of the old school. "Ah, so you're from a military family. Then you'll know that we're different, more austere."

Next day Mr Papadopoulos and I drive out in the Dodge to Grivas's villa. Grey clouds are scudding low above the Athens suburbs, that groundswell of cement spreading to the surrounding hills. A small silver icon dangles from the driving mirror, and another is fixed to the dashboard. Mr Papadopoulos sighs. "You've no idea what my friendship with the General has cost me." This frank speaking of the last three days with me is absolutely unheard of in his experience. Mr Papadopoulos implores me to be careful in what I write. As we draw near the villa in Psychikon, the policemen at the cross-roads stand to attention to salute the car.

The front door is reached up an external flight of steps and inside the entrance stands Grivas, next to a life-size head and shoulders of himself in terra cotta. In his study is a portrait even more fiercely idealised, his eyes blazing, the whole cast of his head defiant, topped by a beret with an EOKA emblem. Here is enshrined the complete romantic conception of a guerrilla. The painter sent this picture without ever seeing him, Grivas says. On shelves are two small bronzes of him. Another picture shows tombstones of the EOKA dead in a setting glowing with the holy colours of martyrdom. EOKA is hardly even a veteran's association, for many who claim membership joined long after everything was over. The children of real EOKA fighters are endowed out of money Grivas makes from his memoirs with scholarships to study at Athens University. More than a hundred of them have benefitted so far, and he is now building a hostel for them. Here he is, after so much gunfire, so little achievement, like other old men in retirement, salvaging what he can from his souvenirs.

From his chair he looks across at a photograph of himself at Athens airport, arriving after the London agreement had abruptly cut short EOKA. There stands Grivas, still not changed out of his sweater and boots, small and passionate at the centre of thick, pressing crowds, and beside him are the chief of police and Averoff, Greek Foreign Minister at the time. Grivas is speaking through a microphone, but his right arm is thrown high in the gesture of conquest. It was, one realises, the one golden moment of triumph, when he was heroically alone, the mob around him, the future open: the moment he would have seized for good, fusing gun and microphone, had he known how.

The EOKA days must have been the happiest in his life, I say. Certainly they were. "The satisfaction was mixed with danger. Without danger you can't do anything. You have to take risks." What if you run risks and lose? "Don't let yourself be disillusioned." There have been attempts to murder him, principally the sabotage in mid-air in 1967 on an aeroplane which Grivas was thought to be taking on a regular flight from Athens to Nicosia. The 66 passengers died but nobody was arrested for the crime. Grivas has no idea who was responsible: "I am afraid of nobody."

194

Yet he lets himself go – baffled beyond endurance by the fanaticism in himself which he has been unable to resolve, but which others more agile than him have turned to their advantage. The London-Zurich agreements, he claims, were kept secret from him by Archbishop Makarios. In Athens he went to the army chief of staff's office for a copy of the text, then to the Foreign Office. They told him they knew nothing – as they were to do again after November 1967, when he wandered forlorn in the corridors of power.

"In 1964 Makarios was gripped with fear of the Turki (as Grivas always calls them). If you want an army, you stay out of this, we told him. As sure as I'm seeing you, we would have beaten the Turki. We would have taken reprisals, turning our artillery on their villages. But Makarios was only wanting a solution to leave him where he is. If he could be Prime Minister of England, he'd say yes."

The window shutters are closed. Coffee is served to us by Madame Elli Christodoulidou who turned her house in Limassol into the EOKA underground headquarters for Grivas. She has flown over to Athens because Madame Grivas is ill and needs nursing. The books of Mao Tse-tung and Guevara are next to studies of desert warfare and guerrilla tactics in a low cabinet. And Lawrence Durrell's *Bitter Lemons*. Grivas believes that telegrams of congratulations to him from Castro and Guevara were suppressed by Archbishop Makarios.

The Archbishop, he returns to the charge, cannot be criticised as head of state without insulting the church. According to convenience, he chooses which hat to wear. Grivas, a deeply religious man, cannot understand how the Cypriots let their Ethnarch get away with it. The church's fortune has to stay intact, a clause in the constitution guarantees it. "Go and look at the church's real estate if you want to understand Cyprus." His voice falls flat, but his energy is still apparent. "If you've worked for years for something and you see that all your efforts are destroyed by others, you are disgusted . . . I am disgusted by everything. They've spoiled so much for me." As he puts it and repeats it: "*Ils m'ont gaché beaucoup de choses.*"

He has his stamp collection, complete sets of every Greek and Cypriot issue, and now those commemorating the Olympic Games. A locked steel cupboard contains some of them, the rest are too valuable to be kept in the house. He opens the cupboard and shows me some sheets from his albums. On his desk lies a half-section of a hand-grenade presented to him by friends and next to it the two volume Yvert and Tellier international stamp catalogue. He has prepared for me a folder of stamps, including duplicates of some he has just received from Cyprus, showing President Kennedy and quoting a speech of his on self-determination for Cyprus. When you are tired, he advises me, it helps to pass stamps through your fingers. On the front page of the folder he signs his name, in a spiky up-and-down hand. When I try to thank him for all his generosity, the words will not come, not in that half-dark room with its forebodings of tragedy.

Grivas shakes my hand in both of his and walks with me down the flight of steps. Before the privet hedge, a magnolia stands bare in the front garden. Grigoriou pulls away in the Dodge and Grivas turns round briskly to hasten indoors. It has come on to rain: the Greek winter has begun.

Nicosia, like Athens, has a new airport. The main road into the city centre connects with Grivas-Dighenis Boulevard. Archbishop Makarios has also built a handsome stone palace just inside the Venetian walls. Standing next to it is the old palace, a few rooms of which have been given over to an EOKA museum, an assortment of photographs, clothing and mementoes. British police methods are particularly recorded.

Trikkomo is 45 minutes away across the plain, almost

Asiatic in its colouring and flatness. A thin blue and white post in the village proclaims a welcome to the birthplace of Grivas-Dighenis. The Grivas family house was sold by a cousin not long ago for £2,000 and pulled down and the site converted into three bungalow shops. The Church of St John, where Grivas's ideas were formed, is a Byzantine monument of the 11th century: a low entrance leads to a dark, suggestive interior. Nobody in the village cafés shows much interest at the mention of Grivas.

Returning to Nicosia down back roads, I have to pass through several Turkish enclaves, the barriers guarded by armed sentries and watched by United Nations soldiers who are mostly Scandinavian students on a bit of a spree. Careering UN jeep are an habitual traffic hazard. In the Turkish enclaves all the men are *mudjabit*, or conscript fighters. They are outnumbered by the Greek Cypriot National Guard whose officers still come under contract from mainland Greece.

Some Turkish areas have been abandoned to the Greeks. Omorphita, a quarter of Nicosia, consists of several hundred Turkish houses looted down to the door-frames. A few dogs stray in the ghost-streets. Refugees have been resettled in new housing thanks to subsidies of nearly £8 million a year from Turkey. The island's Greeks and Turks are now two separate, self-governing communities whose mutual suspicious are voiced in daily accusations and counter-accusations. Talks are held between Glafkos Clerides for the Greeks and Raouf Denktash for the Turks but for the moment this is more of a formality than a compromise.

"You've seen Grivas?" ask Greeks, Turks and UN officials alike. "Is he coming back?" They want to know because the extremist National Front declares its faithfulness to *Enosis* and to prove it throw bombs as if in some outdoor hobby. Former EOKA fighters are making their presence felt, and they look to Grivas. Some of them have found their way into the regular police force, where their patron was Mr Polykarpos Yorghadzis, for a long time the Minister of the Interior. (Those policemen who try to enforce law and order risk being murdered for their pains, and are naturally demoralised.) Implicated in an assassination attempt against members of the Greek Government, Mr Yorghadzis has been forced to resign. Private armies such as his, whether acknowledged or not, are a feature of Cyprus. Talk to Dr Lyssarides, for example, a deputy and the private doctor of Archbishop Makarios whose signed portrait is above his surgery desk, and you will hear how some scores of his friends got arms together ostensibly against the Turks but somehow do not disband. Two cabinet ministers and the chief of police have recently been shot, and the latter is unwilling to resume work. Obscure plots surround Archbishop Makarios: a bomb exploded in the courtyard of his new palace. The Archbishop declared publicly that he has the names of the criminals but his proceedings against them are cautious, indirect.

The Archbishop works in the Presidential Palace, to which he is driven early each morning in his Cadillac by his chauffeur, who is his brother. This building was erected after the previous Government House was burnt in the riots of 1931. A light blue helicopter waits in the grounds. At the end of a mock cloister are the swimming pool and disused tennis courts.

When he receives me in his office, Archbishop Makarios is informal and has laid aside his hat: I am made to feel at ease. A gold pen and a gold crucifix shine on his blue robes. I have had to prepare questions in advance and am handed typewritten answers which the Archbishop discusses without wasting words. He tells me that no comparison can be made between the so-called National Front and EOKA, however similar their views. He deplores the National Front. Their motives are personal not political, and they do not understand the harm they do. They will be controlled – "I am perhaps not a good policeman."

At the mention of Grivas, the Archbishop smiles, showing interest – an all-embracing deep crinkle of the face. His eyes seem to close. It is rather early to make any assessment either of Grivas or of EOKA, he thinks. In 1964 Prime Minister Papandreou had accepted Grivas's own suggestion that he command the Greek forces in Cyprus – the Archbishop did not invite Grivas. At critical moments, explains the Archbishop, Grivas would leave his post or ignore his instructions. He was also liable to see insults where none existed. "I was not personally in contact with him and don't know what he was told from Athens." Would Grivas like to be in Cyprus now, the Archbishop asks? I suggest that he would not be welcome. The Archbishop disagrees. "I don't care very much. When he was here in Cyprus, he tried to overthrow me but he could not. What was he proposing? To be president? If he had not come back to Cyprus, if he hadn't played politics, his prestige would be much higher."

In his view the 1967 event was most unsatisfactory and could have been avoided. "Some people thought that I was pleased that Grivas was removed. I didn't care. He was not a danger to me. *Enosis* cannot be achieved by slogans. The question is not whether we want it, the question is how." Nonetheless, one reflects, Grivas and the Turks ran each other out to leave the Archbishop undisputed master in his own house.

"I don't think Cyprus will become a Russian province," is his dismissal of Grivas's anxieties for the future. "The people are religious and as well they enjoy a high standard of living." Is the Russian Orthodox Church being persecuted, is it an instrument of state, he wonders? In Yugoslavia, the only socialist country he has visited, he conducted services in crowded churches. Turning to the Clerides-Denktash talks, he thinks some solution must evolve.

The Archbishop leans back in his chair. There has been an airport strike; today employers need protection just as trade unions do. Should students be sent to Communist or capitalist universities, in order either to reinforce or reverse their convictions? In a characteristic movement, the Archbishop shakes his head rapidly from side to side, as if juggling every possibility, looking round every corner for the traps. As he summarises these issues, slowly, elegantly, brilliantly, he lets fall an aside: "I consider my job as President temporary."

Opposite his desk is a carved stone relief of the Royal arms, lion and unicorn, *Dieu et mon Droit.* As the door opens to show me out and sunshine filters in down a long passage with a cedarwood ceiling, I draw attention to this survival. "Ah," the Archbishop says, "we don't destroy our history."

The Telegraph Sunday Magazine
March 13, 1970

Postscript: On the day my reportage was published, the Archbishop's helicopter was shot down and the pilot killed. At this level, foreknowledge of events explains coincidence. Afterwards on more than one occasion when I entered Greece for a holiday, a passport official would intimate that they knew all about me, and a customs officer would open my suitcase.

Samarkand

FEW PLACES HAVE the long-flung fierce appeal of Samarkand, city of Alexander the Great, Genghis Khan and Tamerlaine, and for whose possession Asiatic armies were sacrificed. In the 1860s a Hungarian, Armin Vambery, one of the greatest in that great age of travellers, had risked death to make his way there, disguised as a dervish from Turkey. He saw Samarkand in its final years of independence. "At last, on toiling up a hill, I beheld the city of Timour in the middle of a fine country. I must confess that the first impression produced by the domes and minarets, with their various colours, all bathed in the beams of the morning sun – the peculiarity, in short, of the whole scene – was very pleasing." In 1868 the Russians took it, losing two men in the assault and avenging the burning of Moscow by the Mongols.

We drive in from the airport. We have flown from Moscow over the flat green landscape, away across the Aral Sea, above the black sands of the Kara Kum. On the way we have spent a day at Tashkent, capital of the Socialist Republic of Uzbekistan. "Tourism, Passport to Peace," the message is framed on boards in the airport. Everywhere we have been met with a reception, and vodka and Georgian wines and *shampagn* have been lined up for us, the plastic corks popping up to the ceiling. For we are travelling as a group. More, we are an official group, most of whom think Leonid Brezhnev's policy of détente is a vision of money, and one or two who hope to study the KGB – alias Intourist – in action. In any case, the farthest reaches of Soviet Central Asia are to be made available to holders of hard currency.

Now at a level crossing a train passes lengthily, 56 travelling hours from Moscow, its coaches marked to Astrabad, Ferghana, Alma Ata, Dushanbe. The afternoon swelters but there are orchards between the clusters of houses on the outskirts, and they break the dust and heat. Vambery would hardly recognise Samarkand now; the old walls and fortifications have gone, without trace, to be replaced by Russian streets. Where these start, where the buses lurch at a crossroads, rises a gigantic billboard of Lenin in his brown tweed suit and hard collar. Uzbeks are squatting on their heels beneath it.

"These old clay houses will soon be knocked down," the guide says. "The new Intourist hotel will be finished when you're next here." Bulldozers are at work on building sites, rubble piles around small mosques, their fragile eggshell domes broken open. The Zerovshan, the one hotel in town, is Soviet old-fashioned, and it has a garden at the back where jasmine and bougainvillaea bloom. One English tourist is already there, a teacher travelling alone, perhaps the first of the packaged wave planned for the future.

Another Intourist guide arrives, an Uzbek girl wearing the modern version of the *khalat*, a shift cut down to a stripy nylon dress. She says that although she is a Muslim, her religion has no meaning for her, but she becomes touchy when questioned about it. A serious, even sombre, girl. We are taken to the Observatory of Uluk Beg, built in the early fifteenth century and excavated by a Tsarist professor. Although he was Tamerlaine's grandson, Uluk Beg is an approved Soviet hero because he was also a scientist far in advance of his time. Which means – it is explained to us – that in order to measure the heavens he had this stone sextant of his pushed up and down on its steep incline by his slaves. The sextant weighed a ton or two, and whenever it slipped, slaves were crushed to death by the score.

The Shah-I-Zindar is a street of mosques and tombs alongside one another, up a climbing stairway. Mosaics and majolica in the colours that caught Vambery's eye; large inset inscriptions from the Koran in an agile Sunni script; the thin arching doorways and minute tracery of the East. Occasionally a family of Uzbeks is wandering about and staring at its heritage, while here and there on stone benches a few elders sit in silence and stroke their beards as wise men should. The anti-Islam museum dates back to the years when every religion in the Soviet Union was under attack. The door is padlocked. The guide denies that the museum exists; then she says that it is being reorganised; finally that we are anyhow too late to visit.

The Samarkand market is much like the Old Town of Tashkent, but with a back-drop of the Bibi Khanum, an enormous and crumbling mosque built by Tamerlaine's widow, the blue ceramics of its dome glistening bright in the sky. Some aged Koreans, traditionally dressed, are survivors of cheap labour brought in by the Tsars. Through the crowd we slip away from the ever-present guides, for the pleasure of being alone, to wander off into hidden Samarkand where the houses are still made of mud and wattle, hardly more than walls around a courtyard. Women are baking flat bread in clay ovens or fetching water in pitchers from the local pump. Their hens are scattered. Men are sawing wood, or laying the foundations of a new house which will be in a more modern style, and they nod politely. They invite us to sit with them. Family beds, tables, chairs, pots and pans, are out under the vines which grow to shade the small courtyards.

Leaving down the dusty dry paths where refuse is running in a slow channel, we attract some scuffling children. And we are followed. When we stop, this man also stops. This must be the moment for the KGB hand on my shoulder –

my imagination leaps ahead. As we stare, this man comes across some open ground and then into the maze of tiny streets along which we turn bewilderingly to the right, to the left. He speaks German, he begins, because he'd been a long time in Germany, first as a prisoner, then as a labourer. Had we been here a few days ago when a missile division went though? A fine sight, apparently, though not the pastoral picture the Intourist guides liked to paint. This unexpected man offers hospitality in a crowded *chaikhana* where old men are reclining outside on iron bedsteads and sipping green tea as they always did. The young men, I gather, are praising England for her football team.

One of the Uzbeks stroking his beard is willing to show me the anti-religious museum. He pulls the doors back as far as the chain and padlock allow and I peer in at the exhibits and tableaux which are always there – for instance one of a Muslim being beheaded for laxity in his religious observance.

To return to the hotel, I manage to stop a car and get a lift. The driver turns out to be a Crimean Tartar. In the cool of the evening, he drives first to the Gur Emir, Tamerlaine's tomb. In spite of restoration, the limpid browns and green and blue and gold blend. We go on to the Registan Square, once the city's heart, a sixteenth century ensemble of three *medresseh* or religious colleges. Scaffolding is up to repair the tilted minarets and falling masonry of these buildings. There are still Uzbeks to do the work although the necessary skills and craft are in danger of extinction. A rose garden spreads across the wide square and among the flowers a man comes up, announcing that he is Russian, a sailor and drunk. "Geroin," he insists. (In Russian, the English *h* is turned into a *g*.) All Englishmen are drug addicts, he explains, the *New York Times* said so. His friends pull him away.

There is nowhere to eat except in the hotel. We are served

shashliks of the usual size but stuck on to a skewer two feet long. *Plov*, the local rice dish, is plenteous but suspiciously brown in colour. Salads are good and so is the wine from a winery on the edge of Samarkand. Afterwards we sit out, some thirty of us at one long table, under the trellis in the hotel garden. A three-piece band is playing American favourites of 15 years ago, but they pack up at 10.30 sharp – union hours, they say. I am one of the fortunate few in the Zerovshan who do not have to share a room, but there is no bath with it and the shower has been fitted 18 inches above the floor so I have to lie prone in order to use it. The rates for rooms are standard throughout the Soviet Union, and though there are three grades of hotel nothing (as far as I could see) is gained by paying for the higher of them.

Next day, a journey has been arranged to Pendjikent in Tadjikistan, the Soviet Republic on the Chinese Border, with a corner to Afghanistan. The road runs down the valley of the Zerovshan river between the Turkestan mountains and the first Pamirs, immense and snow-capped as they bulk ahead at the end of the long plain where the Asian horsemen once came riding. The air is silver-clean. The villages have quince and mulberry trees, and they have been collectivised. At one of them, Bagizan, the guide is persuaded to stop. Dogs bark and donkeys stand immobile under too top-heavy a load. Cactus has been grown as a fence. On her doorstep a mother is feeding her baby. She waves. In the fields the women and children at work are brilliant in their red *khalats*. Once they would all have been veiled.

An ancient site has just been excavated at Pendjikent and frescoes have been found. A track leads out there over the grass slopes of the mountains so clear-cut and high in the distance. A placard about the Vietnam war stands at the entrance to the site, a placard in Tadjik which like Uzbek is now written in Cyrillic script, a Soviet measure aimed to cut off the culture of the past.

Pendjikent itself has junipers and cypress groves, and acacias planted along its streets, a lake, the charm of a far-away province. But we have to leave, we are units of hurry in an unhurried place where turbaned men are making bricks by hand and women are hoeing as they always have done. Back at Samarkand airport, a send-off awaits us. Each man to his place with a line of glasses. *Shampagn*, vodka, once more the bottles are emptied. Toasts grow wilder, in Russian and in English. The airport manager is in the lead, his face reddening, his goodwill undoubted. When at last the aeroplane for Moscow takes off and swings on the turn northwards, climbing into the blue above Central Asia, the group suddenly falls silent as though aware at last how they had been manipulated.

The Daily Telegraph Magazine
February 12, 1971

THE ESSENTIAL TEST of reform in a communist country is the willingness of the Party to submit itself to the rule of law. So far, not one has done so irrevocably. Few have been so recalcitrant as the Czechoslovak Party. Under a special Soviet protection which was reinforced by the invasion in 1968, the Czech Party bosses have been accustomed throughout their careers to doing whatever serves their ambition, and enforcing it by police methods. The arrest, and trial this week, of Jan Carnogursky is the latest example of the lawlessness at the heart of communist rule.

The irony is that Carnogursky is a lawyer, and the Party's quarrel with him began some four years ago when he tried to defend dissidents according to the Party's own laws. For this, he was barred from practising, and has been unemployed for the last 18 months.

The real reason for such disregard of their own law is that Carnogursky is a Slovak and a Catholic – words which are practically synonymous – and on both scores a target for the Party's repression. As a lawyer, writer and activist, he has many friends and contacts, and earlier this year they reported that the Party was closing in on him. I saw for myself what this was like late in June, when I visited him in his home town in Bratislava.

In his diaries, Kafka describes a tram ride between Vienna and Bratislava, lasting half an hour, through fields and meadows. My journey by bus dragged on almost three hours, thanks to a search by Czech border guards, in which they unpacked the possessions of all the passengers. A high proportion seemed to be Sudetendeutsch, expelled after the war and now aching with nostalgia. The lady next to me was considering applying to settle in her native Bratislava on the grounds that even communism was preferable to the drug-addiction, crime and homosexuality of the Sydney which had taken her in after 1945.

Upon arrival, I shared a taxi with another Sudetendeutsch up to Dubravka, the suburb where Carnogursky lives in one of the many concrete rectangles of approved "socialist realist" housing. He is a thin, calm man in his mid-forties, with a jolly wife and four children rushing in and out. One of the girls was learning German at school, and soon I was drawn into her homework. I also gave Carnogursky paperbacks which earlier had been fingered by the border guards, a novel by L. P. Hartley, another by Iris Murdoch.

A book of mine, *The Closed Circle*, had just been published, and it had been agreed that I was to talk to perhaps a dozen of his friends about it. This book concerns the Arabs, and it argues that their legacy of tribalism and its supporting values has been strong enough to prevent the emergence of those social and political institutions necessary to genuine modernisation. Arab nationalism, in brief, has not worked. Hardly a hot topic in Bratislava, but according to Carnogursky no information of any kind about the Arab world is available outside Party media. I spoke of a Czech scholar who between the wars had recorded Bedouin poetry. No such person could exist today.

We arranged that he would pick me up at half past ten the following morning and do some sightseeing until it was time to meet his friends in the evening. The appointed time came and went. About an hour later I started to resent the two men opposite the hotel entrance apparently so deep in argument that they were rooted to the spot. Over two hours were to pass before the concierge gave me a message: "Our planned meeting will not take place." With the signature "John."

"John" seemed to me an authentic touch, as it were a confidential nod. I had long since understood that he was in trouble with the police; that "John" inhibited my instinct to return to his flat. Instead I visited the Palffy and Mirbach palaces, St Martin's church, the old streets.

Carnogursky was about 12 hours late by the time he arrived at the hotel, walking there as soon as he was released by the police. They had picked him up early, while he was visiting an office in the town centre. During the interrogation, they had mentioned the English writer and his lecture about the Arabs, revealing how he and I had been monitored. After some hours, he had persuaded the police to telephone his wife, who by then needed to know where the car was, as she had to fetch the children. That was also the moment when the police planted the false message on me, with its deceptive "John." Nobody else, as Carnogursky pointed out, could have done it; nobody else knew where he was.

We went for a late-night coffee. We would be under observation all the way, he said. What I should have done, he explained gently and without reproach, was to join his wife and friends, as agreed, and give the talk about the Arabs. Everyone's name would have been recorded by the secret police at the door, but no law had been broken, no consequences would follow beyond an entry in everyone's dossier.

Was he not afraid of being arrested? As composed as ever, he shook his head and replied that he kept strictly within the law. I couldn't have imagined, I said, that the police would play this trick on us, going to such lengths for nothing at all. "You've had an instruction in how we live" he answered.

On 14 August he signed a statement that Slovaks should

lay flowers at appropriate places to mark the 21st anniversary of the Soviet invasion of 1968. The Party bosses are pleased to call this "incitement" and "subversion," they label him a "clerical-fascist," and he faces a prison sentence of between three and ten years for it.

The Spectator
October 7, 1989

ILSE HESS has a certain representative look about her – thousands of German women in their seventies, that is to say, have similar strong faces on which make-up would always have seemed out of keeping; they have that same air of being sufficient in themselves, muscular in body and spirit. Seeing them, one cannot help thinking of what they have lived through, not only the rallies and the flags, of course, but the air raids and casualty telegrams, the collapse of home and hearth. For all German women the ordeal is over, the wounds have healed into scars – for all German women except Ilse Hess, whose husband Rudolf was Hitler's Deputy, sentenced at the Nuremberg trial to the life imprisonment which he continues to serve out in the Berlin jail of Spandau. She is the last woman left whose husband might still come home from the war.

Life for Frau Hess broke completely in half on May 10, 1941, the day her husband so amazingly abandoned his post to fly in a Messerschmitt to Scotland, with the hope, the illusion rather, that such a gesture would enable the British to come to their senses, rid themselves of Churchill and make peace with Germany. Several witnesses have testified to Hitler's rage when he heard of his Deputy having gone absent without leave. Something as politically and psychologically erratic as that was most certainly a Nazi setback. Frau Hess was left to take the blame and from that day she was a marked woman, plummeting in a fall from grace that matched her husband's. "I became *persona non gratissima*. Martin Bormann treated me very badly," Frau Hess says,

pointing her index fingers at one another to indicate dag-
gers drawn – the Martin Bormann whom she had known by
his nickname of *Vater Bo*, when he had been a junior on her
husband's staff, before he became Hitler's right-hand man.
"He was not big enough for the job Hitler entrusted to him.
Often powerful men have secretaries who let them down."

Until then the Hesses had been living in a pretty house
set behind trees in Harlaching, close to Munich. Photographs in an old leather folding frame are fetched to show
what the place which Hess left behind him had been like.
With her small son, Wolf-Rüdiger, then as now affectionately
known as Buz, she moved out, which was just as well as soon
afterwards the Harlaching house was destroyed by a bomb.
To be out of harm's way she came to the Allgäu Alps, to the
Ostrachstal, a valley between two towering ranges of rock,
where Germany, Austria and Switzerland rub shoulders.

As the road loops up to her tiny village of hardly a dozen
houses, the view opens and grows more and more majestic.
This is the kind of place which fits Germanic ideals of com-
muning with nature, with prospects for walking in summer
and skiing in the winter. The Hesses had first come here in
the days of their glory, in 1935, and decided that this should
be their mountain retreat. They negotiated with a Frau
Modersohn for her house, all of wood in the typical peasant
style, with a barn attached. Nothing came of it at the time.

During the remainder of the war Frau Hess rented
another house in the village and here Buz grew up and went
to school so that his German is broadened by the local
accent. For a while Frau Hess was interned by the Allies in a
camp for VIP wives at Goggingen. Then she earned her living by running a tea-room in her village, taking in guests as
well, doing the work more or less single-handed. "I had no
time to think about anything, I was working so hard." In the
Sixties Frau Modersohn at last decided to sell and Frau

Hess acquired a house which her husband had known. If ever Hess is released, it is here that he will come. A certain mute pride can be sensed in the village that celebrities have

come among them.

Modernisation has left intact much of the place's original character, the wooden beams on the ceiling, and the thick doors. For six years the guest house has been in abeyance due to Frau Hess's poor health, but in summer a few old friends are still taken in downstairs (no meals provided), so that the lower level of the house has a slightly spick-and-span impersonality. (The money that she managed to save during the years of running the guest house provides her income now, besides what her son can give, because she is not allowed to claim a pension.) The entrance and the dining room, what is more, form the Modersohn Galerie, for Frau Modersohn's son was an artist well known in the region and many of his landscape paintings have been left on the walls on permanent exhibition. Visitors will also notice a small upright display case of the books which Frau Hess and Buz have published separately at different times to draw attention to the rights and wrongs of the Hess case.

"What do you know about Alexander Simpson of Worksop?" is Frau Hess's opening question to me. Some kind of fortune teller, it seems, this man has just predicted in print that Hess will be released for his 82nd birthday on April 26th. Frau Hess wears an expression of willing belief, but Buz Hess dismisses such fantasies. A matter-of-fact man, with a direct intelligence, he is a civil engineer, trained in Munich and working for the time being in Hamburg. He likes sports and spends the sunshine hours of this weekend out on the ski slopes.

Both mother and son have acquired experience they could do without, of handling press publicity. With ability, they have conducted a long campaign. Buz Hess has been doing the rounds of Allied foreign offices, looking for ears prepared to listen, "It's like having a second career." he admits. To be his father's son, to have these particular sins visited on him, has been "a heavy burden." By and large, the Americans, the British and the French veer from indifference to sympathy, but would release Hess if the Russians would only consent. The four post-war occupying powers must vote unanimously on such an affair, and the Russians always veto any proposal of mercy, with that *niet* of theirs which has put its stamp on the world.

So counting the time he spent in England and on trial in Nuremberg, Hess has been a prisoner for 34 years. Doenitz, Raeder, von Neurath, von Shirach and Speer were sentenced with him to varying terms in Spandau, so that for his first two decades there he had the company of at least some of them. Since the departure of Baldur von Shirach and Albert Speer in 1966 having completed their 20-year sentences, Hess has been alone, in what amounts to solitary confinement. The huge 19th-century prison, complete with modern watch towers, is maintained for this single inmate under the eyes of officers and guards of the four occupying powers, rotating each month with every bureaucratic and military formality that could be devised for this tense little flash point of the Cold War – and at the expense of the Bonn government. This is a unique one-man Gulag maintained, at Russian insistence, on Western territory. In the France of Louis XIV a mystery prisoner was secreted for his lifetime on an island off the coast at Hyères, a legendary victim referred to as The Man in the Iron Mask. Hess is that man in a new guise.

In old age Hess has mellowed. Although members of his family were allowed the regulation monthly visit, Hess had always refused to meet them, on the grounds that it would have been dishonourable all round. As a result, Frau Hess says, he had grown over-suspicious, shut in on himself, ill. When at last he was admitted for treatment in the British military hospital in Berlin – a move which the Russians resisted until his life was in danger – a turning point was reached. The kindness and skill of the doctors and nurses convinced him that human trust need not be forfeit, and at Christmas 1968, at last he broke the spell and received his wife and son and has been doing so regularly since.

Warders supervise these half-hour meetings. Frau Hess says, "The time is very short but also very long. In his last letter he teased me that he was amazed how quickly I talked, and how many subjects I could cram into these moments. You are afraid of a dead minute. Then the guard says five minutes to go, four minutes and so on, there is a count-down. My husband can still get angry and tell the man not to bother with it, and that's a good sign."

So each month Frau Hess prepared the topics for 30 minutes of conversation. Nothing political, nothing about his career, is permitted. Hess is interested in questions of technology and science; a paper on the new mathematics has been put by for him next time; also a paper by a life-long friend, a professor, on the outlook for the world's food. Books he asks for have to be censored, to satisfy the Spandau authorities, which involves Frau Hess in a mass of reading. Robert Lekachmann's analysis of Keynes is his latest request, and there in the index is a single fatal reference to Hitler. Frau Hess has to cut it out. Many details of these dreary years of waiting and prison-visiting are similarly absurd and touching, but Frau Hess does not want them repeated. "My husband might suffer." *Mein Mann*, in German, sounds far more close and elemental than its translation into *husband*.

Not that it can go on this way for much longer. This is what I came to Frau Hess to talk about, but it is difficult, then and there in her quiet sitting room, in the presence of her son, to lean forward and ask what will happen if or when Hess dies in prison.

More than that, I have heard from what is convention-ally described as a reliable source, that the Four Powers are quarrelling in Spandau at the top of their voices on this very question. For if Hess does die in prison what is to be done with his corpse? Those who were hanged at Nuremberg were cremated and their ashes were scattered over a country lane in Bavaria (or according to another version, thrown into the River Isar), the purpose being to avoid any possible future reliquary or memorial round which Nazism could once again gather. Are the Allies, that is to say *us*, to be party to something of the kind with Hess one of these days?

If he were to be buried inside Spandau prison, clearly he would have made some claim on an official site, which is exactly what the Russians do not want. What if the body were to be given back to Frau Hess for burial? Would she then create a shrine for him, thereby providing the one and only monument of its kind, in its way an emblem? For Ger-many may be searched high and low and nothing public, no work of art, neither statue nor ornament, not even a com-memorative tablet, exists to remind the present of the Third Reich. Eagles and swastikas and such-like were naturally smashed as soon as possible. Only a few empty niches and alcoves on the facades of rare surviving buildings symbolise the way the Third Reich was to be stripped out of history.

Frau Hess is shocked when I explain all this to her. She is silent, she turns to Buz, who says, "Perhaps it's right, we must think of these things." At first she limits herself to the thought that he *must* be released before his death and then the problem would be released with him. "The English can find a way to end this situation, they have international obligations, for they handed my husband over to Nurem-berg in the first place." All British governments, one after another, write a little note every so often to the Russians, and leave it at that. Nobody is anxious to stick his neck out on behalf of a man who, had he stayed in Germany and never flown to Britain, in all likelihood would have been hanged as a war criminal.

Well, it would be possible to bury him here in this small village away in the Alps, but provisions to do so have not been made. And if he were to be cremated like the others instead, swept under the carpet so to speak, dust to dust and ashes to ashes without physical trace? "That would be barbaric, something out of the Dark Ages." There would be too great a scandal, even the Bonn government might find a voice. These dead-ends stare everyone in the face.

"Maybe the Modersohn Galerie one day will become the Hess Galerie" I put in, just for the effect, and the idea is resonant enough for Frau Hess to return to it the following morning with good humour. The household wakes early. Purzel, the dachshund, barks at the door. Outside my bedroom, one where the summer guests can stay, the sun rises in brilliance, it floods the mountain tops dispelling the gruesome speculation of the previous evening. Frau Hess is energetic, she does not give the impression that the extraordinary isolation of her plight has pushed her into the margin of life. She is also prepared to recall the past (although Buz has warned me in an aside that this disturbs her).

As Ilse Prögel, in her maiden name, she campaigned for the Nazis when they were a dim nationalistic faction brawling in Munich. The number on her original card was extremely low, which was something chic in the Third Reich. Hess was in on the humble beginnings of Hitler's political career; he took part in the abortive putsch of 1923 and was imprisoned with him in the Landsberg fortress, where he had some secretarial role (exactly how much is debated) in drafting the manuscript of *Mein Kampf*. Shades of the prison house closed upon him even then. The Hesses were married in 1927. "My husband was always close to Hitler, he liked him. He told Hitler what he thought, even if Hitler did not want to hear."

Somewhere in the house she has letters and postcards from Hitler, she says. Not many. I also get her to show me her copy of *Mein Kampf*, the first edition bound in vellum and Number 4 in a limited run of 500 which were specially printed. There in Hitler's scratchy hand is the dedication to his companion in prison – a little tribute which turned out more like a prophecy. Next to it on the shelf are *The Collected Works of Frederick the Great*, in 14 large volumes, bound in red morocco, and given by Hitler as a Christmas present in 1935, again with a warm inscription. Also an anthology bound in vellum again, of Hitler's speeches presented by the editor, Julius Streicher (Gauleiter of Nuremberg, where he was hanged) to Hess on his birthday in 1939. The speeches of Goering. Photograph collections published to glorify the annual Nazi party rallies. A copy of a book eulogising Hitler in French, its binding decorated with swastikas. Some war-time propaganda against England (not that similar English pamphleteering bears scrutiny today). Here, in short, are the remains of a library assembled in the Third Reich.

As for letters and papers, they are upstairs with more books. If there was anything more to be discovered about the origins of Nazism, it might be in this unexplored archive.

The chests are in a terrible mess all over the house. We have private papers, not sorted out, not looked through. After 1941 I brought it all here from Harlaching, with other things – for instance, that piano over there was my husband's. Official papers were captured, these are only personal. I'm keeping them all for my husband. All these years I thought that my husband could write a book and

I could help him. All our film was saved, there are a few
thousand negatives going right back to early days. My
husband always carried his camera with him.

That life, so close really and yet so absolutely remote,
comes into the mind's eye like a snapshot when she tells stories, for instance, how once she took Goebbels to task for
the way his ministry had filmed a novel of Hamsun's and
ruined it. She cannot understand how Frau Goering was able
to stomach living in Karinhall with the memory of the first
wife all around. Nor for that matter, how Eva Braun could
put up with Hitler's maudlin adoration of Geli Raubel, his
niece who shot herself. Hess found the body. Somewhere
upstairs is a red album with photos of Geli, "historically
important," Frau Hess says, and wanders off to dig it out,
with no success, and the thought that it might be lost nags
her for the rest of the morning. Instead she brings down a
pastel portrait of Hess done in 1932 for Buz to take a photograph of it because a man from Spanish television needs
some illustrations for a programme.

"No Galerie Hess here, I could never do that," she repeats.
Hess's memory, it seems, is good. "My only wish is to talk to
him before his death and know how he thinks. Nobody
knows really how he thinks. A huge willpower must be in
him, nobody knows either how he keeps going." She also
assures me that Hess certainly knows nothing of *Barbarossa*,
the codeword for the German attack against Russia which
occurred six weeks after his flight, and has always aroused
Russian suspicions that he came to make an underhand
pact with England on the lines of the underhand pact the
Russians themselves had made with Hitler in August 1939.
"On May 6, five days before the flight, he had seen Hitler for
a *tête-à-tête* lasting over two hours. The SS outside the door
later told me that they had heard shouting and then quiet,

and when my husband came out, Hitler had his arm round his shoulders. What did they speak about? Only my husband can say, and he won't write anything unless he can check it in a library."

"We don't lose hope. I hoped for his release for his 80th birthday, and to be honest I felt really ill afterwards. I had set myself that date as a goal. One has hope and the understanding of hopelessness."

Hess, one realises, must have become the final living example of Nazism to the Russians, and they want revenge to the bitter end – pardon him, and they might appear to be pardoning all their enemies, and that would never do. As a result, the Russians have ensured that the disposal of Hess's mortal remains in one way or another will be a piece of macabre last-minute body-snatching. His drawn-out life-in-death has brought about this issue, and the needless consequence is that the issue will stay alive after he is dead.

The Daily Telegraph Magazine
April 18, 1975

Kurt Waldheim was one of the most despicable – and most despised – public figures in the West since 1945. His whole career was an exercise in craft and evasion. As secretary general of the United Nations from 1972 to 1982, he helped to put in place the standard approach of that body, which is above all to blame the United States for the world's ills, and therefore to obstruct its foreign policy. He and the Soviet Union, needless to say, were mutually supportive in that critical stage of the Cold War. Under him too, the U.N. discovered that anti-Israeli agitation served to broaden the attack on the United States. In 1975, he did nothing to oppose the resolution that "Zionism is racism." The following year, the Israelis rescued passengers on an aircraft hijacked to Entebbe, in Uganda. For Waldheim, this famous blow for freedom was "a serious violation of the national sovereignty of a United Nations member state." Leaving office, he purloined a large amount of silver that he himself had commissioned for the U.N. Now that he has died at the age of 88, these stolen goods must form part of his estate. The shamelessness is characteristic.

From 1986 to 1992, he was the president of Austria. Perhaps the Austrians applauded a statesman with an international reputation; perhaps they approved of his record; and perhaps they appreciated that he was anti-Jewish like they were, and of two minds about Hitler. They knew that in a time of glory they had been enthusiastic supporters of Hitler, but now in a time of loss they liked to deceive themselves that on the contrary they were his early victims. The election of Waldheim squared the circle, sparing Austrians any residual guilt they might have felt about their Nazism and anti-Semitism.

Fatally for the self-image of victimization, however, the truth was emerging that Waldheim was almost certainly a war criminal but refused to answer for it. To their credit, Austrian journalists like the indefatigable Hubertus Czernin were the first to probe. By 1987, the U.S. Department of Justice had enough evidence to place Waldheim on a list of persons denied entry to the country. He therefore found himself unable to attend the celebration in New York of the U.N.'s 50th anniversary. Other countries followed suit. Austrians soon found themselves represented by a president so ostracized that he could hardly travel abroad, and whom virtually nobody visited. His disgrace, his shamelessness was also Austria's.

In interviews and autobiographical books, Waldheim had always maintained that he had not been a Nazi and had played a minimal part in the war. He was dissembling, and – what must have added to his confidence – getting away with it. Ambition made him a natural opportunist. The child of a school inspector, he was born in a village near Vienna in 1918, as the Habsburg Empire was falling apart. Originally the family name was Watzlawik, but the change to Waldheim Germanized Czech origins that would have proved unhelpful in the Nazi era. At the time of Hitler's invasion and annexation of Austria, Waldheim was a law student in Vienna. Three weeks after the annexation, he joined the Nazi Student Union, an affiliate of the Nazi party. At the time of Kristallnacht in November 1938, the Nazis burned 42 of the 43 Viennese synagogues and one week later Waldheim joined the Sturmabteilung, the S.A. or Brownshirts. In 1941, he was sent to the Russian front. Lightly wounded in the ankle, he was brought back home to Vienna, and liked to

pretend that he had spent the rest of the war there complet-
ing his law studies. This lie conditioned everything that
followed.

222   In reality, Waldheim was posted for three years as an
intelligence officer in the Balkans. Officially, he was a translator, an interpreter, and a "special-missions staff officer."
This involved verifying and transmitting orders and making
his own recommendations. Anyone in his position could not
avoid being fully informed about the course of local events.
He served on the staff of two particularly brutal generals:
Friedrich Stahl and Alexander Loehr, another Austrian,
whose specialty was the execution of hostages, for which he
was hanged in 1947. In what was known as Operation Kozara,
and much feared at the time, the Germans and their Croat
allies, the Ustashe, rounded up tens of thousands of partisans, mostly Serb Chetniks under the command of Tito.
Waldheim was quartered close to Jasenovac, the concentration camp where these Serbs were killed. Ante Pavelic, the
Croat dictator commanding the Ustashe, rewarded Waldheim for his work with the Order of Zvonimir, enhanced by
oak-leaf clusters, in the citation praising his "courage in
battle." Waldheim's last posting under General Loehr was to
Arsakli on the outskirts of Salonika, at a moment when
50,000 or so of the Jews living only a mile or two away were
being deported to their death in Auschwitz and Bergen-
Belsen.

     At the end of the war, Waldheim was interned with other
prominent Nazis. He duly became Case No. R/N/684 in the
United Nations War Crimes Commission dossiers, charged
with "murder" and "putting hostages to death." The Yugoslavs wanted his arrest and extradition. The commission
was dissolved as early as 1948, and the case against Waldheim disappeared into thin air. In the cozy Austrian man-

ner, friends pushed him into the foreign ministry and made a diplomat of him. He rose fast, as a delegate to the U.N., an ambassador, director general of political affairs and in 1968 finally foreign minister. That year Soviet tanks crushed the Prague Spring and Waldheim gave orders that the Austrian embassy close its doors to any Czechs seeking refuge or visas to leave – a favor to the Soviets, and all the more unexpected in someone whose original name had been Watzlawik.

An invisible process of lobbying governs the choice of the U.N. secretary general. In 1971 the United States' candidate was Max Jakobson, who was Finnish and Jewish. The Soviet Union was trying to extend its hold on the Middle East by backing Arab nationalism, and Jakobson was therefore unacceptable. Yugoslavia had broken with the Soviet Union by then, but now joined with it in pushing Waldheim as their candidate. So unusual was this démarche that commentators regularly wonder whether both countries had incriminating material on Waldheim – blackmail might explain his readiness to give in to the Communists and their bloc in the Third World. Tito awarded him the Order of the Grand Cross of Yugoslavia. The symbolism was perfect: Waldheim had been decorated by the Fascists and the Communists in the same country.

As his record came more and more into question, Waldheim resorted to the standard Nazi apologia which goes like this: I was never a Nazi; and if I was, then I did nothing bad; and if I did do something bad, then it was someone else's fault. He had never been to Kozara, he began by claiming, and had never heard of any operation there, nor about mass murder at Jasenovac. He was one of only 30 Germans to receive the Zvonimir medal, but said he could not remember what he had done for it, and in any case it had been handed out "like chocolates." As for the fate of the Salonika Jews,

"I never heard or learned anything of this while I was there."

The World Jewish Congress, Prof. F. H. Hinsley (the foremost authority on British intelligence), a team set up by the Austrian government, the talented writer Shirley Hazzard – all are among those who have attempted to establish the degree of Waldheim's war guilt. And all concur that Waldheim had been lying to cover his tracks: An intelligence officer in his position could not conceivably be as ignorant as he pretended to be. In an authoritative study, Prof. Robert Herzstein of the University of South Carolina went further, to conclude that Waldheim was "an efficient and effective cog in the machinery of genocide."

Nobody has yet come closer to proving Waldheim's complicity in crime than C. M. Woodhouse. In his early twenties he was the youngest colonel in the British army and head of the Allied military mission to Greece in 1943. One of the officers under his command, Captain Warren, was captured, interrogated by Waldheim at Arsakli, and then summarily executed. Waldheim drafted a summary and commentary on the interrogation, falsely depicting Warren as a saboteur, and this crucial document with his signature on it is in Washington. In a long article in 1988, Woodhouse explained that much of this document is illegible, inexplicably having "suffered massive deletions with a brush-tipped pen." (Does technology now permit the reading of these deletions? one may ask.) Woodhouse always believed that evidence would come to light one day substantiating that Waldheim was responsible at the very least for the illegal shooting of a British prisoner of war.

Why the prevarication, why the lying? Evidently because it paid off. Case No. R/N/684 moldered in some storehouse, and nobody appeared to examine it or to care. So this unsavory character took his chances to distort the purposes and practices of the United Nations, passing off his innate flaws on to the organization that above all should have exposed him. So Austrians rallied around him because they knew he really and truly was one of their own, and if he could succeed by making his Nazi past invisible, so could they. It is a 20th century story, a parable of its time.

225

National Review
July 9, 2007

Hitler and women – it was a prime topic in the years leading up to 1939. Women, it seemed, longed to immolate themselves before the man. Hitler's appearances in public, even when impromptu, generated an atmosphere of prurient sexuality. Women would scream themselves hoarse, panting, even fainting, for an approach to him. Power is a curious aphrodisiac, and perhaps the effect was heightened in this case by Hitler's evident inadequacies or deficiencies. What was this ill-featured and middle-aged bachelor up to? Commentators tried to link him to the very few women he saw at all often. There never was anything to it. Hitler used to complain that he brought women bad luck. His exact relationship to his niece Geli remains to be cleared up, but he was thoroughly upset when she shot herself in 1931 at the age of 23. Eva Braun, assistant to his official photographer Heinrich Hoffmann, came into his life soon after that. In November 1932, pining for him, Eva Braun also tried to shoot herself but botched it. Hitler felt responsible, and thereafter she had him hooked, though she was kept out of sight at his mountain home of Berchtesgaden.

In its issue of April 7, 1938, *Ken*, a short-lived American magazine, published an article, "Hitler Hunts A Wife." Among several contenders named, besides Eva Braun, was Unity Mitford. Three weeks later this was denied by Unity's father, Lord Redesdale. "There is not, nor has there ever been, any question of engagement between my daughter and Herr Hitler." Of course, this did a great deal to spread the rumor. The public at large scarcely had heard either of Unity or her family.

Lord and Lady Redesdale might have been invented by P.G. Wodehouse. Connoisseurs of English Edwardian eccentricity relish them, and have been given every detail, and much more besides, in the recent memoirs of Nancy and Jessica Mitford, two of the six Redesdale daughters who all became famous one way or another. Lord Redesdale cared for little besides the House of Lords, skating and shooting. Lady Redesdale believed in what she called "the Good Body," maintained by the dietary laws of the Old Testament and unpasteurized milk. Were it not for their children, this innocent-minded couple should have departed the earth, in the fullness of time, with nobody much the wiser that they had ever graced it.

Unity Valkyrie was their fourth daughter, born in August 1914, three years older than Jessica, four years younger than her sister Diana, five years younger than her one brother, Tom. Her names later acquired a prophetic ring, and Unity affected the German spelling *Walküre*, but her mother merely had admired an actress of the day called Unity Moore, while her grandfather, the first Lord Redesdale, a diplomat, had apparently foisted the name Valkyrie onto the baby under the impression that these war-maidens were Scandinavian.

Even by British upper-class standards, Unity's childhood was sheltered. She reacted to it by being naughty, which invited punishment, and that made her naughtier still. This spiral she never managed to break, although in the end it led to self-destruction. Her education, mainly by her mother and a series of put-upon governesses, was pitiful. Two schools, in quick succession, expelled her for total disregard of the rules.

It was difficult in 1932 to enroll with the Bright Young Things, as Unity was supposed to in the wake of Nancy and Diana, both by then established members known for their looks and personalities. The Depression and the coalition government that emerged from it challenged the old order. How was inherited privilege like Unity's to be justified in the face of unemployment and hunger marches? The failure of purpose throughout the governing class was despicable to anyone with a spark of feeling. A section of that generation brought up to peer at the world through country-house windows – Kim Philby, Guy Burgess, Donald Maclean – suffered arrested development because of this urge to turn against themselves and their background. Unity's guilt feelings and desire to escape were similar to theirs but followed the opposite political course, in the wake of her sister Diana, who went off that summer with Sir Oswald Mosley and married him four years later.

Mosley ostensibly had been born to command. He had inherited his baronetcy and a fortune. After the first war, he was elected to Parliament as a conservative, but crossed the floor, and ended up a junior minister in the Labour government of 1929. When his proposals for dealing with the slump failed to become policy, he resigned, he visited Mussolini, and by the autumn of 1932 he had recruited a party of his own, the blackshirts or British Union of Fascists. Mosley's attempt to scrap parliamentary tradition and take to the streets was unprecedented in Britain and proved to be a dead-end. But to Unity it looked like a mass movement which she could join at the top, ridding herself of guilt but keeping privilege. With Mosley and Diana as her leaders, she had great expectations. At the end of August 1933 she went with the official BUF delegation to the first Nuremberg rally to be held after the Nazis seized power. Hitler was in his element, and so was Unity. "The moment I saw him I knew there was no one I would rather meet." So Unity was quoted in a newspaper soon after her return from Germany.

Sixteen more months passed before her wish came true. In that time she lived in Munich, in a finishing school, then in the student hostel of the university. Day after day, she stood on street corners hoping for a glimpse of her Friend, as she referred to Hitler in her letters. She discovered that he was in the habit of lunching with his cronies at the Osteria Bavaria (a restaurant that still exists), so she positioned herself at another table where she could not avoid being noticed. Hitler eventually grew curious and invited her to join him. The classic pick-up gambit had worked.

At the student hostel Unity made friends with another English girl, Mary, whom I was lucky enough to trace. She later married a German, suffered for it and gave me her diaries on condition that her surname be omitted from my writings about Unity. From these diaries we know the exact date of Unity's breakthrough. February 9, 1935 was a Saturday and Mary had been away for the weekend. She returned to hear the news: "Hitler sent for Unity on Saturday and she had lunch at his table – thrilled to death, of course."

For a while afterward Unity and Mary had rooms in a pension near the university. Unity would sit trembling by the telephone in case she was summoned by an adjutant. Then an official Mercedes would arrive to whisk the girls off to tea with Hitler in the Prinzregentenstrasse apartment where he felt more at home than anywhere else. He was politeness itself, according to Mary. On the theme closest to Unity's heart, he would declare only that he was wedded to Germany.

Unity was also received in the Berlin Chancellery. She accompanied Hitler to the opera. She went to the Bayreuth festival (and once returned from it on Hitler's private train, with Mary too). And she never missed one of the monster Nuremberg rallies. She was tantalizingly close to Hitler, close enough for Eva Braun to complain jealously in her diary about "the English Valkyrie." But only very occasionally were the two of them alone together, always to the consternation of his staff, who to a man distrusted her. There is no doubt that Unity was in love with him. He was flattered by the attentions of this blonde in her early twenties and appreciated the way she restrained herself from displays of hysterical hero worship in his presence. Presuming that she had social influence, he also used her to spread rumors and news convenient to him. What she repeated from their talks found its way either through journalists into the newspapers, or through British diplomats into the Foreign Office.

Nazism to her was a simple cause, to be promoted by example alone. As her one-sided crush on Hitler proved more and more frustrating, her only recourse was to violence. Back in England she became a brawler, she marched, she demonstrated. The infamous Julius Streicher, Gauleiter of Nuremberg and publisher of the anti-semitic *Der Stürmer*, realized Unity's propaganda potential and arranged for her to address a Nazi midsummer rally and to write to his paper, "I want everyone to know that I am a Jew-hater." Her Friend might be attracted by her self-sacrifice. More or less on her own initiative, she taunted a huge crowd at a Save Spain meeting in central London by giving a fascist salute, and almost was lynched for it. At a moment of international tension she drove from Munich into Czechoslovakia and got herself arrested, the kind of phony incident that the Nazis hurried to capitalize on.

In the summer of 1939, Hitler arranged for Unity to be set up in a flat in Munich. A Jewish family was evicted to make way for her, which she accepted without qualms. But Hitler also had betrayed her, knowing by then that the attack on Poland was in preparation and Unity would have to either make a run for it as war broke out or stay as a traitor. Like other women personally involved with Hitler, she chose suicide as the way out. On September 3, as the British ultimatum to Germany expired, she put a bullet into her brain, but failed to kill herself. Hitler arranged for her journey back to England, where she remained an invalid until her death in 1948.

In herself, Unity was a woman of no importance. She mattered only as a collaborator. She and Hitler liked to draw up lists of who would have done the dirty work in the event of a successful German invasion of England. As a matter of fact, official lists exist in the archives, which, if published, would create resounding scandals. For example, Walter Schellenberg, in charge of foreign subversion and intelligence, was debriefed after capture by the English in the summer of 1945. He was not a reliable man at the best of times, but supposedly he spilled the names of his English contacts, overt and covert. The embargo on papers lasts for 30 years so this file ought to have been made available in 1975. But the Cabinet Office will not, and perhaps never will, release it. The suspicion must remain that prominent figures are implicated in it.

Unity at least was out in the open and made no secret of the fact that she hoped England and Germany together would rule the world. A significant section of society agreed with her, if more discreetly. For the most part they were conservatives with a concern for property. Year after year the same fellow travelers of Nazism turned up at the Nuremberg rallies and saw in those marching columns their bulwark against Bolshevism. There were members of Parliament like Sir Arnold Wilson, Sir Frank Sanderson, Lord Apsley, Sir Thomas Moore; and there were peers like Lord Glasgow and Lord Eltisley, Lord Brocket and Lord Mount Temple and Lord Allen of Hurtwood; and tycoons like Sir Frank Newnes. Well-connected people were continually touring the Third

Reich during the 1930s. They were received by Hitler, and left enthusing. There were dupes like Lord Rothermere, the press baron, and Viscountess Snowden, widow of the former Labour chancellor of the exchequer. There were boobies like Henry "Chips" Channon, also an MP, who loved the parties thrown by Goering and Goebbels. Lord Londonderry, a former minister of air, even after Munich advocated on the cover of his book about Germany, a Penguin special, that "we should adopt a policy of Friendship with Hitler and a better understanding of Germany's Aims."

Among Hitler's catches was the Duke of Windsor. Hitler, at least, thought so. The Public Record Office has a report by the British consul in Munich of a conversation which the consul had with Unity on September 7, 1937. They bumped into each other at the railroad station, where both had gone to greet the Duke and Duchess of Windsor. By coincidence Mussolini also was in Germany then, on a state visit. Taking her cue from Hitler, Unity was upset by the abdication, and was at the station proving her loyalty. Three days beforehand, Unity told the consul, she had been having tea with Hitler and she reported that he had said, "If Mr. Baldwin had not turned out King Edward VIII I might have been receiving him today instead of Mussolini."

Frances Donaldson, in her judicious book *Edward VIII*, has weighed the evidence about the Duke's dealings with Germany. It was not only a question of staying with Hitler at Berchtesgaden, and wildly blabbing appreciation for him and his policies (an appreciation that apparently remained unshaken for the rest of the Duke's life). After the war started, the Duke left France for Lisbon, and there the dubious Walter Schellenberg arrived. Other clandestine contacts were opened. The Duke's Portuguese host acted as emissary between him and the German ambassador in Lisbon, and through him with Ribbentrop in Berlin. Two weeks after leaving Lisbon to become governor of the Bahamas, the war-time post where he could be no danger to anyone, the Duke was still in communication with the Germans through his Portuguese emissary. "There is no doubt," Frances Donald- son sums up, "that his actions would have earned fierce reprisals in the atmosphere of, for instance, the French Resistance."

As late as August 31, 1942, Hitler in his *Table Talk* can be found mourning the Duke of Windsor's abdication: "To topple over so fine a pillar of strength was both wicked and foolish." But then Hitler was cherishing illusions of a collab- orationist England along the lines Unity had sketched with him. On January 27, 1942 with Himmler as a guest, he said, "If Samuel Hoare were to come to power today as is desirable, all he'd have to do would be to set free the Fascists .... Men like Mosley would have no difficulty in solving the problem, by finding a compromise between Conservatism and Social- ism, by opening the road to the masses but without depriv- ing the elite of their rights." Some in England also thought that Sir Samuel Hoare, a foreign secretary under Baldwin and home secretary under Chamberlain, might play such a role. In his diaries Sir Alexander Cadogan, permanent under- secretary at the Foreign Office, pins the label "Quisling" directly onto Hoare.

Until well into the war Hitler continued to toy with the possibility that Mosley and the British fascists might be useful instruments. The fascist movement endorsed every single one of his conquests, from the occupation of the Rhineland to the dismemberment of Czechoslovakia and the attack on Poland. It continued to agitate against fight- ing Hitler right up to the moment of its suppression at the end of May 1940 during the German blitzkrieg on France.

The membership of the BUF never has been properly established, but 100,000 is a reasonable estimate of the number of subscribers over the seven years of its existence. At most a third of these might have been active collaborators in the event of a German landing. How many actually did commit treason by volunteering with the Nazis on the continent is disputed, but it was only a handful. Several had been Mosleyites. The most notorious traitor of all, William Joyce, the broadcaster Lord Haw-Haw, had been a Mosleyite spokesman until 1937, and had been a BUF delegate to Nuremberg in 1933 with Unity.

Behind the fascists were several pro-Nazi pressure groups, such as *The Link* with a membership of 4,322. Its chairman, Admiral Sir Barry Domville, a former chief of naval intelligence, spent the war in prison, like Mosley. At its head were Professor A. P. Laurie, Professor Sir Raymond Beazley, C. E. Carroll, Lord Sempill, and Unity's father, Lord Redesdale, who lost no chance to praise Hitler in the House of Lords. The Anglo-German Fellowship, sponsored by the German Embassy, was larger and rather more genteel, aiming to persuade opinion-makers of the need to surrender to Hitler's demands. It disbanded early in the war.

Appeasers of course were of all sorts. Some admired Germany's military might and others were panicked by it. Lloyd George, for instance, prime minister in the first war and a keen visitor to Berchtesgaden afterward, argued that England ought gratefully to grab whatever terms were available before defeat became a certainty. In his excellent book on the Polish campaign, *The War Hitler Won*, Nicholas Bethell has described one of many backstairs initiatives intended to help Britain sidle out of a confrontation and into an alliance with Hitler. The Duke of Westminster was one of the richest men in the country. The war was just a week old when "he assembled an impressively titled group and read them a pro-Nazi memorandum." Among his audience were Lord Arnold, Lord Rushcliffe and the Duke of Buccleuch, all of whom were known to favor good relations with Nazi Germany. The Left and the Jews were apparently to blame for wanting Nazism to be destroyed. The Duke's manifesto poured scorn on "the parrot-cry that Nazism as exemplified by Hitler and his entourage is an obscenity so hideous that the world cannot resume its ways of liberty and quiet living until it is destroyed." Nicholas Bethell concludes, "It is terrifying to speculate about what would have been their attitude if Hitler had ever gained control over the British Isles."

Nor was it necessary to be a peer of the realm to have this attitude. After a lifetime of sneering at democracy, Bernard Shaw reached climax with an article in the *New Statesman* of October 7, 1939, before the German guns in Poland had cooled. Hitler, he wrote, ought to be supported in his aims. "Our business now is to make peace with him and with all the world instead of making more mischief and ruining our people in the process."

Support for Hitler in England was wide enough and influential enough for the German leadership to believe that peace and cooperation would be welcomed and accepted, if it were not for the obstructive Churchill, his clique of friends, and the Jews. Hitler himself believed that the English would prove true to their racial origins and make common cause with their Nordic brothers. Unity, the one English person whom he admitted regularly to his inner circle, had always told him that this was so, thereby confirming what he wanted to hear. Hitler's deputy, Rudolf Hess, who also dabbled in racial geopolitics, dramatized the idea when he flew clandestinely to Scotland on May 10, 1941, to contact the Duke of Hamilton, and to appeal through him to what he was sure was a public longing to endorse Germany's New

Order. It was not so bizarre a move. Had he timed it before the Battle of Britain, he might have split the ruling class right down the middle.

236   Hitler continued to seek the key to an England that he felt was being suppressed against its instincts. If the war was to be waged successfully, some suppression of pro-Hitlerite opinion was an urgent priority, but it remains a taboo subject to this day. Those who compromised themselves by appeasing or defending Nazism, and even those who saw it not as a mortal danger but as salvation, were let off lightly afterward. The record shows that in numbers and social position they were not negligible. Unity Mitford was a cheerleader: she would have been standing on the steps of Downing Street waving a swastika at the incoming Reichskommissar. She was not the first, nor the last, to embrace hatred and call it patriotism. She was a flagrant example of the type that could not be trusted in the crunch. For although it was the country's finest hour, a quite different state had also been there for the making, furnished with a tainted ex-monarch, a fully fledged fascist movement, plenty of immoral aristocrats and a few corrupted politicians and intellectuals: altogether a Quisling state in embryo.

The New Republic
May 14, 1977

IN THE AFTERMATH OF World War II, a tide of nationalism
swept over Asia and Africa. It was understandable. Europeans had just devastated their own continent. Bystanders if
not participants in the Holocaust, they could no longer
claim any moral authority to be ruling over others. Furthermore, their political classes had almost invariably maintained that they were preparing their empires for ultimate
independence. For the likes of Nasser, Nkrumah, Sukarno,
Ben Bella and Boumedienne in Algeria, Nehru and Gandhi,
and Ho Chi Minh, the time for self-rule had arrived. The
Third World duly took shape on the international stage.
One central element was systematic resentment against the
West, a resentment ably attacked by Ibn Warraq in his
*Defending the West.**

Third World leaders were mostly military men ready and
willing to resort to violence. To mobilize the masses in support, they denigrated the previous European administrations
as so many embodiments of the white man and his manifest
faults. "Imperialist," "colonialist," "racist" served as so many
collective curse-words. It is doubtful that they really believed
the sloganeering and stereotyping so useful to them. As
soon as they themselves were securely in power, they hurried
to westernize their countries as best they could, evidently
wanting similar universities and hospitals and armies, sports
and even pop music. So far-reaching has imitation been that

---

*   *Defending the West: A Critique of Edward Said's Orientalism*, by Ibn Warraq; Prometheus, 500 pages, $29.95.

some of the new nationalist rulers incorporated second-hand the fascism, Communism, and anti-Semitism that had wrecked Europe.

238   The British responded to Third World nationalism in a welcoming phrase about "the winds of change," as though those mobilizing enmity towards them had simply blown in with the weather. Only the French made determined efforts to resist, and then in vain. Defenders of empire had always been few and far between. Treasurers resented the expense – research shows that the imperial powers all had to pay out immense and unaffordable sums on maintaining possessions abroad, and the money would have been better spent at home. The calculations are uncertain, but it appears that Britain alone may possibly have enjoyed some small financial benefit from empire. Military staffs resented the posting abroad of troops needed in the European theater. Empire-builders such as Lord Cromer, Lord Curzon, and Alfred Milner, or Jules Ferry and Marshal Lyautey in France, could only advance arguments about responsibility for others and a *mission civilisatrice*. Hard-headed colleagues listened to these abstractions with skepticism.

Intellectuals in Europe went much further, pleading guilty to all the accusations leveled against them by Third World nationalists. They and their predecessors had always been constant and enthusiastic critics of empire, and now were thrilled to have their diatribes against their own countries thrown back at them, as it were, by clever students and disciples. Violence committed by the ruled against the rulers won their applause. This attitude of opposition starts with the delight so widely expressed in Britain over the loss of the American colonies – even the conservative-minded Edmund Burke supported the colonists. Innumerable nineteenth- and twentieth-century writers treated whatever reflected badly on the imperial power as a running scandal –

the Indian mutiny, the Governor Eyre episode in Jamaica, Denshawi in Egypt, Amritsar, the Arab revolts in Mesopotamia and Palestine, partition in India, and so on. Following Marxism-Leninism, leftists everywhere took it for granted that imperialism was the ultimate by-product of capitalism, to be extirpated accordingly in the glorious and imminent world revolution. Bernard Shaw and the Fabians, Sir Roger Casement, J. A. Hobson, Bloomsbury and the *New Statesman*, Arnold Toynbee, and other opinion-makers all over Europe acquired reputations as they savaged not just the British but the Belgians in the Congo, the Dutch in Indonesia, the French in the Maghreb or Indochina. Jean-Paul Sartre and Frantz Fanon recommended the murdering of Frenchmen as a measure that Arabs owed themselves if they were to be free.

The outcome of this long-drawn anti-imperial campaigning has worked its way into today's truism – taught in classrooms everywhere – that Europeans were exclusively vicious oppressors while those they ruled are exclusively virtuous victims. This incarnation of the myth of the Noble Savage overlooks, or carefully ignores, that imperialism brought far-flung peoples into contact with European languages, law and culture, a necessary prerequisite if East and West were to meet on equal terms.

The United States is not an empire, but its intellectual elite has so resented its rise to the status of superpower that they have adopted the self-same contempt for their own country, now exemplifying the West as a whole. In these circles, the United States is depicted as guilty of unmitigated racism and imperialism, while also responsible for triggering the Cold War and a course of outrageous events from My Lai to Gitmo. In common with Sartre, Norman Mailer recommended murder as the key to personal freedom from racism. Mary McCarthy, fresh from admiring Communist

Hanoi under American attack but still enjoying royalties that paid for her large country house on Cape Cod, agreed with Hannah Arendt in their exchange of letters that they both would soon have to flee a fascist America. Among many similar media stars, the likes of Noam Chomsky, Gore Vidal, and Michael Moore have proved as determined as their European counterparts to show everything to do with the West in as bad a light as possible, and everything to do with others in as good a light as possible.

Such alienation culminates in the morbid gloating that on 9/11 America "had it coming," and it spreads infectiously too. As I write, the Archbishop of Canterbury, by name Rowan Williams, and self-described as an intellectual, a Druid (of all things in a Christian primate), and a "hairy Lefty," is reported giving an interview to a Muslim magazine in which he compares the United States unfavorably to the British Empire in its imperial heyday. Its response to 9/11, he opines, has been gratuitous violence.

Edward Said was an outstanding example of an intellectual who condemned the West root and branch while taking every advantage of the privileges and rewards it has to offer. In its dishonesty and exercise of double standards, his was truly a cautionary tale of our times. Born in Jerusalem in 1935, he laid claims to be a Palestinian, dispossessed by Zionist Jews, and therefore an archetypal Third World victim. In sober fact, he was the son of an American father, a member of a prosperous Christian family with extensive business interests in Egypt. Undoubtedly an intelligent and civilized man with one side of his personality, he became a professor of comparative literature at Columbia University. Yet with his other side, he wrote speeches for Yasser Arafat in the 1970s, and was far and away the most vociferous advocate for the Palestine Liberation Organization. Although he knew the history of persecution that lay behind Zionism, he could not accept Israel as anything but an injustice that had to be put right in bloodshed. On the pretext of victimhood, but from the safety of New York, he urged others to kill and be killed. When Arafat professed (falsely as it turned out) to be willing to make peace with Israel, Said broke with him, insisting on armed struggle. At the end of his life, this professor of a subject within the humanities was photographed throwing a stone from Lebanese soil against the boundary with Israel.

The contradictory aspects of the man came together in *Orientalism*, a book Said published in 1978. The thesis was that every Westerner who had ever studied or written about the Middle East had done so in bad faith. From ancient Greece through the medieval era to the present, the work of historians, grammarians, linguists, and even epigraphists had been "a rationalization of colonial rule." There was no colonial rule in the lifetimes of the majority of these scholars, so they must have been "projecting" what was to come. For Said, these highly eclectic individuals were all engaged in a long-drawn conspiracy, international but invisible, to establish the supremacy of the West by depicting an East not only inferior but static and incapable of change. At bottom, here was the vulgar Marxist concept that knowledge serves only the interest of the ruling class. Said had also latched on to Michel Foucault, with his proposition – modishly avant-garde at the time – that there is no such thing as truth, but only "narratives" whose inventor is putting across his point of view. This reduces facts to whatever anyone wishes to make of them.

Omitting whatever did not fit, misrepresenting evidence, and making unwarranted generalizations, Said committed the very sin for which he was accusing Westerners – of concocting a "narrative" to serve his purposes. As he summed up: "Every European, in what he could say about the Orient, was consequently a racist, an imperialist." The "narrative"

242

shaped a conclusion particularly crucial to Said. Europeans included Jews and later Israelis, and they were therefore integral to the conspiracy to do down Orientals and ensure that Palestinians were prime victims of racism and imperialism. Palestinian violence and terror was therefore natural and legitimate.

Orientalism owed its éclat to fashion. Here was someone within a prestigious American university making the nationalist case in an approved high-brow idiom that the West was really to blame for the misfortune of Arabs and Muslims, including harm they had done to themselves. The timing of the book was also propitious. The balance of power was already tipping against the West, and in favor of Muslims. The public was ready for instruction about the encounter with Islam, this rather shadowy novelty suddenly looming on the horizon. The whole range of intellectual guilt-mongers and masochists, stretching out to Middle East lecturers, area specialists, experts of one kind and another, and not least those with anti-American and anti-Jewish prejudices, eagerly promoted Said to be their champion and hero. In these circles, Said earned further immediate praise by welcoming Ayatollah Khomeini's Islamic revolution because it was anti-American in principle and practice. Universities instituted courses deferring to Said, who was invited to present his bright new "narrative" to one prestigious audience after another. Orientalist, the portmanteau term for every Westerner with a scholarly, literary, or artistic interest in the East, is now firmly in the almanac of curse-words. Said succeeded in widening animus against Israel by folding it into generalized anti-Westernism. More than that, he had politicized the study of the Middle East in its manifold aspects.

Discussion of inconvenient facts soon began to expose piecemeal Said's "narrative." An Israeli scholar, Justus Reid Weiner, uncovered the extent to which Said had been romancing his own victimhood. Leaving Jerusalem as a young boy before Israel became independent, he had grown up in Cairo and been educated at its most prestigious British-run college. His credentials as a Palestinian refugee and a spokesman demanded more than a stretch of the imagination. It was not the Zionists who had dispossessed the Said family, it turned out, but Nasser when he expropriated the property of all foreigners including theirs. The victim of Arab nationalism, Said was nevertheless its most ardent defender, and this psychological inversion is the most mystifying thing about him. Perversity of the sort may perhaps illuminate the psychological process whereby so many kindred intellectuals misplace hatred and guilt, admiring those who injure them and condemning those who might protect them.

Said did not live long enough to read Robert Irwin's book *For Lust of Knowing*, published early in 2006. This thorough rebuttal of Said is a monument of genuine scholarship, examining who the Orientalists were, how historically they advanced their disciplines all over Europe, and what their achievements have been. At the outset, Irwin calls Said's book "a work of malignant charlatanry," and he demonstrates the point calmly; in contrast to Said, he is free from either spite or arrogance. (Stephen Schwartz, another informed critic, also deploys the words "malignant charlatan" to describe Said.) Irwin's account of the founding of chairs in European universities for the sake of studying and translating Eastern languages and literary texts is particularly strong. Dedicated scholars handed down to their successors a tradition of learning and research. Even Christian churchmen and apologists among them were prepared to pursue knowledge objectively.

Some of Said's critics have had Arab or Muslim origins, for instance Sadiq al-Azm, Fouad Ajami, and Kanan Makiya, and Said treated them all as though they were traitors. He would surely have issued another personal fatwa in his usual style of bluster and insult against Ibn Warraq, whose *Defending the West* further demolishes in close detail the Saidian "narrative."

Originally from the Indian subcontinent Ibn Warraq is the author of a previous book, *Why I Am Not a Muslim*. This is a scrupulously documented examination of the life and teaching of the Prophet Muhammad, of the Qur'an and its sources, and the resulting culture. As he sees it, intolerance and ignorance, and all manner of taboos, have been deliberately preserved and cultivated down the centuries, doing the faithful no service, and creating what he openly calls the totalitarian nature of Islam.

Like the earlier book, *Defending the West* rests on very wide reading in several languages; there are almost a hundred pages of footnotes. The impact is all the more solid because the tone expresses neither ridicule nor anger but only determination to get at the truth. The book mounts its demolition of Said from several angles. To begin with, Said's pseudo-Foucault style often descends into meaningless verbiage and contradiction. Said's selectivity and failure to take historical context into consideration also lead him astray wildly. Out of laziness or carelessness, he makes egregious historical blunders. For instance, at the time when Said is accusing the British of imperialism in the Middle East, the actual overlords were the Ottoman Turks. And if British and French Orientalists were imperial agents by definition, how come Germany had no Middle East empire when its Orientalists were the most distinguished and original of all? And what about Ignaz Goldziher, the founding father of modern Orientalism and ready to consider converting to Islam, but Hungarian, therefore from a country with no imperialist aims in the Middle East?

As common sense suggests and Ibn Warraq substantiates, the interest of Westerners in the East from classical antiquity onwards was motivated by intellectual curiosity; they wanted to find out about the other human beings with whom they were sharing the world. To seek knowledge for its own sake is the special and wholly beneficial contribution the West has made to mankind. "Only the West" in one of Ibn Warraq's lapidary judgments, "seems to have developed the notion that the natural world is a rational and ordered universe, that man is a rational creature who is able to understand, without the aid of revelation or spiritual agencies, and able to describe that universe and grasp the laws that govern it." Rationalism, universalism, and self-inspection are Western traits which expand civilization. Said's cultural relativism leads only to a dead-end.

More than that, intellectual curiosity on the part of only a handful of Western scholars was the indispensable prelude to the rescue and revival of cultures – Muslim, Hindu, Buddhist among them – that were on the edge of extinction. Henry Rawlinson in Persia, Austen Layard in Mesopotamia, Sir William Jones and Henry Colebrooke in India, and Max Müller the great Sanskrit philologist, restored to the local peoples the pasts that had once been theirs, giving them pride in their ancestors, and the self-respect without which there could have been no nationalism. Nationalist historians now concur, and even the more extreme among them are able to praise a figure like Lord Curzon for salvaging the monuments of India in his years as viceroy.

The final hundred or so pages provide an account of various artists, writers, sculptors and even musicians who either worked in the Middle East or used themes and subjects from it. From Herodotus to Kipling, and from Gentile Bellini to Delacroix and Gérôme – to Said, all such at all times and in all places were collaborators with one or another imperialism. In reality, as Ibn Warraq has no difficulty showing, they were reporters and observers, enthused by unfamiliar customs and colors, and any social or political opinions they might express were in sympathy with the local people. They were actually celebrating everyone and everything that Said believes they were injuring.

Defending the West might seem a specialist book with a narrow focus on someone who made a spectacle of himself by absorbing uncritically the Third Worldism of his day, a lost soul who perhaps ought to be pitied rather than exposed. That would be quite wrong. The purpose here is to reinvigorate the humane and universal values without which there is no civilization worth the name. Ibn Warraq is anxious because these are bad times for the West: its culture is in decay, its achievements denigrated, its citizens everywhere demoralized and therefore in a weak position to defend themselves against militant and mindless Islamism. It is a source of hope and some sort of historic milestone as well, that a Muslim by birth should now be the free spirit calling on the West to be true to itself.

The New Criterion
January 2008

Over a long period prior to World War II the British Foreign Office was a principal institution in defense not of Britain alone but of the international order. Success against Nazism in the war should have strengthened the skills and morale required to deal with the spread of Communism in its aftermath, but in fact the Foreign Office proved virtually helpless, paralyzed by a strange new conviction that the breed of dictators rising abroad was indeed representative of their people and of their age and therefore irresistible. Confronted by post war nationalists of the Nasser and Nkrumah type, British diplomacy suddenly looked incompetent, rooted in illusion or worse.

Of all species of British diplomat, perhaps none had been so celebrated as the Arabist, the man who "understood" the Arabs and who on their behalf had fashioned federations and pacts, unity and independence. When, in the post war period, these measures led to chaos, the Arabist passionately advocated more of them. It has never been clear quite how tradition, character, and chance combined to form these Arabists, but Sir Evelyn Shuckburgh's diaries – intended as a document for posterity, and much shortened for this first publication – give us a welcome and fascinating insight into the process.

Between 1954 and June 1956, Shuckburgh was head of the Middle East department of the Foreign Office. By his own frank account, he was a complete failure, brought by the job to the verge of nervous collapse. Where the Arabs were concerned, he sought ceaselessly on their behalf for fresh concessions, only to discover that no concession was ever enough for them. Where the Israelis were concerned, his attitude developed into hostility which was often fantastical, not to say paranoid. In his surprise and dismay over unfolding events is heard the melancholy but authentic sound of the breaking of the British Empire.

Privately, Shuckburgh and his beautiful wife had high social connections, and they shared tastes in the arts and in music in particular. Here was someone cultivated in the best sense. Also he was following a family tradition, in that his father, Sir John Shuckburgh, had been Under Secretary in the Colonial Office, with special responsibility for Palestine between the wars. In an early posting to the Cairo embassy, in 1937, the son was already writing to ask his father, "How can we risk prejudicing our whole position in the Arab world for the sake of Palestine?" Then and since the Foreign Office has been unable to see beyond that simplified, one-side-or-the-other formula. In fairness, it should be said that the indecisiveness of Shuckburgh *père* and his generation over Palestine and the Arabs had fully prepared the miseries of Shuckburgh *fils* and his generation.

The diaries begin in 1951, when Evelyn Shuckburgh was promoted to private secretary to Anthony Eden, then Foreign Secretary in Winston Churchill's last government. Initially impressed by Eden, Shuckburgh in the end perceived him as vain and egocentric, a poseur who liked to conduct business in his bedroom and addressed him and others as "dear." As the anxious heir-presumptive to the ageing Churchill, Eden lacked the courage to be his own man, lest he somehow forfeit his claim.

Presumably it was a matter of temperament that both Eden and Shuckburgh were so much occupied with daily trivialities. In these diaries, long-term policy assessments are nowhere suggested, and nothing indicates that either Eden or Shuckburgh were making such assessments. Both men were busily, and sometimes hysterically, responding around the clock to rumors, to gossip about colleagues, to articles in the press, or to the absence of articles in the press.

Unkind words pierced Shuckburgh. His first two big occasions were at the United Nations debate on Korea in 1952 and at the 1954 Geneva Conference on Indochina. At the former, Andrei Vishinsky, formerly the chief prosecutor at the Moscow Trials and now the Soviet representative at the United Nations, gave an anti-Western speech that was "very disagreeable." At the latter, the Chinese came "preaching hatred of the white man and confident in the massive forward march of their nation and reckoning to throw us out of Asia altogether." Shuckburgh recorded: "I am upset – what is it? Frightened." It was axiomatic to him that "it would be folly to try to save Indochina by force of arms." He did not consider what effect it would have upon Russians, Chinese, and the Vietminh to observe someone so palpably upset by speeches alone.

American robustness in the face of these opponents was so alarming to Shuckburgh that it seemed almost indistinguishable from Communist aggression. Hearing Dean Acheson say that the Western nations would have to "fight their way out," Shuckburgh took no heart at all: "The fact is that when you scratch this elegant and civilised Acheson, he turns out to be just another tough guy." Chinese rage itself seemed to him primarily the fault of the Americans "for being so damned contemptuous of them." Secretary of State John Foster Dulles, openly displaying "almost pathological rage and gloom," at what he had to hear from allies and enemies alike, becomes a favorite bugbear in these pages. Encounters between Dulles and Eden were embarrassing, as

Eden withheld even moral support because of his conviction that the Americans wanted only to replace the French
in Indochina and the British in Egypt.

"One gets a terrible impression of the United States and
Russia as two unwieldy, insensitive prehistoric monsters
floundering about in the mud," wrote Shuckburgh. Which is
the more strikingly false in this phrase – the political perspective which reduces the United States and Russia to one
and the same mud pile, or the assumption of superior British sensitivity.

Taking over responsibility for the Middle East, Shuckburgh had to contend with the fallout of the Mossadegh crisis in Iran, the Baghdad Pact and its repercussions, a dispute
with Saudi Arabia (which had invaded the desert oasis of
Buraimi), and above all Egypt's President Nasser. At that
moment, Nasser was consolidating his power by eliminating those who had helped him to achieve it, as was only to
be expected. Eighty thousand British troops were stationed
in the Canal Zone, and if Nasser could succeed in removing
them on his terms, he could hope to justify himself to the
Egyptians as their leader. To that end, he directed the usual
terrorist campaign.

Typically, Shuckburgh nowhere discusses whether with-
drawing or maintaining the garrison would serve British or
Egyptian interests, or both, or neither, all of which is as
debatable today as it was then. Churchill and Field Marshal
Montgomery are among those recorded here as advocating
the use of bayonets in the circumstances. Churchill hoped
for a fight, after which the British would withdraw leaving
Nasser to learn his lessons the hard way. Reflexively, Shuckburgh mocked and rejected this line. It was a foregone conclusion to him that Nasser could not be resisted. Principle
was not involved. No pacifist, he merely considered that
force was too public, too ungainly.

Shuckburgh's conception of the nature of Middle East politics was too shallow to have any practical application. His inability to grasp that the Arab socio-political system owed nothing to British sensitivities, let alone to democratic values, condemned him in advance to defeat and loss. The limitation in his thinking often led to unfounded suppositions – for instance, that Syria might meaningfully merge with Iraq, or that the Sudanese, split religiously and tribally, and at that point uncertain of independence from either Britain or Egypt, "have it in them to become a really independent and stable nation." Egypt was a society without defenses against a man of Nasser's ambitions, yet Shuckburgh imagined offering him a "carrot" to desist from the pursuit of power, and fondly hoped that "sense" might be put into him. In the event, Nasser and his Free Officers could hardly believe their luck at the terms proposed by the Foreign Office for the evacuation of the Canal Zone. The Egyptians signed on the spot and not even their grins of delight alerted Shuckburgh to what lay ahead.

How, the British wondered, was it conceivable that Nasser, who had been ceded what he wanted, was still not friendly to Britain? Would more concessions do the trick? Perhaps something should be done about the Arab-Israeli dispute, one of the "unnecessary irritants" that in Shuckburgh's judgment needed to be eliminated in order to improve relations with the Arab states. It was to this, at any rate, that he turned his attention. Together with Francis Russell, his opposite number in the State Department, he worked out "Plan Alpha," a fine example of diplomats' geometry that involved complex territorial concessions by Israel, with land going to Jordan and Egypt and British guarantees to follow.

The discovery that the Israelis would not allow their boundaries to be thus whimsically reduced embittered

Shuckburgh. His thoughts turned to using force against *them*, for their own good. He persuaded himself that the Israelis did not appreciate their own true interest, and that if they did not obey, then they could only expect to be killed one day: "They seem to have some sort of ghetto instinct." It was a short step from there to losing his temper with Israeli representatives, telling Prime Minister Eden that the *Guardian* was a Jewish newspaper, making reckless accusations about agents and lobbies. By November 1955, he "half hoped that the secret reports [of impending war] were true, and that the Israelis would attack Egypt, and have a good fight before going under for good and all."

Plan Alpha had no basis in reality. It coincided with the launching by Nasser of guerrillas from the Gaza Strip, and Israeli retaliation. By contrast, Nasser's interest in raising the stakes was very real, for by this means he was able to oppose the Baghdad Pact and secure Soviet arms, thereby opening up the maneuverings between East and West which finally made him the uncontested Egyptian leader. To Shuckburgh, as apparently to the whole Foreign Office, these developments were quite beyond prediction. In bewilderment, Shuckburgh came slowly to perceive that British policy had created the very Soviet opportunity in the area which it had been designed to preclude. He bemoaned the ingratitude of the Arabs, rather than blaming his own timidities and misconceptions. "How they hate us really," he wrote in his usual vein, when the true lament should have been, how deftly the power-seeking Nasser has taken advantage of us.

Like Shuckburgh, Eden himself was soon swinging between alternative reactions of abject surrender and violence, whose climax was reached in the disastrous Suez campaign of 1956. "Poor England! We are in total disarray," Shuckburgh was exclaiming at the end of his term in office, and these sentiments earned him a transfer as Chief Civilian Instructor at the Imperial Defence College, of all posts and places.

The profound defeatism so vividly exposed in these diaries no doubt was the guiding disposition of many influential Foreign Office officials at that moment, when the fate of many former colonial peoples was in the balance. Unable to recognize their own interests, officials of this cast of mind could not recognize anyone else's either. Refusing to pay the price for order, they handed the costs of disorder to others, in this case the Arab masses left at the mercy of any dictator now able to capture the state.

Commentary
July 1987

Here be Dragons: Robert Fisk at Loose in the Gulf

WHEN SADDAM HUSSEIN ordered the invasion of Kuwait on August 2 last year, he was immediately perceived in this country as a monstrous aggressor. Opinion polls revealed a majority – which was to grow – in favour of resisting this dictator's ambitions, by sanctions first, but should these prove inadequate to the task, then by force. Within a time-span measured in months, moreover, Saddam was due to acquire nuclear weapons, thus creating a balance of terror which would have allowed him to have his way in Kuwait and elsewhere if he chose. Mature and steadfast, the public response was all the more impressive in view of the voices maintaining that panic, indifference or surrender would be more appropriate.

As was likely, the Foreign Office pioneered the blind eye, providing information contrary to all reality up to and even beyond August 2, that Saddam was merely "sabre-rattling" and British people in Iraq and Kuwait need take no precautions. Many hundreds of these people soon found themselves hostages as a result, and some still in hiding were to have the bitter experience of being advised by William Waldegrave, a junior minister at the Foreign Office, to give themselves up to the Iraqis. This pre-emptive cringe surprised even the Iraqis, who had not prepared to receive them. "Sanctions are the world's only answer to Saddam," was the unforgettable title of an article to that effect in *The Times* of August 3, by that Bourbon of a former diplomat, Sir

Anthony Parsons. Plenty of other retired ambassadors and Chatham House squaddies urged that force should not be considered an option for fear of the consequences.

Presumably Denis Healey and Edward Heath had reasons – or at least calculations – known to themselves for the alarm they spread. Both advocated outright appeasement. Had either politician been listened to, Kuwait today would still be in Saddam's hands and Iraq's nuclear capacity that much closer. To serve their purposes, these "two misguided old missiles," in the *Sunday Telegraph*'s phrase, conjured up the purest fancies about world-wide Muslim agitations to come, imminent Turkish or Iranian invasions, the tractability of Saddam and the extension of sanctions indefinitely, the political and economic collapse of the West, unprecedented casualties, in the style of Nostradamus.

As Minister of Defence, Healey in 1968 had taken the decision to withdraw the British presence from the Gulf, probably the worst mistake of post-war British foreign policy, and certainly the most unnecessary. Heath had then won an election on a manifesto which included the firm promise to overturn this decision to withdraw, but no sooner was he Prime Minister than he speeded it up. Both men, then, bear their full share of responsibility for creating the power vacuum in which the Shah of Iran swelled up, and Ayatollah Khomeini, Saddam and local oil-price manipulators. As this vacuum was extending into a yet wider regional disorder, we were obliged to return to the Gulf in circumstances more difficult and costly than they need have been. It was particularly galling to be given by Healey and Heath more of the prescription which had proved itself so harmful.

Know-nothings and proud-of-it-too, like Auberon Waugh, felt that Arabs have nothing better to do than kill each other, and nobody else need be in the least concerned by that. The Left, especially its CND component, might have been expected to welcome the prevention of a future nuclear war at Saddam's behest, not to mention the promotion of freedom and liberation for tyrannised Arabs. Instead, the Left's emotional anti-Americanism rose in full spate. America was stated to be fighting for oil, for imperialism. This marxoid notion had no substance. Had Kuwait chosen to unite voluntarily with Iraq, or for that matter if any or all Arab oil-producing countries were to merge by choice under a single ruler, then that would be their business, as it is for European countries to set about building a common future by consent. The Church, which by and large is CND in a surplice, provided an alarmist chorus. Fourteen bishops and three theologians, for instance, signed a letter to *The Independent* on December 12, 1990, in the hope of avoiding "this potentially terrible conflict," which could "make a graveyard of the Middle East" no less.

Even against this background, Robert Fisk, the Middle East correspondent of *The Independent*, stands out for the wild errors of his judgement throughout the Gulf crisis. In everything, in matters great and small, he was plain wrong. His general outlook was typically that of the Left, to be sure, in that to him "the decisive factor" was oil, and the United Nations enterprise was only American aggression and short-sightedness in disguise. However, a political outlook of that sort does not fully account for Fisk's performance, whereby he was able to present a timely and well-executed Western policy as a mirage of despair and defeat. He lost no chance to mock American and Arab leadership or to cast doubt on the morale of the troops; to know better, in the loftiest assumption of omniscience, than the likes of President Bush, General Schwarzkopf and King Fahd; to belittle American weaponry as something in which faith was "unwarranted" and even to speak of "this Disneyland of technology." Upon complex political and military operations, he placed his

own simple spin of doom, by exaggerating mishaps and difficulties, and by inventing all manner of campaigning or
ideological dangers where none existed. Not just wrong,
Fisk was hysterical.

To judge by letters published in *The Independent*, a number of readers seem to have caught this hysteria. If any soldiers or members of their families paid attention to Fisk,
they can only have been distressed and to no purpose at all.

Fisk first came before the public as a reporter for *The
Times* covering events in Ireland in the Seventies. Whatever
the government then did by way of coaxing out a solution
for Ulster, he decried. Evidently, he takes it for granted that
governments are there for everyone else to be their adver-
saries. Journalism, to someone of this temperament, has the
duty, even the sacred duty, to expose and oppose what can
only be bad if not scandalous, with the result that its practi-
tioners are not reporters concerned with news and facts, but
rather clerks of high calling and moral purpose, a clerisy, a
priesthood.

In Beirut since 1976, for *The Times* and later for *The
Independent*, this particular clerk or priest sought to refine
his vocation. His experience as a reporter in the Middle East
has been resumed in *Pity the Nation*, a book he published
in 1990.

In its preface, he has a conceit about the journalist "at
the edge of history" as a man might sit on the lip of a smoking volcano, recording "as honestly as we can." Far from following this pontification, on the page Fisk is busy selecting
whatever helps to build some case according to his temperamental and moral preconceptions, whether or not the
facts fit.

Over the last fifteen years Lebanon has disintegrated
from a democracy, albeit imperfect, into a free-for-all whereby
its several religious or ethnic communities have withdrawn

from such agreed arrangements as existed, each into his own identity. Each seeks to survive at the expense of the others, and all employ the same means of offence and defence. However regrettable it may be, moral distinctions between the communities are vain and irrelevant. This is customary or tribal warfare, and it illustrates the central dilemma of Arab politics today. No political structures or institutional mechanisms exist to permit some form of power-sharing, with pluralism and rights, and in the best case, democracy. To the strong the spoils as ever, and to the weak disposses-sion, flight and finally massacre. The Lebanese plight is to be found in reality or in potential in every Arab country, all of them despotisms where one man and his kind hold power at the expense of everyone else.

Unwillingness to address this central dilemma makes *Pity the Nation* tendentious to the point of untruthfulness. Ever the adversary, ever the priest on the trail of wickedness, Fisk ignores the defective structure of Arab politics by laying the blame for everything on foreign intervention, primarily American and Israeli. The pretence that such intervention is the cause of present troubles – rather than yet another effect of them – opens the way to moral hysteria against the West. Fisk never notices how condescending it is to depict Arabs as people without a decisive say in their own affairs, not agents but only passive objects of others. The Victorian imperialist ascribed bad character to the native whom he did not like and good character to himself. The target is reversed for Fisk, who ascribes bad character to the West because he dislikes it, and good character to the native, but the emotional need to be moralising at other people's expense remains constant.

This is the mind-set which led Fisk so astray in the Gulf crisis. In his reports the tone of delicious gloating over the Western calamity which he anticipated was as unmistakable as it was other-worldly. The priest had talked himself into a belief that the hour of retribution was at hand.

At this point, something must be said about Fisk's technique. The standard practice in filing a newspaper report is to minimise selectivity and bias. This involves opening with a statement which resumes the event in question, then following up with supporting evidence, including quotations from witnesses or those affected by it. The reader is provided with substantive facts upon which to base an informed opinion of his own.

This will not do for Fisk. Instead, he prefers, if possible in the first sentence of his story, to select some individual, then to append a splashy purple description of him or her, and the circumstances of their encounter, finally extrapolating from that encounter some generalised conclusion. What he has seen and heard has been used to paint his mood. Here is the exact opposite of recording "as honestly as we can." More often than not, Fisk's conclusion cannot bear the weight of extrapolation from the individual encounter and amounts to nothing but a personal statement which may or may not be valid. The net effect is that Fisk habitually places himself not at all on the edge but at the centre of his story, not really reporting on others but on himself.

This is not a style in which the truth can be told. Readers are instead being invited to admire the panache of Fisk's approach, the advantage with which he is able to observe the bit-parts played by those fortunate enough to be converting themselves into his copy and finally the superior morality which allows him to absolve or to condemn, even as he leaves the scene. How he depicts himself tripping over corpses (his phrase), imagining Israeli jets passing through the windows of his bedroom one foot above his bed (his dream), screaming four-letter words at those alleged to be preventing him carrying through with his calling. Pocketa-pocketa, as Walter Mitty had it. Self-dramatisation like this is a branch of fiction, not journalism.

260 From the beginning of last August, when he turned up in the Gulf, until early in December when he seems to have taken a break lasting into the new year of 1991, Fisk set about establishing as best he could that a victorious war could not be waged by vulnerable Western troops against the formidable Iraqis. The political and military costs would be unbearable. The West, which he sometimes likened to "crusaders" or even "Christendom," had no conception of the revenge Arabs and Muslims would exact. He appealed to history as justification for some highly dubious but *ex cathedra* generalisations. It would be well, he had already jumped to the conclusion by August 9, for "the West to remember that history in the Middle East rarely rewards the just. It never favours the foreigner .... Not once has a military adventure in the Middle East achieved its end. For it is also an irresistible trap.... Mr Bush urged his people yesterday to go to church and pray for the young Americans who are on their way to the Gulf. It was a wise precaution."

Evidence for these pre-conceptions then had to be furnished. The seamen of HMS *York* were duly "expressing the nonchalance of frightened youth." The ship itself "looked a very fragile vessel," and he continued, "had not its sister ship Sheffield been hit by an Exocet missile? Did the Iraqis not have 1,000 Exocets?" Day after day, he imagined new fields for hysteria. The Iraqis had struck the USS *Stark* in an unprovoked attack in the Gulf in 1987. The US Navy had little protection against mines, and – pocketa-pocketa – "Any location west of 50.5 degrees would place American ships in range of Iraq's Mirage fighter bombers and their Exocet missiles." Two Italian ships off course threatened the US fleet.

Most of his stories were in the give-away mould, for instance on August 20: "Sami Ahmed Abdullah and Tahir Juma Mohamed were yesterday rejoicing in the sobriquet of 'rightful soldiers of Saddam Hussein, thanks to the US Navy.' ... They were the first Iraqis to brave US gunfire in the Gulf .... They proved how seamen can make a mockery of a naval blockade .... US naval operations had earned a definite failure mark." What they proved in fact was how Fisk manages to extrapolate whatever he needs for his temperamental ends from the insignificant actions of insignificant individuals.

It was the same on land. "He was every mother's son, tall, strong, handsome, enjoying his status as a soldier in a foreign land. He stood on the ramp in an artificial way, rifle in hand, bag over his shoulder, feet apart, an image on a hundred front covers and a thousand war memorials." Or again, "truth is not the first casualty in war. Soldiers are. There are enough portents already that this crisis could end in tragedy without confusing the issue." There were fistfights in Marine units, he informed us, and infantrymen were chastising their officers for lack of command-and-control procedures. A private soldier asked Fisk if he could borrow a tourist map "to see where we are." The "unhappiness of the Americans" prompted Fisk to advise them to "train and move at night; clean and maintain engines, generators and weapons constantly, initiate a postal system," and so on.

Granted the mentality which disposed him to blame the West for Arab shortcomings, Fisk devoted numerous reports to the incompatibility as military allies of the West and Arabs. What with their insensitivity and ignorance, the Americans were alienating Arabs, and bound to do so more and more. The armies could not integrate their commands. Press conferences allowed him to create the mood for which he was searching. American spokesmen or organisers were "sweating … truly awful," while the message for the Saudis was "watch out." Right to the end, such conferences reinforced Fisk's anti-Americanism. "Uninformative and embarrassing" in his words, briefings served to confirm in Arabs their "suspicion and hatred" of Americans as people intoxicated with their technology and blinded by naivety.

Actually, the Egyptian and Syrian leadership was more eager than anyone to draw Saddam's claws by enforcing his departure from Kuwait, by a land campaign if necessary, but Fisk sought to show the opposite with stories about their alleged insincerity. One such story opened typically, "General Mohamed Bilal says that his primary military mission is to defend Islam's holy places. This is, of course, a terminological inexactitude." When he asked of Arab armies, "Will they fight?" the question was merely sarcastic. By September 26 he had convinced himself by these means of "the catastrophe that may soon befall all the armies of the Gulf."

Beyond that, one of his articles of faith was that Arabs, as Muslims, could not possibly accept any American presence on Saudi soil, especially not to wage war against an Arab country. It is part and parcel of his condescending attitude that Arabs must be considered people who cannot think through what exactly their interests are, but confuse politics and religion so irrevocably that they can have only a single and unanimous response to a given situation; in short, they are creatures of frenzy. In a staggering inversion of the facts on the ground, he wrote, "The greatest threat to Saudi Arabia is not Iraq. It is America." Proof of this? A Saudi sheikh and Khalid, a Bedu, both doubted that America would really evacuate its troops after the war.

Since Arabs seemed unaccountably reluctant to oblige Fisk by splitting the coalition and breaking the new "crusaders," he press-ganged the Israelis to bring this about. Under the bald heading "The Gulf alliance is gunned down," on October 10, he discussed at length the horrible incident which had just occurred in Jerusalem. At the bidding of Saddam, the PLO had attempted to instigate a mass uprising there. Caught by surprise, Israeli police lost order and regained it only by firing into the crowd, killing 19 people. Fisk's predictions arising from this event bore not the least relation to what was to happen. "At the very moment when those Western armies desperately need to maintain a broad measure of Arab support for their stand against President Saddam, the Israelis have done more damage to this new alliance than all the radical leaders combined .… If ever a sword was thrust into a military alliance of East and West, the Israelis wielded that dagger." President Mubarak could now not contain Egyptian dissatisfaction for much longer, the Syrians would not be contributing armour, the Israelis had allowed Saddam to undermine America.

Let it be conceded that Fisk was sincerely worried by the prospect of Allied casualties; and also that he, like others, was taken in by the Pentagon's brilliant campaign to dampen everyone's expectations. Even so, anyone with a fifteen-year experience of the Middle East ought to have understood that Iraq was a fragmented country ethnically and religiously, and for dreadful years had been in the grip of terror, that its soldiers embodied the fragmentation and feared the terror, and had as a result performed poorly in the Iran war, and now had no intention of engaging the Allies in a hopeless war fought solely for Saddam's aggrandisement. Nor is this hindsight. Hazhir Teimourian of *The Times* was only one among many informed commentators to publish (on December 12) an accurate forecast of the likely course of events under the title "Arab generals say war against Baghdad could be won on the first day of battle." The Egyptian chief of staff, Field Marshal Abu Ghazzala, described in a definitive and much-quoted speech how for many years he had co-ordinated Egyptian-Iraqi military endeavours, and from his knowledge he declared that the war would be over in three days. Informed commentators also observed the common Arab-American aims which solidly underpinned the coalition. Fisk's fears were groundless.

Returning from his leave (if it was) at the beginning of this January, Fisk took up all his themes on a still higher note of hysteria. War was evidently approaching. On January 14, Fisk found the Iraqi anti-tank "berms" of piled sand to be "frightening revetments" – the armour was to cross them without ado – and he observed soldiers wiping tears from their eyes at the prospects ahead. Stormy weather may have granted "a few extra days of life to the tens of thousands of young men who are likely to die in the coming weeks." General Disorder rather than General Schwarzkopf, he already thought, was likely to be in command and now he repeated that "wars destroy the best-laid plans." Instead of factual or first-hand reports, speculative anxieties poured out of him. The Iraqis might use gas and biological weapons, the Israelis might expel the Palestinians, Jordan might disappear. He worried deeply about such things as Islamic scholars asking why Muslim armies had been beaten back from Vienna in 1683: "was it because they lacked faith or because the armies of Christendom possessed better weapons?"

On the day when the UN ultimatum expired, Fisk asked where American confidence sprang from. "Patriotism? America's characteristic and dangerous trust in technology? Or was it the war-speak of military colleges?" Saddam was speaking in just that vein about America. Fortunately, Fisk reassured himself by finding soldiers "who suspect the war which now seems inevitable will lead to disaster." For once hearing a soldier say that the war would end in seventy two hours, Fisk criticised him for "dangerous euphoria." To his own satisfaction, he established that Allied air successes were nothing of the kind. "Pilots have noticed Iraqi planes flying on a non-combat status around them over Iraq," he wrote, whatever this might mean. There were no Iraqi defectors either, he thought, because those "truly awful" organisers had not produced any for him.

Under the fascinating heading, "Tanks bogged down in unmapped mud and confusion," Fisk on January 23 depicted "a logistical nightmare," in which the mass of troops and armour heading for the front-line were unable to find their way. Summoning once more the full military skills he must have gathered as a newspaperman, he explained how convoy discipline was to be restored, secrecy of unit location maintained, and medical standards bettered. Medical staff might be unable to do much about gas attacks, but he could instruct how to suck teeth out of a throat wound. Self-dramatising as usual, he was able once more to donate maps to commanders who were "hopelessly lost." Judging from the response in *The Independent* and elsewhere, this story marked the turning-point when readers began to wonder what confidence could be placed in Fisk.

The very next morning, he was reporting how Saudi Tornados had taken off on a sortie, as a result of a decision "taken personally by King Fahd and applauded privately by President George Bush." It was heart-warming, naturally, that these two leaders should have interrupted their schedules to confide their personal and private thoughts and deeds to Fisk; perhaps they had been moved by his contribution to the war of those maps, or his alarm at what might be happening west of 50.5 degrees. No less imaginatively, Fisk was still warning that the Arabs were on the side of the Americans only because of three conditions. The war had to be concluded victoriously and swiftly, Iraq had to survive as a strong nation and the Israelis had to keep out. "The trouble, of course," as Fisk summarised it with guesswork erratic even by his own standards, "is that the first condition can no longer be met, the second is unlikely to be fulfilled and the third could collapse within days."

Brand new anxieties were surfacing right up to the liberation of Kuwait. For instance, "Arab reaction to the relentless bombardment of Iraq could now cause as many fractures in the Arab coalition as if Israel became involved in the war."

Then it was over, as informed people knew it would be. Just a few hours of the land war, and Fisk was exposed as someone whose obsessive self-dramatising had led him into a gaping and obvious dead-end which was far more uninformative and embarrassing than anything American press officers might have provided. Just a few hours, and Fisk's preconceptions and analyses and predictions burst like soap bubbles. Once it was over, and he was in Kuwait City, on February 28, he discovered what the Iraqis had actually done there, and hey presto! he sensed "that something very wicked, at times evil, had visited this city." Were these by any chance the same Iraqis whom it had been utter madness to think of attacking all this while, the same men who behind their "frightening revetments" had been about to set the Muslim world marching in righteousness against the West? The priestly purpose remained the same, but just a few hours were enough for the target of the moralising to be reversed.

Did he apologise for his hysteria? Did he ask himself why he had outrageously misled readers of his newspaper and done so much to confuse public opinion? Did he question the total mismatch between what he said would happen and the actual unfolding of events? Did he reflect on the American performance west and even east of 50.5 degrees, and go on to wonder why Arab anti-Americanism was not as he had anticipated? Might he think through his misconceptions about the structure of Arab politics? Oh indeed not. Nothing of that sort. By March 15, back in Beirut he had settled down to the same old obsessions, reaching a conclusion about the war which was surely the extrapolation to end them all. "President Bush is now facing the prospect of something not unlike defeat." 267

Plenty of reporters *à la* Claud Cockburn or Walter Duranty have been liars and fantasists, but at least they knew they were, and gloried in it. What other reporter has ever projected his own self-drama as though it were reality? Who else has been unable to distinguish between a priestly purpose and the facts? No precedent for Fisk springs to mind.

Salisbury Review
June 1991

THE SURRENDER AND EXIT of the Palestine Liberation Organization from Beirut after its shattering military defeat is the kind of event that has an air of finality about it. Things can never be the same again. The meeting in Amman of Yasir Arafat and King Hussein – enemies for more than a decade – suggests that politics may at last be replacing armed struggle. It is now beyond question that the policy of armed struggle has been an unmitigated catastrophe for the Palestinians – and now, perhaps, some of them may be ready to say so out loud. With each trial of strength, Israel secures land it otherwise might have had to concede, and becomes more implacable, while the Palestinians are dispersed and diminished. The PLO's 15,000 men could offer nothing but destruction and death to people who had never asked to be associated with them. What kind of Palestine could have been built at the expense of Lebanon? The murder of Bashir Gamayel and the ensuing massacre of the Palestinians at Sabra and Shatila provide the desolate answer.

At the port of Beirut in the last week of August, an extraordinary demonstration took place. Driven to the docksides by the truckload under the watchful eyes of an international police force, the PLO as a body appeared under arrest. Among the PLO men obliged to evacuate Beirut, there were no doubt deluded idealists along with the motley mercenaries – Bangladeshis, Somalis, Nigerians, and Turks. But in the end, not even fellow Arabs could show much sympathy for their ideals and would agree to receive only limited numbers of escapees.

Since this scene unfolded, many have wondered how it could have been witnessed so passively by the people the PLO claims to represent. A million Palestinians live under Israeli occupation, another million in Jordan, and hundreds of thousands more in Syria, the Gulf states, and Lebanon itself. They could have disrupted their societies by every tactic from passive resistance to open revolt. Yet none did so. As in earlier cases, Palestinians declined the PLO's appeals to action. In part this is because the Palestinians, though they may well resent Israel, Jordan and the Lebanese Christians alike, have been under much more immediate and sustained threat from the PLO itself. It was PLO "officers" who visited the refugee camps to press-gang Palestinian youths, extort money from merchants, and abduct and murder anyone who questioned these methods – associating the word "Palestinian" not only with victimization but also with brutality and hatred. To suppose that Palestinians have been incapable of understanding this is to patronize them. But to many who have not been personally threatened, and so cannot imagine what it is like to be Palestinian, terror acquires positive value once it is labelled a national movement.

Yet it is not only the immediate physical threat of the PLO's methods in the camps that explains the curious – to many Westerners – passivity of the Palestinian masses. The answer is also to be found in the history, both recent and remote, of the relationship between the miserable Palestinian people and the militant Palestinian leadership.

After the Six Day War, the PLO, armed with slogans about fish swimming in home waters, tried to set up on the West Bank in order to oppose the initial stage of the Israeli occupation. Fewer than a hundred local volunteers joined it. Instead West Bankers accepted jobs offered by Israel that they continue to fill today by the tens of thousands. Far from being able to start guerrilla operations in the occupied territories,

the PLO evacuated within weeks. Yasir Arafat himself is said
to have had to escape to Amman. Ever since, the PLO has
had little success in inciting public disturbance on the West
Bank and in Gaza. Consciously or not, the population may
be considered to be reconciled to co-existence with Israel.

In Jordan, where the PLO tried to reorganize after this
fiasco, support from the masses once again did not materialize.
The PLO's option of armed struggle was quickly paralyzed by
Israeli reprisals, menacing Jordanians and Palestinians alike.
The armed struggle degenerated into internal lawlessness. In
1970, when King Hussein decided to curtail the PLO in his
country, ordinary Palestinians almost without exception fled
to avoid being caught in the crossfire. I will never forget how
refugees in Baqaa camp outside Amman were in such despair
at what the PLO had brought upon them that they proposed
marching across the Jordan River, shouting that they would
throw themselves upon the mercy of General Dayan. About a
hundred PLO survivors did seek refuge in Israel.

Lebanon was the PLO's last resort. Its avowed objective
there was still the pursuit of armed struggle against Israel,
but it dishonored its agreements with the host government
and erected a state within a state. Every means was used to
bully and brutalize Palestinians, and even Lebanese citizens,
to give money to the cause and to enroll their sons. Since
the Lebanese Army was too weak to emulate King Hussein's
troops, law and order could be restored only by outside
forces. The Syrians failed in their attempt; the Israelis succeeded. The physical elimination of the PLO in their strong-
hold of Tel el-Zaatar in the summer of 1976, by the Phalange
but under Syrian auspices, stands in hideous symmetry to
its elimination from Beirut under Israeli auspices. On both
occasions, the Palestinians did their best to stay at a distance from the PLO.

For fifteen years, in one country after another, the PLO

has been inflicting unmitigated punishment on the very people it pretends to be saving. If this continues, the entire Palestinian nation will be left in ruins.

In my experience almost every Palestinian will admit this in private, elaborating with bitter personal detail. But to speak aloud is to deliver oneself as a hostage to fortune. Dozens of honorable Palestinians, including religious leaders, have been assassinated by PLO gunmen for expressing the wish to live in peace with their neighbors. Metaphorically and sometimes literally they have all been held at gunpoint. This is also what incites Lebanese Christians to seek revenge, even though that revenge spares the terrorists and can only fall upon the innocent.

Of course there is always the possibility that the PLO, encouraged by Western politicians and intellectuals with no firm grasp of Middle Eastern realities, might somehow carry the day. The intentions of presidents and foreign secretaries of state are inscrutable – or to put it another way, these powerful leaders could not really be as ignorant and foolish as they seem. Who could tell what plans Arafat might be privy to? In the unlikely event of the PLO one day seizing power, every Palestinian has taken care not to expose himself or his family to revenge. That possibility now looks remote indeed. There are other ways to proceed.

There were always other ways, and the vast majority of Palestinians have sought them to the best of their ability. Exactly one hundred years have passed since the first significant Jewish immigration into Palestine confronted the Arab population with the choice of resisting or compromising. The inclination to compromise was predominant. The rich were prepared to sell land to the Zionists and the poor to obtain employment from them. Grievances were localized and could be resolved. Palestinians at the time were a settled people, emerging from the torpid centuries of Ottoman

rule; they were hard working and law abiding and conservative (as they still tend to be), prepared to seek advantages
that might be available to them through accommodation.

272 As the country developed, Arabs as well as Jews immigrated
into Palestine. Fred M. Gottheil has shown, in an essay in
Palestine and Israel in the 19th and 20th Centuries, edited by
Elie Kedourie and Sylvia C. Haim, that Arab immigration
accounted for an astonishing 36.8 percent of total immigration into Israel prior to statehood.

Palestine's religious leaders and intellectuals (of whom
there were then only a handful) were alone in advocating
violence against the incoming Jews. The first call to stamp
out Zionism seems to have been made in a book written in
French by Negib Azoury, published in Cairo in 1905. The
historian Neville J. Mandel credits Azoury with "the distinction of combining both Arab nationalism and opposition to
Zionism with anti-Semitism." Latter-day Azourys continue
to present the case as though nothing can be learned from
history. Nineteenth-century nationalism, with its romanti-
cizing of violence, held such intellectuals in its grip; and to
that extent they too were victims of circumstance. Militant
nationalism, as they perceived it, had made Western powers
what they were: to be hated and feared, but emulated for the
sake of obtaining parity with them. The end of the Ottoman
Empire in 1918, and the installation of the British Mandate
in the former Turkish province of Palestine, offered a chance
to put these ideas into practice.

At the outset of the Mandate, Haj Amin el-Husseini
emerged as the spokesman for nationalistic violence. The
son of the Mufti of Jerusalem, he was appointed Mufti himself by the British High Commissioner, Lord Samuel, inci-
dentally a Jew. As Mufti, he represented the highest religious
authority in the land, and as a Husseini he was a member of

one of Palestine's foremost families, one that had filled such posts as mayor of Jerusalem under Ottoman rule.

In his clerical robes and turban, with his sharp gaze and trim beard, Haj Amin was an impressive figure. His manner was calm and dignified. His policy, however, was to concede nothing to the Jews. In default of dialogue, violence was to be the one and only instrument of the Arabs. The Mandate administration was to be coerced either to throw the Zionists out or to create conditions in which the Arabs could do so. Throughout the 1920s Haj Amin built up his position, moving forward from one well-organized riot to the next. He whipped up the religious feelings of ordinary Palestinians, playing upon their fears and aspirations until he could be sure of generating the collective violence he wanted. A British police officer, Colonel Main, considered that "holy war" had been aroused. Haj Amin, he wrote, "mixed religion with politics so cleverly that it is impossible to say where the one begins and the other leaves off." It is still impossible to separate Haj Amin's fanaticism from his opportunism. Douglas V. Duff, another police officer of the Mandate, has described in his autobiography *May The Winds Blow!* the kind of fanatic whom the Mufti gathered around him and who terrorized the peasantry. "There is an Arab word, *faszad*, which describes their tactics; there is no single-word equivalent for *faszad* in English. By it is meant all the evil, perjuring, malicious, lying Machiavellian intrigue which will do anything to achieve its end."

Under Haj Amin there was to be no election of representatives, as among the Zionists; no participation in joint legislative councils or assemblies; and constant boycotting of efforts to reach agreements with the British or the Zionists. His noes constitute the history of the Palestinians under Mandate.

Some Palestinians were still brave and civic minded enough to oppose him. The Nashashibis in particular did so, partly because they were as prominent a family as the Husseinis, quite as accustomed to public office, and partly because they were convinced that political options could be entertained and even rewarded. Eventually the Nashashibis and their supporters were to throw their lot in with Jordan (still a realistic solution today), but not before they had been thoroughly victimized by the Husseinis. Anyone who showed a willingness to compromise was accused of treason. Haj Amin's gunmen murdered all who dared to stand against the Mufti, not only the Nashashibi faction but also moderate mayors, Arab trade unionists who supported class solidarity with Jewish workers, indeed any independent spirit. In the end the Mufti's men were to kill King Abdullah of Jordan because he was willing to consider peace proposals with Israel.

Once Arab–Jewish cooperation, such as it was or might have been, was paralyzed, there could be only a trial of strength. Hitler's rise to power in 1933, which resulted in the large Jewish immigration to Israel, gave Haj Amin the opening for which he had carefully prepared. Having sent into the field the various guerrilla bands that he had financed and armed, he gave orders for the general strike of 1936, hoping to capture control of the state.

The "Arab rebellion" lasted for the next three years. In its first phase, the Mandate administration's response was to set up the usual commission of inquiry. Lord Peel, its chairman and an experienced civil servant, ruled that Palestine ought to be divided between the two communities, with a small Jewish enclave dominated by a much larger Arab area. It was a rejection of the exclusively military option, and the Mufti would have none of it. He promised a Palestine without Jews. He redoubled his guerrilla efforts. His bands in the Galilee numbered about 15,000.

As Nicholas Bethell says in *The Palestine Triangle*, "The British gradually realized that the most violent aspect of the revolt was not the rebels' attacks against themselves, or even their attacks against Jews, but their treatment of fellow Palestinian Arabs who defied them or were lukewarm in supporting them." Palestinians were kidnapped, marched blindfolded to commandeered houses, taken before a "general" to be told what "crime" they had committed, and sometimes executed on the spot. If kept prisoner, they would be flogged, thrown into makeshift prisons, or moved from place to place, handcuffed in pairs, ahead of organized search teams. Bethell concludes that the vast majority of the Arab population would never have dared to oppose the rebellion publicly.

The Mandate authorities dealt summarily with the second and final phase of this rebellion. By the time the British Army had finished, collective punishments had been imposed on the Arabs, a number of villages had been destroyed, the 15,000 guerrillas were dead or scattered abroad, defenses had been erected around the borders to prevent their return and the Mufti and his associates were exiled. This was a dress rehearsal for horrors ahead. But the PLO has constructed out of these events a myth of a national uprising yet to be consummated. Memories are short and easily distorted. In a recent PLO propaganda film, an elderly Palestinian bemoans the present and wishes she could return to her native Galilee when all was harmony just before the World War, which of course is when this vicious spiral of violence began.

The Arab rebellion attracted the attention of the Nazis, whose policy then was limited to expelling Jews from Germany. The Mufti wished to persuade them otherwise, and he received in Palestine such emissaries as Adolf Eichmann, later the official responsible for the logistics of the enlarged

Nazi policy of mass murder. On the principle that the enemy of one's enemy is one's friend, in the aftermath of his abortive rebellion, the Mufti turned to Hitler, whom he called "the great leader and teacher" and at whose victories, he claimed, the Arab nations everywhere had feelings of "the greatest happiness and the most profound gratitude." Haj Amin spent the war in Berlin, where he was welcomed by Hitler and Goebbels in particular, as a valuable propagandist who exhorted Moslems to volunteer for S.S. units, and who toured concentration camps, eagerly endorsing the extermination of Jews. Of all the major collaborators and quislings, he alone escaped the death penalty after 1945.

Discredited as Haj Amin was by then, his influence in the Arab world continued. Post-war proposals for partition were rejected as intransigently as ever, in the face of irresistible pressure to accommodate in Palestine those Jews who had survived Nazism. In frustration, the British turned the issue of partition over to the United Nations.

In 1947 the United Nations' partition plan was accepted by the Jews but rejected on behalf of Palestinians (who were not consulted) by the surrounding Arab nations, who invaded the new-born Israel, in May 1948. Their various leaders, in true Mufti style, promised to kill the Jews and restore Palestine to the Palestinians, though it is questionable whether they would have done so at the end of a successful campaign. After their unsuccessful campaign, the Egyptians administered Gaza as their own, and the Jordanians annexed the West Bank.

For the Palestinians, the option of armed struggle at this juncture amounted to asking to be excused from the consequences of the twentieth century. Inhibited by Arab leaders from reaching agreement and unwilling to wage war, Palestinians made a third choice: they fled. (For the very few cases in which they were encouraged to do so by the victorious Israelis, see *A Political Study of the Arab-Jewish Conflict* by Roney E. Gabbay, published in 1959.) In the event, a mass vote had been taken by the nation to be elsewhere while its destiny was in the balance. This lack of confidence, though understandable, was evidence of the state to which these unhappy people had been reduced by those who claimed to be arriving to their rescue. How many times have I heard since from refugees that they ran away under orders from leaders whom they now curse. Once I was escorted in a PLO car to Bourj-el-Barajneh, not far from Beirut, to watch some of Arafat's men in training. They were apparently practicing killing Jews, but my PLO guide whispered that I should not be deceived by appearances. His brother had stayed behind in Jaffa, quietly prospering down the years, he said, and now he and every Palestinian understood how they had been tricked by false promises.

The 1948 fighting left Israel independent, though larger by force of arms than any partition plan had envisaged. Israel's continuation of the 1967 fighting left Israel in possession of the whole of Palestine west of the Jordan, and now there is scarcely scope for partition. In a metaphor first used by the Peel Commission, half a loaf would have been better than no bread, but now there are hardly even crusts to retrieve.

This pitiful history must be recalled not in order to point to folly which cannot be undone, but because nothing changes in the continuation of armed struggle except the Palestinian personalities. The methods of Haj Amin have been adopted in their gruesome and suicidal entirety by Arafat's PLO, and the disaster visited upon the Palestinians is now all but complete.

The PLO was brought into being by a decision of Gamal Abdul Nasser in 1964. He envisaged a militia, under his control, to be used for subversion and other purposes of

Egyptian policy. How ordinary Palestinians lived, and how
their national tragedy might be concluded, were of little or
no concern to him. After the 1967 war, precipitated by
Nasser, every Arab nation conceived that the Israelis could
still be fought by some other means, namely the Palestinians.
As proxies, accordingly, small factions of Palestinians – or
failing them, of assorted Moslem and Arab mercenaries –
were financed and armed by most of the Arab nations. The
communal struggle was said to be directed against Israel, but
soon the various factions were enacting among themselves
the quarrelsome policies and rivalries of their sponsors.
Israelis have died by the hundreds in this process, but Arabs
by the tens of thousands, exactly as in the 1920s and 1930s.

Yasir Arafat's particular genius has been to gather around
him these disparate militias so he would appear to be speaking on behalf of a representative organization. Like Haj
Amin before him, Arafat's ambition has been to gain control
of a state, and he has adapted the means to achieve the ends.
Which Palestinians have been killed by which faction, and
why, are questions that have preoccupied the police and
security forces of a score of countries. Moderates are supposed to exist within the PLO, but their language is scarcely
distinguishable from that of the extremists, either because
they are terrorized by them or because they secretly agree
with them and are playing devious political games. What
the PLO likes to call national unity is no more than the climate of terror around it.

Ironically, through his mother Arafat is a Husseini, a
relation of Haj Amin's. The PLO program of armed struggle
to destroy the Zionists differs from Haj Amin's only in that
revolutionary rhetoric has been substituted for (or joined
to) religious fervor. The violence is unchanged. Just as Haj
Amin's demeanor concealed from many his real intentions,
so Arafat's contrived and almost picturesque presentation

of himself has attracted Western admirers, who will greet the outrages perpetrated by the PLO with cries of apology.

Who stops to ask why this self-proclaimed leader of his nation has only 15,000 followers – and many of them not even Palestinian? Why do Palestinians *en masse* leave the PLO alone? Are they supposed to be too benighted to know what is good for them? The PLO has so often been treated at its own valuation that the real sufferings of Palestinians at its hands have been ignored. As long ago as 1968, Arafat was idolized on the cover of *Time* when he had just been driven off the West Bank, and had lost the one battle for hearts and minds that he might have won. He has since been received with a standing ovation in the U.N. and embraced by the likes of Gandhi and Kreisky and Papandreou. Whenever he looked as though he were being jettisoned by his backers, a Senator Percy or a Lord Carrington or a Prince Fahd or someone else for whom Palestinians are only political pawns, has devised a plan to give the PLO a further lease on life. Most recently it was the Vicar of Christ in Rome.

This extraordinary public relations success has no popular base, and would have been inconceivable if Arafat had not brilliantly exploited a gap in the cold war. Where Haj Amin offered himself to Nazi Germany, Arafat has been able to turn to the Soviet Union. More than a sign of the times, this is a measure of the change in the world's distribution of power. The Soviet Union also cares nothing for the Palestinians, and early in the struggle showed only such deference as was due to any brainchild of Nasser's. Nasser's collapse in 1967, however, obliged the Soviet Union to rescue and re-equip Egypt, thereby unexpectedly increasing Soviet leverage in the whole region. In this context, the Soviet calculation that the PLO might be profitably backed and armed was logical. Nasser's death and Sadat's political evolution then unpredictably switched Egypt from a client into an opponent, leaving the Soviet Union with the PLO on its hands. Just as ordinary Palestinians had nothing to gain from the Nazis, so now they receive no advantage from the Soviets. They have watched the PLO slipping under Soviet control out of expediency, and this may have frightened them off as much as any PLO terror tactics.

No means exist of discovering what public opinion may be today on the occupied territories, which are the eye of the storm. The drama of Beirut will seal the fate of Nablus, Hebron, Jenin and Gaza, whose inhabitants now face the Israelis on their own. Perhaps as the shock of events wears off, Palestinians there will be able finally to reject the unending Haj Amin-Arafat armed struggle, publicly choosing instead to accept the compromises that in fact they are living. Something may still be salvaged – an entity, autonomy, a confederated state extending to Jordan.

President Reagan's latest proposals could implement the PLO's military defeat by bringing about its political isolation within the Palestinian community. There is a not unreasonable hope that spokesmen for the Palestinians under occupation will come to agree to whatever is left of the concept of partition. If the recent talks in Amman between King Hussein and Arafat mark another stage in the demilitarization of the PLO, and a possible political reconciliation with Jordan, then these Palestinians for partition might make themselves known. If they do, Begin and Sharon can go no more adventuring into the night, and President Reagan's plan loses an element of wishful thinking.

Will some Palestinian intellectual at last argue in favor of compromise along such lines, legitimizing a course that is realistic and honorable, thus helping his nation to break out of its wretched history of negation? Are there leaders in the occupied territories capable of standing up and taking responsibility for their people, no matter what Prime Minister Begin hysterically proclaims, and irrespective of the shadow of Israeli settlements? Undoubtedly they exist. There is Anwar Nusseibeh, the former defense minister of Jordan who lived in East Jerusalem. There is Elias Freij, the moderate Mayor of Bethlehem, who recently accepted the Reagan plan (that is, the Labour plan) for peace. (There were other mayors in the occupied territories such as Rashid Shawa of Gaza, who were genuinely willing to deal, but they were egregiously dismissed from their posts by the Israelis.) And there is even Mustapha Dudeen, a former Jordanian cabinet minister, now head of the so-called Union of Village Leagues, who has met with the disdain of self-appointed Western tribunes for the Palestinians. He was prepared to state in an interview to the London *Times* on September 7: "What we should do at least is to secure our existence on the ground." In addition, there are former notables, heads of families, men with distinguished records. To one such personality who could well lead a government, I once presented a copy of my book, *The Face of Defeat: Palestinian Refugees and Guerrillas* (1973). He looked himself up in the index, and then turned to the entry under Arafat, whereupon he handed the book back with the words, "I do not wish to read what you wrote. Who is Arafat?" What he meant was that Arafat's standing was not something he was prepared to take seriously.

If such Palestinians do not declare themselves, then the cowed and demoralized remnants of their people are likely to be submerged into a Greater Israel comprising all of Palestine west of the Jordan, with the prospect of lingering national demise, annexation, or worse. Then the Palestinian people will have paid in full for the faults of their leaders.

The New Republic
November 8, 1982

ANYONE WHO LIKES games of chance should be watching
President Hafez Assad of Syria. He is a most consummate
player in the casino which passes for Middle East politics,
and right this moment his mixture of cunning and force and
luck is weaving rings around everyone in sight. Not since
Gamal Abdel Nasser in his flush of youthful intrigue has
anything quite like it been seen in that part of the world.
Lebanon was the public arena in which Nasser then chose to
wage the Arab cold war. Western intervention saved Lebanon at the time, but in today's changed world the blind eye
rules. If the destruction of Lebanon is still the price to be
paid for inter-Arab feuding, then that's just too bad. In 1958,
Egypt might have picked up the pieces; in 1976, Syria.

Perhaps Assad deserves to succeed, simply for having kept
a cool head so far. Most of his predecessors in office would
have been irresistibly tempted to annex Lebanon outright, no
matter what the cost, in the conditions prevailing since April
1975, when fighting between Christians and Moslems first
offered a pretext. Piecemeal, tragically, the Lebanese state as
it has evolved since independence from French rule in 1943
has been expiring. More than 30,000 people have died. (Algerian sources estimate at least 50,000 dead or nearly two percent of the population.) Central institutions, including the
army, have ceased to function. The country has reverted to a
primitive anarchy in which local leaders and their followers
or dependents pursue narrowly defined interests.

In practice this means that the historic conflict of Christians and Moslems flares up in modern guise. Labels of right

wing and left wing are falsifications imposed by Westerners who assume that other people's politics must be like their own. It is possible to transfer allegiance from one confession to another, but those who do are numerically and politically insignificant. The Rejection Front, for instance, the radical grouping of dissident Palestinians who altogether reject Israel's right to exist, is led by Christians, but that only makes it even more suspect to Moslems. Partition along religious, and even clan, lines already exists on the ground. Traditional sectarian loyalty is really all that a Lebanese has by way of identity, and it does not extend far. The senior civil servant in charge of the administration of Palestinians in Lebanon, himself a Sunni Moslem, once told me that he did not mind where the Palestinians went so long as they left his country.

The Christians made a mistake which there is no retrieving; they believed that they were militarily stronger, better prepared and more cohesive than they were, with influential friends in the West to fall back on. They set to battle with light hearts. The Moslem opposition turned to Syria as to a natural protector. Syria had always argued that Lebanon was one of its rightful provinces. Was not Assad of their faith and in the forefront of revolutionary progress as well, allied to the Soviet Union in the struggle against Western imperialism and capitalism? Assad prevaricated brilliantly. He has under his control and pay some Palestinian clients, the Saiqa guerrillas and the so-called Liberation Army, and he released them to police Lebanon. Not enough, in other words, to stop the situation worsening, but too little to upset his Arab rivals, Israel or America.

Notice having been served in this way that Syria respected the nuances of power politics, the Christians did their best to rise to the occasion. Suleiman Franjieh, president of Lebanon and a Christian as by constitutional arrangement he has to be, was obliged to give way, though kicking and

screaming to the last as hard-liners do, to Elias Sarkis, a man
approved of in Damascus. But political compromises of the
kind were not what the Moslem opposition had in mind at
all. They had smelled blood. A strange alliance they have
been too, of the Shia minority, Communists, self-appointed
mercenaries, Palestinian groups financed by Iraq and Libya –
if they have a nominal suzerain, it is Kemal Jumblatt, who
has long been a frustrated maverick in his ambitions, and
has much to answer for in this crisis. As a Druze, he is condemned to be leader of a small but hardy minority, and cannot aspire to the highest offices. He is not the first millionaire
landowner who has tried to broaden his base by declaring
himself a Socialist and obtaining a Lenin peace prize for it.
Confident that the Syrians, and behind them the Russians,
could be manipulated into supporting him, he made one
ceasefire after another unworkable.

Yasser Arafat calculated along parallel lines. His Palestine Liberation Organization had been obstreperous enough
to cause civil war already once, in Jordan. He was anxious
that the same disaster should not overtake the PLO in Lebanon, the one and only country which still offered a base for
operations. Clashes with the Lebanese authorities had been
violent in the past. It was the armed and apparently uncon-
trollable Palestinian presence which had thrown out the
delicate Lebanese balance in the first place. What the Christians and conservative Moslems resented was the way Arafat had involved Lebanon in his fruitless skirmishing and
terrorist endeavors, not only attracting Israeli reprisals but
disturbing such settled fabric as there was in society with
his sloganizing. He sensed the danger of leading an unloved
minority, but decided to make the most of his prominent
position in the Moslem opposition bloc. It may have seemed
inconceivable that the Syrians could really discard him and

the PLO, which they had sponsored and exploited so often and effectively in many a tight spot before.

That is what has happened, and a fine Byzantine *renversement des alliances* it is too. Christian morale collapsed in almost South Vietnamese style after several massacres of their community; they were no longer able to give as good as they got. Refugees took to the boats and flights out. None of the Western powers, traditional protectors of Christians in Islam, lifted a finger for fear of reprisals through an oil embargo. Even the Pope, who managed to correspond with Bishop Capucci in a Jerusalem prison for smuggling arms on behalf of the PLO, had little to say about developments in Lebanon, save the proffering of his love – which may not in the circumstances have been a useable commodity. Having exhausted their stockpiles of weapons and ammunition, the Christians failed to find adequate suppliers outside Eastern Europe, which leads to the suspicion that the Russians may be playing one side off against the other. Frightened for their lives, the Christians had only Syria to turn to for protection and so it is that Assad has Lebanon where he wants it. For entirely different reasons, Christians and Moslems have appealed to him. He can act the impartial statesman. Regular Syrian troops have invaded, ostensibly to protect a beleaguered minority of Christians facing slaughter. It is in fact a simple extension of Syrian influence, violently executed.

Kemal Jumblatt has had the spoils removed from under his very nose, and for the first time in months he has had to forget the smell of blood and make approaches to the Christians, suddenly pretending to care at this stage about Lebanese independence. Yasser Arafat is also far from welcoming his Syrian brothers-in-arms, linking them now with Zionist conspiracies and worse. He too has been driven toward hated rivals, in his case George Habash of the Rejection

Front, in order to see whether the two of them can salvage anything for the irredentist Palestine cause. They cry betrayal, they assume militant postures. Perhaps they really did deceive themselves that the Syrians were nothing but fraternal crusaders. The moral is that when Syrian national aims are at stake, the restoration of Palestinian rights must look after itself. At the United Nations Arafat may be a celebrity, but in Beirut he is a leader of busted street-gangs. And to be on the safe side, Assad arrested over a hundred Palestinians and their sympathizers in Damascus who might accuse him openly of treachery.

By reflex action, the Palestinians have appealed to Cairo for succor, a procedure which ended by obtaining the comforting words of the United Nations. President Sadat may chuck them a bone or two; his misgivings over Syria's military and political enhancement remain to be tested. Iraq has a grievance that Greater Syria is a step closer to reality. Some sort of *club des réfusés* between Iraq, Libya and Algeria may emerge, all in the name of Palestinian solidarity and with Russian blessing. In the normal co-ordinates of the inter-Arab cold war, all these governments will no doubt try to reanimate their various friends and factions in Lebanon. The whole country has been a training ground for every Arab ideology. It is miserable whenever the opportunities of a democratic structure, even one so imperfect as Lebanon, are used to ruin it.

In the short run Israelis may consider that this clash between Syria and the PLO is a happy spectacle. But just as it suddenly came about as a matter of expediency, so it may vanish. Every Lebanese sect and confession has lost out in these 15 dreadful months of civil war. All of them have been at the mercy of their sponsors and backers. Should Syria manage to find some face-saving formula all round and establish itself as the permanent governing presence in

Lebanon – as seems likely for the time being – it may wish to help the PLO again, if only for fear of any other Arab government doing so. In any case, a Lebanon subordinated to Syria is not in Israel's wider interest. Put simply, Jews dare not expect to fare better than Christians in the Arab Middle East. Minorities are all under sentence. That's, of course, why the Israelis may seem skittish; they would not be wrong to see the Lebanese death happening as an indication of what their enemies would do to them if they could.

Over the past year Israel has been threatening in certain circumstances to take protective action by invading southern Lebanon. Some imaginary "red line" is supposed to be the point beyond which Syrians should not approach. Dropping the Palestinians, Assad has had the extra triumph of calming, or more properly neutralizing, Israel. The risk he ran in respect of the "red line" probably never matched the noises made by the Israeli government. Condemnation of any Israeli movement across the Lebanese frontier in self-defense would have been absolute – in marvelously ironic contrast to the tacit shrug of world approval to Syrian movements across the Lebanese frontier.

President Assad's future approach to Israel will be that much the stronger if he can keep the lid on everybody and everything in Lebanon. In order to try conclusions, he can take advantage of his new position to negotiate a deal *à la* Sadat. Security in Damascus, he might reason, no longer depends on the immediate or full recovery of the Golan Heights. But a further irony: he might demand as part of some bargain that Israel make concessions to the Palestinians which he himself would never contemplate, and so recover the Palestinian goodwill lost through *realpolitik*. What if he proposed non-belligerency with Israel on condition that a Palestinian state on the West Bank was set up without delay? And would he necessarily share the fetish of fashionable commentators that the PLO is the chosen vessel for the hopes of those in the territories?

The West Bank is the last place where the PLO can make a bid, its final throw. Whether the West Bank is more or less vulnerable to outside Arab interference than Lebanon will soon be seen. Many of the new mayors of the West Bank towns have certainly made public pronouncements favorable to the PLO. The process whereby they were chosen as candidates was connected with the Lebanese fighting in the sense that the older order was giving way everywhere, and the West Bank also wanted to be keeping up appearances. For all the rhetoric and radical top-dressing, however, this is still a conservative society. The mayors may be new, but they are not quite the break with the past that they proclaim themselves to be. They are representatives of their clans or families, as usual, and for another factor they show no willingness to forego the subsidies from Jordan which enable them to hold the Israelis at arms' length. In private, they are in the same relation to Jordan and Israel as the outgoing mayors were.

PLO funds on any large scale would certainly alter the sophisticated give-and-take which everyone has perfected since 1976 but even so, as recent West Bank disturbances and riots have shown, the only available weapons are stones and burning tires. Nine people have died there, distant casualties of the Lebanese fighting (and of the ritual hysterics at the UN) rather than of the Israeli occupation. There may well be more, sadly, for as the PLO and the extremists in Lebanon are brought under Syrian control, they will have no other outlet. They are in the habitual Palestinian position of being able only to call down a curse on everybody. That much at least is unchanged.

The New Republic
June 19, 1976

KING HUSSEIN has now been on the throne of Jordan for 25 years and that is a jubilee altogether more remarkable than Queen Elizabeth's. His has been a perilous reign, so perilous that it has been easy at any moment to mark the King down for the scrapheap of history. Jordan, so the argument has run, was never much more than a desert emirate concocted by the British Colonial Office when it had already lost its touch. There has never been, and never will be, a sound economic basis for this state whose sole resources are phosphates and tourism, and which has only one port, Aqaba on the Red Sea, alongside Israel's Eilat, where everything is better handled. Who needs kings anyhow? Pan-Arabism, or Nasserism, or Palestinians, or some such progressive notion is invariably about to cook the King's goose.

In spite of everything, the King continues to survive his neighbors, his enemies, and – sometimes most dangerous of all – his friends. He has survived three wars, one civil war, several incursions by Syrian, Iraqi or Saudi forces and at least three serious coups. In 1958 he was warned what to fear when his cousin King Faisal of Iraq was brutally butchered along with that whole branch of the Hashemite family, and their corpses then were degraded. Two prime ministers, Hazza Majali and Wasfi Tell, have been murdered in office. Ten or by some counts 12 assassination attempts have been made on the King's person and more than once he has picked up side-arms to shoot his way out of a tight corner. And still he comes up smiling. His position would long have been intolerable if he were merely an imposed or antique figurehead. His courage and style are admired in Jordan, and in general his popularity is genuine, which is the point overlooked by the armchair diplomats who keep writing

him off. This monarchy was never as fragile as it seems.

Jordan, to be sure, is an autocracy. Its parliament is designed to express the wishes of the ruler, not the electorate, which is limited strictly to men with property qualifications. There is also a most efficient police and intelligence apparatus, American-aided, and its chief, Mohamed Rasoul Kilani, became a bogey in Palestinian myth. Without this internal security system, the King might indeed have foundered in one of the endless secret plots against him, but it is not – it does not need to be – an engine of oppression as for instance the Syrian Deuxième Bureau is, or as Nasser's police was. By the standards of the region, Jordan is merciful and even relaxed. People do not vanish there as in Iraq, nor are they publicly executed, nor are their limbs lopped by the hangman as in Saudi Arabia or Libya.

The King has his people, of course – the Bedouin, or tribesmen of what is Transjordan proper, the Adwan, the Anizeh, the Howeitat, the Beni Sakhr, in all the ramifications of nomadic genealogy and lore which Western travelers have so romanticized. Some of these tribes enjoyed ancient and hereditary feuds which have not been quite extinguished by a modern policy of urban settlement, but the King is their man. He counts as one of them, a great-grandson of the Sherif of Mecca, descendent of the Prophet. It is a bit of fiction to see King Hussein as a desert Arab when his education at Harrow and Sandhurst made a decent English public schoolboy of him, but all the same it is a fiction which works to give him a constituency.

The Palestinians, around half a million of them (census figures are unreliable), are outnumbered three or four to one by the Bedouin, and they exist in Jordan on tolerance, a fact of which they need no reminding. Historically the way Jordan assumed guardianship for Palestinians is clear. In 1948, as the British Mandate was limping to its sorry end, the Foreign Office under Ernest Bevin turned a blind eye when King Abdullah, Hussein's grandfather, invaded Palestine, or the West Bank, to be precise – that part of the country which the United Nations had voted to partition and allot to the Palestinians as their independent state, with Israel similarly established alongside. King Abdullah had no love for the Palestinians, nor hatred for the Israelis, for that matter, but he had been brought up in the old school which taught that a man ruled what he could conquer and hold. With the exception of Britain, the world did not sanction this annexation of the West Bank. King Abdullah certainly aggrandized his territory but it proved, frankly, not worth the trouble, and soon cost him his life. The West Bank was a rump, its peasant population shattered out of their ways, and swollen by refugees escaping the fighting.

In order to come to terms with circumstances, West Bankers and refugees alike were given Jordanian citizenship; they could enroll in the army and the bureaucracy. Some of them did well in commerce. Some made fortunes. Some rose in the King's service to the highest offices – the Rifai family, his intimate and faithful friends, are originally Palestinians from Safed, and his late wife Alia Tuqan belonged to one of the most notable families of Nablus. But disturbances on the West Bank were frequent and perhaps inevitable, especially when fomented from outside. Nasser built his early career by arousing expectations in these poor people. To counteract him, the King did once experiment in democratic elections, which threw up as prime minister Suleiman Nabulsi, a Palestinian and a rich man who veiled his power-urge by describing it as left-wing. The resulting crisis, with Nasser and the Russians agog in the wings, was perhaps the closest of Hussein's many shaves, and he is not likely to risk experiences of the kind again. By and large, the Palestinians were governed firmly but not too unfairly between 1948 and 1967. Then the Six Day War put an end to King Abdullah's patchwork. With the Israelis left in possession of the West Bank, Greater Jordan was over and done with. In a sense Hussein was freed from his grandfather's ambition.

For Hussein to see it in that perspective, it scarcely need be said, is hard. To the maintaining of his inheritance, he brings emotion. While still a teenager, he had the trauma of witnessing his grandfather's murder by agents of the Mufti of Jerusalem. A conventional man in any case, he feels under family obligation toward the West Bank. As the Six Day War opened, he chose not to listen to Israeli warnings to stay out of hostilities. In this he was really the victim of Nasser, who kept him in the dark, as well as of his own temperament. *Sharafa* – that concept of honor in which the Arab mind bogs down with all manner of military fantasy – dictated that he enter a war which could lead only to ruin. Had he remained inactive, he would have had a crisis of confidence in Jordan only for those few tumultuous days, at the end of which Nasser's destructive lies and consequent humiliation would have been evident. The King could have been the statesman of the hour, with the West Bank and the Old City of Jerusalem still his and intact, and the Palestinian question would have taken a very different course these last 10 years.

On the face of it, this was the most painful misjudgment of the reign. Yet as so often happens, things may have worked out unexpectedly for the good, in that Hussein was obliged thereby to have no share whatever in the Palestine national movement. The Palestine Liberation Organization, Fatah, Saiqa, the multifarious loggerhead groupings, were so many instruments variously forged by Egypt, Syria and other Arab states to advance their ends when their armies could no longer do so in the aftermath of 1967. The Palestinians were there to be paid and exploited as mercenaries. But Jordan was the base for these shallow intrigues. Jordan, not Israel, was vulnerable. From 1967 to 1970 Yasser Arafat and George Habash and Yahya Hammoudia and Naif Hawatmeh had it their separate ways in Amman. They looked to be the real powers in the land, and were reported as such by Westerners who ought to have known better. In fact they were operatives for their paymasters, and had behind them no mass support.

When King Hussein finally moved against the PLO and the PFLP in the events of Black September, he proved what an artifact the Palestinian national movement is. Here was the chance of a Palestinian uprising, indeed for taking over the whole country, if some Western observers were to be believed, but instead the Palestinians in Jordan, the rich and the refugees alike, remained loyal to the King. In part they were little motivated against him; in part, they were afraid of the Bedouin. Some months beforehand, I had been in Zerqa, where the army has its main barracks, and I remember a conversation with Arab Legionnaires in which they were contemptuous of the Palestinians as faint-hearts who had fled their homeland when they should have stayed and fought the Israelis like men. To the Bedouin, the Palestinians have only themselves to blame, and had better cause no more trouble. It was said that the King's mind was wonderfully concentrated for him when the Beni Sakhr chiefs arrived in a deputation to ask him to put the Palestinians in their place or be thrown out in favor of someone who would.

The loss of the West Bank, then, cemented traditional tribal Jordan. The Israelis had acquired the troublesome onus of dealing with the West Bank, and it may be doubted

that they could ever have done so without Jordanian acqui-
escence, which was in the form of the Open Bridges policy.
By means of the open bridges between Israeli-occupied territory and Jordan, the West Bankers were able to buy and
sell in their established markets and in general to live as
normally as possible. Without such a safety valve, grievances
would almost certainly have flared into non-cooperation
and civil disobedience and violence. But the policy for which
Israel tends to receive credit has really depended for its
smoothness upon Jordan, which could have closed the
bridges at any time, thus emphasizing the claustrophobia
and precipitating reactions against the Israelis, leading to
curfews, martial law and horrors all too readily imagined.
King Hussein has had the ultimate responsibility for the
comparative amicability of Israelis and Arabs on the West
Bank, and he has not abused it.

So far Israeli and Jordanian interests have coincided.
The net effect has been to underline how neither party really
wants the West Bank badly enough to be aggressive about
it – we will have to see about the Likud party – but cannot
think how to shed the burden gracefully. The King continues to pay salaries to teachers and administrators there,
which is only bidding for their loyalties just in case a solution one day should turn upon plebiscites or public opinion,
and their votes would be handy. It's the stopgap that endures,
but all the same this West Bank limbo can hardly last for
ever, amen. In the vacuum the PLO operates. Arafat wants
the West Bank badly. He wants whatever is going, and it is
altogether convenient to suppose that he and the concept of
a Palestinian homeland can be tidied away simultaneously.
Neither Syria nor Egypt believes in such a homeland, but
pay lip-service to the idea in order to gloss over how they
actually treat the Palestinians. If a Palestinian homeland
were to be created, both Egypt and Syria would not cease

from conspiring until one or the other controlled it. Syrian support for a homeland for Palestinians is glaringly self-seeking in the light of Syrian elimination of what little vestiges of free maneuvering the PLO had in Lebanon.

It is something quite else when an American president comes out recommending a Palestinian homeland. That President Carter muffed it and had to backtrack into the old mumblings about Resolutions 242 and 338 means perhaps that speaking with two tongues is not confined to the White House of the Nixon era. But President Carter had received King Hussein in Washington earlier in the year and seems to have given him no clue to the blow to expect. The King has been caught by surprise that the Americans feel so free to dispose of a West Bank which is still nominally his. To Amman, it appears as though the King has been deliberately and senselessly rebuffed and he is furious at the loss of face.

A Palestinian homeland, if it were to be realized in Washington or Geneva or anywhere, would be understood in Jordan as approval by the powers that be of anti-Hussein steps. The verdict of Black September would be queried by higher authority. The immediate consequence of ensuing Palestinian agitation would be to unleash the Bedouin to settle the score finally. When extremists, or even well-wishers, advocate that Jordan should become a Palestinian state, or endow its Palestinians with autonomy in some form, they ignore that the Bedouin have the arms and the will to go massacring.

Unwisely encouraged by this turn in American policy, Yasser Arafat has seen his chance, and late last month he offered to meet King Hussein in Amman. Presumably he wishes to impress upon the King how sober the American-sponsored Palestinian homeland would be. The King naturally refused the indignity of having Arafat gloating about how the Americans, of all people, have given him one more

296

throw of the dice. Nor is this the only pressure upon the King. The Syrians have been proposing a formal alliance with Jordan, which has been rejected as though it were an invitation from a boa constrictor. Since the death of their preposterously bigoted King Faisal, the Saudis have recognized the common interests of Israel and Jordan in preserving the *status quo* in the Middle East where the Russians are trying everything to expand their influence. But then the Saudis have a view of politics at all levels as conspiracy by any other name, and so they also pay the PLO as well as making good the deficits of the Jordanian budget. Their signals to Amman are confused and confusing.

Among other signs of the times is a bizarre rumor about the King's suspicion that Western intelligence agents contrived the helicopter crash in which Queen Alia was killed, the purpose supposedly being to expose Jordanian isolation. This is a perfect illustration of the Arab literary device of inventing a false story for the sake of crystallizing something assumed to be true. The King also refused to allow the BBC to make a film celebrating his silver jubilee and this is interpreted as the disgust and scorn against the West that followed President Carter's homeland speech. Meanwhile a Soviet military mission arrived in Amman at the end of May.

The situation is reminiscent of the period between the Suez Campaign and the build up to the Six Day War. In 1956 President Eisenhower compelled the Israelis to withdraw, and the Arabs were therefore spared responsibility for their actions, and in effect Nasser was encouraged into actions which could only be hostile to American interests. This is happening again, but with the Palestinians. President Carter's Palestinian homeland pronouncement is not just an inept betrayal of an ally but an Eisenhower-like refusal to accept that the Palestinian national movement, like Nasserism before it, by its behavior has unfitted itself for power in the eyes of Arabs who must live with it. That is how to prepare for bloodshed.

The Syrian-Egyptian tangle is also much as it was in the early '60s, though Hussein can rejoice that Nasser is no longer plaguing him. But he has in Hafez Assad a master-conspirator who is likely to dominate the next stage of his reign as Nasser did its formative years. Israel has one further option not available in those years, in that it is now in a position to annex the West Bank. If President Carter keeps on moralizing off the point, if Hussein were ever to see advantage in closing the Jordan bridges, the Israel of Menahem Begin might be provoked to repeat exactly the mistake of King Abdullah, and hope to digest what is indigestible. That would be a ridiculous irony, but who knows? It might guarantee Hussein's Golden Jubilee. The years till then will be neither dull nor trivial.

The New Republic
June 25, 1977

THE POLITICAL RECOVERY of Europe since 1945 has been a story of unprecedented success. Communism has been brought down, and without a shot, let alone the sort of all-out war that earlier had been required to defeat Nazism. Democracy, where it existed already, has been strengthened; where it did not exist, above all in Germany and Italy, it has struck deep roots. In Britain and France, the loss of empire has led not to revolution and ruin but to higher standards of living. No West European country has serious irredentist claims upon any other and external threats are more imaginary than real.

And yet, instead of consolidating and enjoying these gains, the entire continent is in the grip of uncertainty and rising instability. Once again, as between the two world wars, ordinary people face a restructuring of the whole European order which they are virtually powerless to affect. The cause of this self-inflicted crisis is European integration, a fraught and long-drawn-out process now inescapably coming to a head.

The West European countries are already taking measures to "converge" their economies according to what were originally quite strict criteria. This is a preliminary to the next step: as of January 1, 1999, all national currencies are to be replaced with a single European currency, to be known as the Euro. "The coining of money," in the words of William Blackstone, the founding father of jurisprudence, "is in all states the act of sovereign power." A common currency is inconceivable without common political institutions to support it, and these common institutions are the end toward which Europe is moving.

Down the centuries, the shifting relationships of Britain, France, Italy and Germany have determined Europe's fate. Now, through the apparently benign and thoroughly boring technicalities of a common currency, a new relationship is struggling to be born. The final goal is a choice among several potential forms of political federation, some loose, some tight, the most grandiose of which is a United States of Europe. But if any one of them is to become a reality, the historic nation-states of Europe will have to surrender their sovereignty and change out of all recognition.

Partitioned throughout the cold war, Germany was "one nation, two states." Every German government had the long-term objective of reuniting the two states. French foreign policy, by contrast, looked upon partition as a lasting and valuable constraint on German power. What the French were afraid of was a revival of "European" ambitions on Germany's part of the kind they hoped had been defeated in World War II. In 1950 a left-wing French deputy, François Billoux, spoke for many of his countrymen when he said, "Europe was Hitler's idea."*

But there were others in France – Jean Monnet and Robert Schuman most notably among them – who clung to an old pre-war conviction that only genuinely supranational institutions could keep the peace in Europe; and as West German economic power grew by leaps and bounds in the '50s and '60s, French policy began to reverse itself. With growing panic, successive French governments sought to create the common institutions which might permit them

---

* A new book by John Laughland, *The Tainted Source* (Little Brown, London), elaborates informatively upon what its subtitle calls "The Undemocratic Origins of the European Idea."

to share in the gathering strength of Germany and who knows, even direct or surmount it. By 1962 General de Gaulle was explaining to his colleague Alain Peyrefitte that European integration was the means by which their country not only could "prevent domination by the Americans or the Russians" but could "become what she has ceased to be since Waterloo: the leading power in the world." Germany, it was clear, needed friends, and in its chastened post-war mood also held out the hope that a constructive relationship with other European powers would preclude further warfare.

From small acorns great oaks do grow. One Franco-German initiative led to another, and one treaty to the next. The result was the European Economic Community, which became the European Community, and is now the European Union (EU), a supranational construction of a type never before seen. In addition to France and Germany, its fifteen countries include Italy, Britain, Ireland, Spain and Portugal, Denmark and Sweden and Finland, the Benelux nations, Greece, and Austria. About the same number again – mostly in Eastern Europe but also Israel, Morocco and Turkey – seek terms for membership or association. Norway, Iceland and Switzerland have chosen to stay out.

Admission has been an erratic process. Those already inside have demanded their pound of flesh, while petitioners must decide what and how to pay. Once in, member governments have bargained fiercely for "opt-outs" and "derogations" without which they would never have been in a position to jump through the hoops of the next stages of integration, as called for in the series of treaties that culminated in the Maastricht Treaty of 1991.

That treaty commits the European Union to a single foreign policy, with a single defense policy to follow, and to a common citizenship with rights and obligations still to be defined. The agreed single currency, the Euro, is to be managed from a new European central bank, in Frankfurt, which will control the gold and dollar reserves of all countries in the EU. (This means that no country could again finance a war in its own interest, as Britain did in the Falklands in the early '80s) The bank will also set a single continent-wide interest rate, the effect of which will inevitably be to benefit some regions and industries and hurt others. On the central-bank board will sit former heads of national banks, now reduced to the role of national spokesmen.

Such is the forum where the interests of member countries of Europe are to be fought out. What this will be like in practice can be observed in the institutions already operating in Brussels, the capital of the EU. To anyone brought up to value democratic essentials like the separation of powers, checks and balances, and accountability, today's European Union is a bewildering improvisation imposed from the top, without the legitimacy conferred by popular consent. Its supreme body is the European Council, consisting of the fifteen heads of state or government, who meet two or three times a year for private discussion behind closed doors. Councils of Ministers then convert the ensuing agreements into policy.

These Councils consist separately of the ministers of foreign affairs, finance, transport, social affairs, and so on of their respective countries, and they too meet at regular intervals. Each such Council enjoys both executive and legislative powers, and may, in the words of an authoritative work on the EU,* "convene in any configuration it chooses." The same source goes on to observe that the individual Council "remains the most secretive as well as the most

---

* *The Penguin Companion to European Unity*, by Timothy Bainbridge with Anthony Teasdale (revised edition 1996).

powerful of the institutions of the Union"; it is the only legislative body in the democratic world which meets and
deliberates in secret.

The legislation generated by this process is then passed
to the European Commission for execution. The Commission consists of a president and twenty commissioners, who
are appointed to office and cannot be dismissed. They
divide among themselves portfolios for trade, agriculture,
the environment and so on. Under them are some 20,000
bureaucrats who enjoy, again in the words of the same
authority, a "unique combination of administrative, executive, legislative and political activities and responsibilities."
A civil service, the European Commission is in fact unique
in two respects: it may initiate and pass legislation, and it is
accountable to nobody and nothing but itself.

In Brussels, some 700 standing committees do the work
of government, of which about 400 are meeting on any
given day. Decisions may be taken according to several different procedures, but the most usual involves what is called
"qualified majority voting" – a euphemism for horse-trading
and rigging.

Still another body is the European Court of Justice, or
ECJ. This was set up with the specific mission – a political
mission, not a judicial one – of furthering the ends of European integration. Commission and Court together are
empowered to promulgate law through a variety of instruments, including regulations (which are absolutely binding
on member states), directives (also binding but allowing
each nation to implement them in its own way), recommendations, opinions and resolutions.

Finally there is the so-called European Parliament, with
some 600 members. Elected in their own countries, usually
on a list system or by proportional representation, they really
represent only themselves. European-wide parties do not

exist. Without genuine legislative or even revisory powers and hobbled by the official recognition of eleven different languages with all the attendant difficulties of interpretation and translation, the Parliament is a figurehead in the style of the Russian Duma. Its energies are devoted, in vain, to the wresting of power from Council and Commission.

In this state of things, "Europe" still has no sovereignty, in the true meaning of that word, but is rather a stew of German federalism, French *dirigisme*, protectionism, corporatism and mass welfarism – all enshrined in an Orwellian language naturally known as Eurospeak and intelligible, if at all, only to the presiding Eurocrats. Key phrases such as "subsidiarity," "proportionality," "non-paper," "*engrenage*," and "co-decision procedure," as well as acronyms like Coreper and Ecofin, hide the human reality: here is a set of rules whose whys and wherefores can neither be anticipated nor readily grasped but from which there is no appeal. The Eurospeak for *that* is "democratic deficit."

This whole structure arose within the confines of the cold war, which imposed limitations of its own on the European political scene. At least as long as that conflict lasted, the notion of an eventual political integration seemed to most European countries a secondary consideration, even chimerical, and whatever was happening in Brussels appeared to escape close analysis. Even so, however, the mounting costs of Brussels soon loomed larger than any benefits.

On the one hand there was the single market, designed to facilitate the movement of people and goods and to encourage free trade; to this, all could assent. But on the other hand there were such things as the Common Agriculture Policy (CAP) and the Common Fisheries Policy (CFP), which, as even the commissioners in charge were forced to agree, were open-ended disasters. Without regard to cost, every profession, trade, and industry had to adapt to standards dictated by the bureaucracy in Brussels, and this created a paradise for lobbyists and special-interest groups, as well as big business with enough clout to obstruct competitors. Intervention-buying led to surpluses: the notorious mountains of European butter and lakes of European wine. Impenetrable to the outsider and all in Eurospeak too, a highly complicated system arose to block the free market through all manner of subsidies, grants, quotas, transfer payments, and special funds. Inventive command-bureaucracy like this is a novelty in the free world.

During the '80s, the project almost strangled to death in contradiction and red tape. The media and the public began to mock the weighty decrees from Brussels dictating the exact bulge of a strawberry, the precise degree of straightness of a cucumber, the impermissibility of a double-decker bus. No satirist could have had the inspiration that, in the name of free trade, animals and even plants should be obliged to have passports, or that whole breeds of dogs might be suppressed on account of the shape of their nose and the texture of their fur. (Canine racism!)

And then in 1989 the cold war came to its abrupt end and every supposition changed. Margaret Thatcher, then the British Prime Minister, and President François Mitterrand of France were quick to perceive that a new balance of power had emerged. Increasing its territory by 40 percent and its population by 25 percent, Germany was back in size to what it had been before World War II, and Russia was no longer there to provide a counter-balance. For the first time in its history, Germany could now settle relations with the rest of the world peacefully and on its own terms. As for the United States, successive American administrations, though they no doubt thought the prospect unlikely, had always argued in favor of German unification and President George Bush waved it through without a second thought.

Chancellor of Germany since 1982, Helmut Kohl was convinced that he was the man fitted to shoulder the responsibilities of the new situation. A more dependable ally of the United States than his immediate predecessors, Kohl conceived of Europe as a bloc in the making, and he was able to push through his idea from a position of economic and political strength. By means of the Maastricht Treaty, he proved himself far and away the most influential politician anywhere outside the United States. Maastricht may be seen as the European treaty that was never signed after the conclusion of the war; it is, to the contemporary order of Europe, what the Versailles Treaty was after World War I.

But why should anyone want this new arrangement? Why should the Germans, of all people, want it? The guilts and atonements of Nazism are on the ebb; the German constitution, the Bundesbank, the deutsche mark are rightly seen as solid achievements. To surrender these things for the sake of Europe must seem an almost saintly act of abnegation, if not of national martyrdom.

And Germany also has its hands full at the moment. At the time of reunification, East Germany was reputed to be the tenth or perhaps eleventh largest economy in the world; in fact, it was a bankrupt rust-belt whose goods were fit only for a command economy. With East German industry uncompetitive, much of it simply closed down, raising unemployment to 30 percent or more. Since then, sums on the order of 100 billion marks have been transferred every year from West to East to pay the costs of reunification, and some experts calculate that twenty more years of such payments will be necessary.

Germans, in short, have already found it hard and expensive to integrate with other Germans. Unemployment stands officially at 4.7 million – about the number just prior to Hitler's takeover – and this figure is almost certainly understated. German wages are already the highest in the world, and taxes and social charges add 90 percent to employment costs. Moreover, Germany's difficulties have had consequences for other countries in Europe, which, given the criteria imposed by the goal of a common currency, have had to adopt the high German interest rate and have suffered deflation and recession for their pains.

To Helmut Kohl, however, these are only trifles on the way to the goal of integration. Where Bismarck united Germany by force, he is determined to go one better – to resolve the German question by uniting all of Europe, and with strokes of the pen rather than the sword. The reason, he maintains, is that aside from the manifest good that is to be found in federation, his countrymen must be tied, locked, bound, embedded, and contained. A strong Germany needs weakening, not only to appease its rightly anxious neighbors but for its own sake.

At times Kohl even invokes the threat of a resurgent German nationalism, with all the fears this specter can arouse in Europe. In February 1996 he warned that "the policy of European integration is really a question of war and peace in the 21st century." A policy paper issued by his party was even bleaker: "If European integration were not to progress, Germany might be called upon, or tempted by its own security constraints, to try to effect the stabilization of Eastern Europe on its own and in the traditional way."

To be sure, it is possible to argue – as some of Kohl's critics do – that he cannot be sincere. Is all this not just a brilliantly expedient dressing-up of German imperialism as altruism, taking measures calculated to achieve supremacy under the pretense of forgoing it? But Kohl is no conspirator. Like many Germans of his generation, he genuinely conflates nationalism with Nazism, and therefore believes that nationalist sentiment has to be submerged and then suppressed by means of a supranational structure. Kohl's rigid conception of ultimate European union is the price to be paid for his rigid conception of the German past.

In any event, the German chancellor insists on pushing through his policy no matter what political and economic realities might suggest. The slightest postponement of the timetable will, he prophesies, wreck the peace of Europe, and there can be no turning back "unless we wish to challenge fate." In this he is seconded by the new President of Europe, Jacques Santer of Luxembourg, to whom any resistance either to the Euro or to the timing of its introduction is the work of "pessimists against whom I declare war." Under pressure, they and their officials also mutter that the Euro will enable Europe to resist the dollar, as if that were self-evidently a sensible thing to do.

Others, however, hold a different view of these matters.

Germans themselves have become increasingly nervous and doubtful about the rewards that will crown the sacrifice asked of them. Why, they have begun to ask, should they incorporate into the hard mark a number of soft currencies debauched by unscrupulous foreign politicians? Do they really have to pay for inherent economic backwardness or mis-management elsewhere in Europe? Why must they placate the whole range of eager supplicants and subsidy hunters – backward peasant farmers, industries protected from competition by socialist governments, inefficient producers and retailers in other lands?

In a recent survey, 79 percent of Germans said they wanted a referendum before going farther and the same survey indicates that the outcome of such a referendum would be close, with only 43 percent in favor of abolishing the mark and 44 percent against. In another poll, only 14 percent of German businessmen believed that monetary union would be beneficial to them and 55 percent expressed doubt. It cannot reassure the Germans that opinion polls in Spain, Italy, Belgium, Ireland and elsewhere show large majorities there in *favor* of monetary and political union. These populations visualize European federation first as an escape from their own internal weaknesses and then as fairy-gold prosperity, backed by all that good German discipline and hard work.

In France a number of intellectuals and politicians are now saying openly that Germany has grown into the outright winner of World War II, while France has been revealed as the outright loser. For such people, only the capture of the mark can halt the German drive to power and gain the French a disproportionate influence in the order set up by the Maastricht Treaty. When President Mitterrand consented to hold a referendum to approve that treaty, he, like other European leaders in the same circumstances, went to extreme lengths to fix the result; nevertheless, he obtained national assent to its terms by less than 1 percent. President Jacques Chirac is not prepared to allow either a parliamentary vote or a referendum on the next steps toward union. Polls, however, show that the country is split down the middle. Unemployment running at 12 percent and deflation, which many Frenchmen see as German-led, are causing demonstrations and low-level violence, of which foreigners are usually the victims.

The British, albeit acrimoniously, have gone along with the drift of things over the years, while unilaterally opting out from particular EU policies they have not liked or have been unable to keep. One of these was the Exchange Rate Mechanism, or ERM, the prototype of today's Euro-convergence criteria. On Britain's entry to the ERM in 1990, the pound was overvalued against the mark and the money markets could not take the strain. The government of John Major had no choice but to abandon the ERM regime altogether in 1992 and other countries then followed suit. The surviv-

ing inner group of France, Germany, and the Benelux countries, bogged down in the recession brought about by their
collective monetary policy, remains resentful of what looks
like Britain's lucky escape (and of its current economic
well-being).

Since then, arguments for and against the Euro and ultimate federal union have engaged British politicians and
businessmen in fierce hand-to-hand combat. Opinion polls
reflect public awareness of the upheavals in store. In 1995,
61 percent were voting to stay in Europe, 29 percent to leave;
by early 1997, only 42 percent were voting to stay in and 38
percent to leave (20 percent were undecided). In the run-up
to this May's general election, most Conservative-party candidates declared themselves against the Euro and other
obligations under Maastricht, and in this respect at least
they seemed to have the agreement of British voters, some
two-thirds of whom were now expressing the wish to have
no more European integration.

Mainly, however, British policy toward Europe has been
marked by hypocrisy. The assumption is that union is any-
way impossible, and federation an idle dream, so that the
prudent thing is to stand aside as the project sleepwalks to
its doom. But what if, instead, it comes into being? Although
a recent government White Paper asserted that even within
a federal Europe, Britain would remain an independent
nation-state, both major political parties tacitly conceded
that this cannot be true. Sizeable minorities seem to believe
that in the end Britain will take a Churchillian stance, and
back out of the European Union altogether. Yet these political minorities have also remained comparatively silent,
even as Britain's national interest, its identity, and the
whole reading of its history hang in the balance.

In the meantime, every European country, Britain
included, already has two heads of state – its own and the

EU president, Jacques Santer – two capitals, two parliaments, two flags, and above all, two systems of law: national law and the law decreed by the European Court of Justice. In 1990 a British judge in a British court ruled that entry into the Union (then still known as the Community) under the terms of the previous Treaty of Rome had indeed meant that "Parliament surrendered its sovereign right to legislate contrary to the treaty on the matters of social and economic policy which it regulated." And those "matters" are constantly proliferating. Mutually reinforcing one another, the European Council and the ECJ decree continually enter new fields, fortifying the Maastricht order and steadily diminishing the place of national law.

The war of laws has brought the rule of law in Europe altogether into disrespect. European elites increasingly treat public life as a vast patronage system, there for the plundering. National courts now hear scandalous cases in which heads of governments, ministers, leaders of industry, parliamentary deputies, even the one-time Secretary General of NATO, are charged with theft of public funds, profiteering from office and even murder – yet somehow the prison doors never quite close on them. In all of this, Brussels sets the pace.

For Brussels with its bureaucracy is an extraordinary swamp of systemic fraud and crime. The total EU budget is 55 billion pounds (approximately $89 billion), for which there is no proper accounting. Perplexed auditors admit that in 1995, the last year for which official figures exist, almost $10 billion disappeared through corruption and mismanagement, and between 4.3 percent and 8.5 percent of the budget was lost through error (no attempt is made to explain why the margin is so wide). According to unofficial sources, a quarter of the EU budget goes missing somewhere in the channels of disbursement. Like the old Soviet *nomenklatura*, the bureaucrats award themselves tax-free salaries and privileges. None of this, however, concerns the ECJ, which is too busy promulgating new law to prosecute violations of the old.

No wonder, as the outlines of a supranational Europe become visible, that another law – the law of unintended consequences – has begun to make itself felt. As the nation-state surrenders to something larger than itself, it is leaving behind a vacuum and ethnicity is filling that vacuum fast. A number of European countries contain ethnic minorities; claiming to represent these minorities, small groups have started movements of "national liberation" on the third-world model. Rejecting assimilation as "oppression," they resort to terror. Basques in Spain, Flemings in Belgium, the IRA in Britain, Corsicans in France, all threaten the social and political cohesion of their respective nation-states.

As ethnic consciousness rises, so does its counterpart, nationalist xenophobia. Nobody knows the figures for sure, but in Europe there seem to be around twenty million immigrants, legal and illegal. Almost without exception, those legally in Europe have rights equal to those of native citizens. In the main they have arrived from Africa and the Muslim world, and lately from the former Communist bloc as well. Popular opinion often blames these foreigners for diluting the old identity of the nation-state.

Historically the nation-state has satisfied but also controlled nationalism, which otherwise builds up like underground gas, to explode when it can. The Maastricht order, however, *encourages* the build-up of noxious pressures. If national parliaments and institutions no longer represent the sentiments of large numbers of people, some of them will make up for the "democratic deficit" in the only way available, through new political formations and parties which express and give form to their grievances.

Nationalist, willing to be strong-armed though not exactly fascist, these strange new groupings – the Northern League in Italy, the Flemish Bloc, the National Front in France, Jorg Haidar's Austrian Freedom party, the Scottish Nationalist Party – are the inadvertent products of the European Union, which after Nazism and after Communism is the latest would-be usurper of national sovereignty in Europe. They have been capturing ever-larger shares of the vote, up to a third in some elections and they have prospects of power. And there may be worse to come. Historians unanimously maintain that the reparations imposed on Germany by the Treaty of Versailles gave rise to a German desire for revenge and helped make Hitler possible. What will the backlash be when Germans come to believe that the dissipation of their economic strength to other countries is a policy of reparations in a new form?

Motivated by emotional and ill-considered attitudes to the past, lured on by the mirage of a Grand Design, the Kohls and the Santers and their kind are embarked upon a utopian experiment which is mustering the very same destructive forces it claims to be eliminating. The national interests of Britain, France, Italy, and Germany remain what they were. On the day these interests collide, there will be nothing except the Euro and a half-formulated anti-American ideology to hold together the artificial scaffolding that is Brussels and ward off a general collapse in anger, disillusionment and violence.

Commentary
June 1997

ONLY A FEW YEARS AGO, mass-murder attacks on the West in the name of Islam, like those of September 11, would have seemed like a thriller writer's fantasy. Nor would anyone have imagined that a bombing by Islamists could swing a general election in a European country, that a Dutch movie maker might be shot dead on the street for a film about the abuse of women in Islam, or that one might find oneself watching, on television, the beheading of Western hostages by men crying out *Allahu Akhbar!* over their savage deeds. Pakistan now has a nuclear bomb, and this weapon is widely described as an Islamic bomb. To judge by their pronouncements, the Islamist leaders of Iran can hardly wait to perfect and use their derivative of it.

At present, it is not clear whether the religious/ideological rage that is the motive force behind these developments has any limits, whether it may yet succeed in mobilizing truly huge numbers of Muslim masses, or whether it can be deflected or crushed. What is clear is that a phenomenon that at first looked like a cloud no bigger than a man's hand has lashed up into a crisis with global implications.

Does this crisis amount to a "clash of civilizations"? Many people reject that notion as too sweeping or downright misleading. Yet whether or not it applies to, say, the situation in Iraq, or to the war on terror, the phrase has much to recommend it as a description of what is going on inside Europe today. As Yves Charles Zarka, a French philosopher and analyst, has written: "there is taking place in France a central phase of the more general and mutually conflicting encounter between the West and Islam, which only someone completely blind or of radical bad faith, or possibly of disconcerting naiveté, could fail to recognize." In the opinion of Bassam Tibi, an academic of Syrian origins who lives in Germany, Europeans are facing a stark alternative: "Either Islam gets Europeanized, or Europe gets Islamized." Going still farther, the eminent historian Bernard Lewis has speculated that the clash may well be over by the end of this century, at which time, if present demographic trends continue, Europe itself will *be* Muslim.

Today's situation has been a very long time – centuries – in the making. For much of that time, of course, the encounter between Muslims and the West remained stacked in favor of the latter, both militarily and culturally. Which is not to say that Europeans of an earlier age were blind to the danger posed to Western civilization by a resurgent Islam. One watchful observer was Winston Churchill, who wrote about Islam – or Mohammedanism as it was then called – in *The River War* (1899):

> No stronger retrograde force exists in the world. Far from being moribund, Mohammedanism is a militant and proselytizing faith. It has already spread throughout Central Africa, raising fearless warriors at every step, and were it not that Christianity is sheltered in the strong arms of science ... the civilization of modern Europe might fall, as fell the civilization of ancient Rome.

Hilaire Belloc had similar premonitions 30 years later in *The Great Heresies* (1938):

> Will not perhaps the temporal power of Islam return and with it the menace of an armed Muhammadan world which will shake the dominion of Europeans – still nom-

inally Christian – and reappear again as the prime enemy of our civilization?... Since we have here a very great religion, physically paralyzed, but morally intensely alive, we are in the presence of an unstable equilibrium.

To these early observers, nevertheless, it did seem that Western cultural and military superiority could be counted on to prevail, at least for the foreseeable future. (Belloc is better remembered for his boast, "We have got the Gatling gun, and they have not.") And prevail it did throughout a good part of the 20th century. In the last decades, however, another historical process has been at work drastically revising the calculus of power.

Contemporary Islamism might be summed up as the effort to redress and reverse the long-ago defeat of Muslim power by European (i.e. Christian) civilization. Toward that end, it has followed two separate courses of action: adopting the forms of nationalism that have appeared to many Muslims to contain the secret of Western supremacy, or promoting Islam itself as the one force capable of uniting Muslims everywhere and hence ensuring their renewed power and dominance. In the hands of today's Islamists, and with the complicity of Europe itself, these two approaches have proved mutually reinforcing.

In Europe, the world wars of the last century finally undid and discredited the idea of the sovereign nation-state, the engine of the continent's pre-eminence and self-confidence. In place of this tried and tested political arrangement, now suddenly seen as outmoded and dysfunctional, institutions like the European Union and the United Nations were thought to offer a firmer foundation for a new world order, one that would be based on universal legal norms and in which sovereign power would be rendered superfluous. It has been the resulting decline of the European nation-state that has helped provide a unique opportunity for Islamism, itself based on a world-wide, transnational community that has been united by faith and custom since its inception and that traditionally has drawn no distinction between the realm of faith and the realm of temporal power.

A number of ideological movements have spread and fortified the modern projection of transnational Islam. Perhaps the most successful has been the Muslim Brotherhood, founded by Hasan al-Banna in Egypt in 1928, with branches today in some 40 to 50 countries. Yasser Arafat and Ayman al-Zawahiri, Osama bin Laden's deputy, are among those formed by the Brotherhood. Its more recent inspiration derives from the Egyptian-born Sayyid Qutb, whose three-year stay in the United States in the late 1940s and early 1950s convinced him that the West and everything it stood for had to be rejected, while Islam already provided every Muslim with state, nation, religion, and identity all in one. Saudi Arabia has spent billions of its petro-dollars financing groups, including terrorist groups, that promote this idea.

The 1979 revolution led by Ayatollah Khomeini in Iran was an opening test of the new balance of forces between a rising transnational Islam and the declining Western nation-state. European countries, which in the postwar period seemed largely to have lost the will to respond to aggressive challenges from without, presented no opposition to the totalitarian Khomeini regime and no barrier to its aggrandizement. That left the United States, still a nation-state very much committed to defending its sovereignty. Indeed, to the ayatollahs and their allies, the U.S. represented a final embodiment of the Great Satan, fit to be confronted in holy war.

This remains the case today. In the meantime, though, a battle of a different but no less decisive kind has been taking place within Europe, where some 20 million Muslims have settled. Thanks on the one hand to their high birth-rate, and on the other hand to the sub-replacement birth-rate that has become the norm among other Europeans, the demographic facts alone suggest a continent ripe for a determined effort to advance the Islamist agenda.

In its global reach and in its aggressive intentions, Islamist ideology bears some resemblance to another transnational belief system: namely, Communism. Like today's Islamists, Communists of an earlier age saw themselves as engaged in an apocalyptic struggle in which every member of a Communist party anywhere was expected to comport himself as a frontline soldier, and in which terror was seen as a wholly permissible means toward victory in a war to the finish. Compare Stalin's "If the enemy does not surrender he must be exterminated" with the refusal of the leader of Hizbollah in Lebanon to negotiate with or ask concessions from the West because "We seek to exterminate you." To Sheik Omar Bakri Muhammad, a Syrian with British citizenship who until recently led a group called al-Muhajiroun, the terrorists of September 11 were "The Magnificent Nineteen" – or, as he explains, the advance guard of an army of "our Muslim brothers from abroad [who] will come one day and conquer here."

Throughout the Cold War era, the European democracies under threat from Soviet expansionism were themselves home to Communist parties, as well as to an array of front organizations ostensibly devoted to peace and friendship and culture but in reality manipulated by and for Soviet purposes. In addition, many people from all walks of life accommodated themselves to Communism with varying degrees of emotional intensity and out of various motives, including the wish to be on what they perceived as the winning side and the converse fear of winding up on the losing side.

Each of these elements, in suitably transmuted form, is

present today. The pool of local recruits upon which Islamists draw is itself very large. Of Europe's 20 million Muslims, it is estimated that 5 or 6 million live in France alone, at least 3 million in Germany and 2 million in Britain, 1 million in Holland and Italy, and a half-million apiece in Spain and Austria.

It is true that most Muslim immigrants to Europe come simply with hopes for a better life, and that these hopes are more important to them than any apprehensions they might entertain about living in a society ruled by non-Muslims – something historically prohibited in Islam. Indeed, large numbers have assimilated with greater or lesser strain, and, in the manner of other minorities, have become "hyphenated" as British-Muslims, French-Muslims, Italian-Muslims and the like. Religious life flourishes: if, a half-century ago, there were but a handful of mosques throughout Europe, today every leading country has over a thousand, and France and Germany each have somewhere between five and six thousand. Muslim pressure groups, lobbies, and charities operate effectively everywhere; in Britain alone there are 350 Muslim bodies of one kind or another.

Among these various organizations, however, a number function as Islamist fronts. Inspired by Saudi Arabia or Khomeinist Iran, by the Muslim Brotherhood or al Qaeda, they work to undermine democracy in whatever ways they can, just as Soviet front organizations once did. They push immigrants to repudiate both the process and the very idea of integration, challenging them as a matter of religious belief and identity to take up an oppositional stance to the societies in which they live. Issues of Islamic concern have been skillfully magnified into scandals in the attempt to foment animosity on all sides and thus further deter or prevent the integration of Muslims into mainstream European life.

The notorious 1989 *fatwa* condemning the novelist Salman Rushdie to death for exercising his right to free speech as a British citizen was an early example of this tactic of disruption and agitation. Another has been the attempt in Britain to set up a Muslim "parliament" that will recognize only Islamic law (*shari'a*) as binding, and not the law of the land. Still another has been the insistence, in France, on the wearing of the *hijab* by girls in public schools, a practice that clearly contradicts the ideals of French republicanism and is in any case not an Islamic requirement. The tactical thinking behind such incitements was well articulated by an al-Qaeda leader who, calling upon British Muslims to "bring the West to its knees," added that they, "the locals, and not foreigners," have the advantage since they understand "the language, culture, area, and common practices of the enemy whom they coexist among."

Still another phenomenon familiar from the Soviet era has lately made a repeat appearance in the West, and that is voluntary accommodation, or fellow travelling, among non-Muslims. Leftist fellow travelers once helped to create a climate of opinion favorable to Communism. Many knew exactly what they were doing. Others merely meant well; they were what Lenin called "useful idiots." In like manner, Islamist fellow travelers and useful idiots are weaving a climate of opinion today that advances the purposes of radical Islam and is deeply damaging to the prospects of reconciliation.

As in the '30s and throughout the cold war, intellectuals and journalists are in the lead. Books pour from the presses to justify everything and anything Muslims have done in the past and are doing in the present. Just as every Soviet aggression was once defined as an act of self-defense against the warmongering West, today terrorists of al Qaeda, or the Chechen terrorists who killed children in the town of Beslan, are described in the media as militants, activists, separatists, armed groups, guerrillas – in short, as anything *but* terrorists. Dozens of apologists pretend that there is no connection between the religion of Islam and those who practice terror in its name, or suggest that Western leaders are no better or are indeed worse than Islamist murderers. Thus Karen Armstrong, the well-known historian of religion: "It's very difficult sometimes to distinguish between Mr. Bush and Mr. bin Laden."

One form of Islamist fellow travelling masquerades as a call for "tolerance," or "diversity," and has penetrated right through the world of European opinion and European institutions. The British Communist historian Christopher Hill once concluded a book on Lenin with a worshipful recital of the epithets the party had devised to glorify him. Pious Muslims follow the mention of the Prophet Muhammad with the invocation, "Peace be upon him." This practice has now crept into a biography of the Prophet written by a British writer not ostensibly a Muslim. To encourage such acts of deference, there has been a complementary effort to stifle contrary or less than fully respectful opinions. When the outspoken French novelist Michel Houellebecq pronounced Islam to be hateful, stupid and dangerous, Muslim organizations and the League for the Rights of Man took him to court, just as the Italian writer Oriana Fallaci was sued for her book tying the 9/11 attacks to the teachings of Islam. Although both writers won their cases, the chilling effect was unmistakable.

The institutions that have been affected by Islamophile correctness run the gamut. In Britain, a judge has agreed to prohibit Hindus and Jews from sitting on a jury in the trial of a Muslim. The British Commission for Racial Equality has ordained that businesses must provide prayer rooms for Muslims and pay them for their absences on religious holidays. In a town in the Midlands, a proposal to renovate a hundred-year-old statue of a pig was rejected for fear of giving offense to Muslims. The British Council, an international organization for cultural relations, fired a staff member who published articles in the *Sunday Telegraph* arguing that the roots of terror and jihad were nourished in the soil of Islam, while the BBC cancelled the contract of a popular television journalist for allegedly using negative language to describe the Muslim Arab contribution to mankind.

Commercial society has likewise rushed to accommodate real or imagined Muslim sensibilities: a British bank boasts that it will comply with *shari'a* prohibitions on the uses of money, and the German state of Saxony-Anhalt has become the first European body to issue a *sukuk*, or Islamic bond. Religious society is not far behind: even as bin Laden speaks of wresting Spain ("al-Andalus") from the infidels by violence, the cathedral of Santiago has considered removing a statue of St James Matamoros ("the Moor slayer"), lest it give offense to Muslims. For the same reason, the municipality of Seville has removed King Ferdinand III, hitherto the city's patron saint, from fiesta celebrations because he fought the Moors for 27 years. In Italy, where Islamists have threatened to destroy the cathedral of Bologna because of a fresco illustrating the Prophet Muhammad in the inferno (where Dante placed him), thought has been given to deleting the art-work from the walls. Even the Pope has apologized for the Crusades. In secular Denmark, the Qur'an (but not the Bible) is now required reading for high-school students. And so forth.

The lengths to which apologists for Islamism are prepared to go is nicely illustrated by the case of Tariq Ramadan, a professor of Islamic studies at the University of Fribourg in Switzerland and a popular writer and speaker. As is well known, the American university Notre Dame recently offered Ramadan a professorship, but U.S. immigration authorities have so far rejected his application for a visa. This has elicited some classic examples of fellow-travelling obfuscation from both Americans and Europeans outraged on his behalf. A letter to the *Washington Post* protesting Ramadan's treatment undertook to explicate his supposed message to Western Muslims: they "must find common values and build with fellow citizens a society based on diversity and equality."

Not quite. What Tariq Ramadan has really proposed in his writings and teachings is that Muslims in the West should conduct themselves not as hyphenated citizens seeking to live by "common values" but as though they were already in a Muslim-majority society and exempt on that account from having to make concessions to the faith of others. What Ramadan advocates is a kind of reverse imperialism. In his conception, Muslims in non-Muslim countries should feel themselves entitled to live on their own terms – while, under the terms of Western liberal tolerance, society as a whole should feel obliged to respect that choice.

Ramadan happens to be a grandson of Hasan al-Banna, founder of the Muslim Brotherhood, but he is also a guarded writer. In fact, his is a relatively "moderate" and qualified expression of Islamic reverse imperialism. More overtly, and with an implicit threat of violence, Dyab Abu Jahjah, a Lebanese who has settled in Antwerp, has denounced the Western ideal of assimilation as "cultural rape," and aims to bring all the Muslims of Europe into a single independent community. He, too, needless to say, has his defenders and apologists among European liberals.

Or consider the European reception of Yusuf al-Qaradawi, heir to Sayyid Qutb as the religious authority of the Muslim Brotherhood. Wanted on charges of terrorism in his native Egypt, al-Qaradawi now lives in Qatar. Like Tariq Ramadan in Switzerland, he emphasizes that Muslims must keep apart from liberal democracy as it is practiced in the West while also availing themselves of its benefits and advantages. But he goes much further. Unlike Ramadan, he approves of wife-beating in the forms sanctioned by the Qur'an; as for homosexuals, he is agnostic on whether they should be thrown off a high cliff or flogged to death. Yet this year, in an official ceremony at London's City Hall, al-Qaradawi was welcomed as "an Islamic scholar held in great respect" by the mayor of London, Ken Livingstone. "You are truly, truly welcome," gushes Livingstone, an otherwise enthusiastic supporter of gay pride.

Also appearing this year in London was Sheik Abdul Rahman al-Sudayyis, a senior imam of the Grand Mosque in Mecca; among his distinctions, al-Sudayyis has vituperated Jews as "the scum of the human race, the rats of the world, the violators of pacts and agreements, the murderers of the prophets, and the offspring of apes and pigs." Standing beside *this* apostle of "diversity and equality" was a junior minster in the Blair government.

The Islamic Foundation, one of Britain's numerous Muslim bodies, has an offshoot called the Markfield Institute. In July, the London *Times* linked both the foundation and the institute to terrorism. An offended reader with an English name wrote to protest: "I hope that Markfield ... will be allowed to help individual Muslims to practice their faith with peace, and respect, in a multicultural Britain." Another reader, an Anglican canon in the Diocese of Leicester (a city with a Muslim majority today), asserted that the institute was simply trying to teach imams and Muslim youngsters alike to work within British institutions.

In just that spirit, even in that vocabulary, the fellow-travelling Beatrice Webb used to advance the transcendent virtues of the Soviet social model. Gullible, false and dangerous statements of this kind are now as common as rain.

In the realm of classical Islam, Christians and Jews once

324

lived as *dhimmis* – that is to say, minorities with second-class rights, tolerated but discriminated against by law and custom. Many contemporary Muslims appear to idealize this long-lost supremacy over others, and aspire to reconstruct it. One way to work for this end is through violence and terror. Another way, the way of Tariq Ramadan and Yusuf al-Qaradawi, is through words. One way and another the project is advancing. Summing up the collective achievement so far, Bat Ye'or, the historian of "dhimmitude," has written that "Europe has evolved from a Judeo-Christian civilization with important post-Enlightenment/secular elements to … a secular Muslim transitional society with its traditional Judeo-Christian mores rapidly disappearing." She calls this evolving entity "Eurabia."

If that is the case, or is becoming the case, is it any wonder that some Europeans are switching sides, so as to be on the winning one? The sheer élan and cultural confidence displayed by Islamist spokesmen may have something to do with the fact that every year, thousands of people all over Europe convert to Islam. Some of these converts, from Britain, France, and Germany, taking the direct route from words to action, have gone on to play a disproportionate role in terrorism and Islamist militancy. Thus, at a rally organized in London last year by a radical offshoot of the Muslim Brotherhood, a high proportion of demonstrators were clearly not of Middle Eastern origin. At a recent trial in Cairo in which three British citizens were condemned to prison for subversion and intended terrorism, two were English born, with English names. They were led away shouting defiance of the West.

There are certainly Muslims in Europe who look with horror upon what is being done in their name, and who wish to have nothing to do with the notion that they are entitled to live in the West as, in effect, conquerors. For wholly understandable reasons, few of them have the courage to speak out. One of the exceptional few recently wrote a letter to the London *Times*, giving his name and address and saying that he defines his community as the people with whom he chooses to interact. He went on: "We do not all subscribe to the same way of being a Muslim, neither do we push our beliefs into the civic and political sphere." But he continued, "Sadly the public does not always get our point of view, because the only Muslims who are consulted are those who choose to drag Islam into the political sphere."

One could not ask for a clearer repudiation not only of all Muslim Brotherhood-style proselytizers but, even more bitingly, of the patronizing and indulgent attitude adopted toward them by the European establishment. Those in Europe who have striven in ways great and small to extend special privileges to Muslims while subtly deprecating their own national identity and culture have indeed helped open the way to Islamic separatism and Islamist agitation. They have thereby hastened the very clash of civilizations that they (or some of them) foolishly claim they are avoiding. If Bassam Tibi is correct in stating that "either Islam gets Europeanized or Europe get Islamized," powerful forces are at work to foreclose the question.

Commentary
December 2004

THE OLD BALANCE of power between the United States and the Soviet Union is no more and tensions hitherto latent but contained have rushed into the global political vacuum. Muslims in particular, especially in the Middle East, experienced a freedom from foreign interference that they had not enjoyed for centuries. But freedom is one thing, consensus another. The relationship that Muslims will eventually reach among themselves – as Sunnis or Shiites, Islamists or nationalists or anything else – is as indeterminate as ever. At the same time the world of Islam has been in the process of deciding whether to accept Western modernity in whole, in part, or not at all.

Western Europe might well have been an uninvolved bystander to these dilemmas of other peoples' identity, except for the fact that since the 1950s and 60s, Muslims have been immigrating in large numbers into all European countries. On account of incomplete census-taking and persistent illegal immigration, statistics are unreliable; but the figure of twenty million is widely accepted. European countries welcomed these newcomers, at first as workers, later as prospective citizens. Recently, under the banner of multiculturalism, they have been encouraged to build institutions to maintain their faith, their languages, and their customs.

Unconscious assumptions of superiority may well have misled Europeans into treating the phenomenon of Muslim immigration as purely a matter of economics. The advantages of living in Europe appeared so obvious that it was expected immigrants would naturally assimilate. Nobody of influence in public life paused to analyze what might be the social and political consequences of such a large-scale influx of people accustomed to defining themselves through a faith and a culture with a fierce history of war with Europe.

Organizations representing Muslim interests are now officially recognized in every European country. Also informing Islamic communal opinion and fortifying internal solidarity are mosques. In France there are 1,600 or so mosques, in Germany 2,200 and in Britain, according to one Islamic website, 1,689. Some of these organizations, and some imams of mosques, work for assimilation; others for separatism. In certain notorious cases, they seek to impose their faith and culture upon those of other faiths and culture. Obeying a traditional concept of jihad – imperialism under an exotic cover – some Muslims have committed acts of terror, notably in Britain, France, Germany, and Spain, killing and wounding many (though fewer than were killed in America on 9/11). According to intelligence sources, over 1,000 potential jihad terrorists are under surveillance in Britain alone.

In several European countries, Muslim groups seek to influence and even to dictate foreign policy. Some also assert the right to determine what may be published about Islam itself, and demand the death penalty for those exercising free speech in ways they disapprove of.

In 2005–6 cartoons of the prophet Muhammad published in a Danish newspaper were the pretext for demonstrations in one capital after another. In London, Muslims brandished placards inciting murder: "Behead those who insult Islam." In France, legal action was initiated (unsuccessfully) to stop reproduction of the cartoons. Following the lead of advocates like Tariq Ramadan in Switzerland or the extremist Abu Jahjah in Antwerp, some Islamic spokesmen have demanded the creation of a "sacred space" under which European Muslims will be ruled by *shar'ia* rather than the law of the land. Presumably this would protect, for instance, the many Muslims opposing the freedom of women, some of whom have been killed for choosing their own husbands or friends.

Ideas of this kind not only block assimilation but oblige non-Muslim majorities to consider at what point they will have to take measures in defense of their own identity. In the late 1930s, Winston Churchill had few supporters when he warned that appeasement of Nazism was a policy for which a very high price would have to be paid. What he called a "terrible transformation" was then taking place in the world. Obviously, Muslim extremism today lacks the leadership and the power of the Nazi state of the 1930's. But it already exhibits a dynamism, and a potential for mass mobilization, that bring within the realm of possibility another lasting transformation of Europe.

One determining factor here, about which much has been written, is that native Europeans have too low a birth rate to reproduce themselves. Demographic extrapolations suggest that Muslims could become a majority in some places within the foreseeable future. The British towns of Bradford and Leicester, for instance, as well as the cities of Rotterdam in the Netherlands, Antwerp in Belgium, Marseilles in France, and Malmö in Sweden are among many in which an immigrant minority may soon outnumber the native population. Libyan president Muammar Qaddafi, articulating the hopes of numerous Muslim preachers and activists, has declared: "There are signs that Allah will grant Islam victory in Europe – without swords, without guns, without conquests. The 50 million Muslims of Europe will turn it into a Muslim continent within a few decades."

In the face of facts like these, many European policy makers have taken refuge in appeasement – an option that postpones examination and hard choices. As one Swedish politician has put it, we must be nice to the Muslims while we are the majority, so that they will be nice to us when they are the majority. Being nice, indeed, has become the order of the day.

Thus, on the grounds that the Qur'an sanctions wife-beating, a German judge refuses to grant a divorce to a Muslim woman abused by her husband. British schools are advised not to teach the history of the Holocaust or the Crusades, for fear of offending Muslim children who will have learned at home that the former is an invention of the Jews to extract money and sympathy, and the latter a Christian crime. For the same reason, municipalities redesign Christmas celebrations to purge them of religious content. Hospitals remove crucifixes from their walls. Apologies are extended to Muslims who object vocally to the Pope's theology, or to statues or artistic images deemed *haram* or forbidden, or to the design on ice cream said to look like the Arabic spelling of Allah, or to observances of Holocaust Memorial Day, or to innumerable other practices and details of life taken for granted by everyone else in the society.

Scattered across Europe today are perhaps over a million Jews, outnumbered by Muslims by a factor of twenty to one, probably more. Many Muslims, perhaps most, accept traditional stereotypes of Jews based on a few unquestioned verses in the Qur'an. Such customary prejudice is reinforced a hundredfold by the Arab and Muslim campaign against the state of Israel.

Indeed, the fate of the Jews of Europe has become linked to the fate of Israel in a way that virtually nobody seems to have anticipated. In 1996, the British historian Bernard Wasserstein published a book, *Vanishing Diaspora*, subtitled "The Jews in Europe since 1945." It was a sober piece of work, but the perspective, however sorrowful, was essentially trouble-free. No danger was foreseen from the Right: Wasserstein quite correctly dismissed fascist relics of the past as having no general appeal. As a result of assimilation and intermarriage, Jews were destined simply to fade away in Europe until, he concluded, nothing would be left of them save "a disembodied memory." Muslims rated no more than two or three passing mentions in the book, and Islamism did not feature at all.

Today it remains true that, with minor exceptions, the principal threat to European Jews does not emanate from the Right. It emanates instead from a confluence of sources: a resurgent Islam, augmented powerfully by the culture of the European Left and the force of institutional opinion as embodied in the United Nations.

In theory, the UN ought to be the forum in which it would become established once and for all that Israel is a victim of aggression rather than the aggressor. In practice the UN is the agency that more than any other works to enshrine the reversal of reality, and it has done that with increasing openness ever since the General Assembly's "Zionism is racism" resolution of 1975. Today, analogies between Israel and Nazism are as widespread as ever, if not more so, lately embellished by the charge that Israel practices a version of South African apartheid.

In one international forum after another, the Left has picked up and run with these vicious accusations, remodeling for contemporary purposes the anti-Jewish militancy of the Right in the 1930s. And not just of the Right. Indeed, the ideological pedigree of today's anti-Israel campaign in Europe can be traced less to Nazism or fascism than to the work of the Soviet propaganda machine that sprang into frenzied action after the Six-Day war of 1967. (Here, as so often, totalitarian systems become indistinguishable.) It is the Soviet-inspired condemnation of the United States and its allies, according to which the poor and oppressed everywhere are victims of American capitalism and culture, that the Left has perpetuated and revived time after time in the ensuing decades. By definition, then, Israel is in the wrong, and on two counts: as an ally of the United States, and as the alleged oppressor of Palestinians, a certified victim group of the third world.

Today's anti-Israel Left in Europe is a massed phalanx of German and Irish bishops, Anglican canons and Catholic priests, journalists from the leading papers of Europe, broadcasters (in particular at the BBC, which has gone so far as to suppress an in-house report of its bias against Israel), parliamentarians like George Galloway and Jenny Tonge, school and university teachers and trade unionists pressing for a boycott of Israel, and many others.

The Portuguese novelist José Saramago, winner of the Nobel Prize for literature, judged that a 2001 Israeli incursion into the West Bank city of Ramallah was "a crime that may be compared to Auschwitz." Gretta Duisenberg, wife of the Dutch former head of the European Central bank, sought a symbolic six million signatures for a petition to be presented at pro-Palestinian demonstrations in the Netherlands. Jan Guillou, president of the Swedish Association of Journalists, walked out of a meeting to commemorate the victims of 9/11 in protest that there was no mention of Muslims killed by Israel. According to the German socialist Oskar Lafontaine, "We must constantly ask ourselves through which eyes the Muslims see us." And so forth. Especially helpful to today's Left are Jews who themselves denigrate Zionism and the Jewish state. Such Jews, especially those with reputations in their professional fields, are featured prominently as signers of petitions and speakers at mass demonstrations where Palestinian and Hizbollah flags are waving and the Israeli flag is likely to be burned.

As if all this were not alarming enough, the internal workings of the European Union have made things worse. At its core, the EU is bedeviled by a contradiction. If it is to survive and prosper and become the homogeneous international body it aspires to be, then its component nations must be re-conceived as local regions or states in the American sense. By the law of unintended consequences, however, this homogenizing impulse has led to its opposite: namely, the reassertion of intense nationalist feeling among ethnic minorities long suppressed by the local majority. Basques, Burgundians, Bretons, Catalans, Corsicans, Welsh, Scots, Lombards and others, their grievances nursed down the centuries, have all laid claim to their historic territories, and the EU has striven to accommodate these claims.

But that leaves Muslim immigrants and Jews as two minorities in Europe without a territory, pitted against each other by the EU in a competition for social space. Compounding the problem, the EU has chosen between them. The consistent condemnation of Israel by Brussels, alongside the EU's enormous and unaccountable subsidies to the Palestinian Arabs, has virtually institutionalized the polarization of these two landless communities.

Realizing too late the flaw in its doctrine, EU legislators have passed a range of laws designed to criminalize and punish both anti-Semitism and "Islamophobia." These laws are at best an expedient rather than a genuine remedy. For the most part, they have had the effect of choking off honest debate about the reality of the Muslim condition in Europe, and of encouraging Islamic extremists to take matters into their own hands and to cry "Islamophobia" when criticized.

True, the EU has also set up a unit to monitor all aspects of racism; until recently, however, its reports were suppressed and re-edited to blur the fact that the high incidence of anti-Semitic behavior is closely tied to Muslims themselves. When Brussels does not wish to hear something, it simply closes its ears.

Countries define and report anti-Semitic incidents differently, so statistics are only suggestive. But, without doubt, they correlate with developments in the Middle East – and with the media's presentation of those developments. The latest, uncensored findings of the EU monitoring unit show that anti-Semitic incidents rose more or less steadily during Yasser Arafat's second intifada after September 2000. In 2002, for example, an Israeli raid on a terrorist base in the West Bank town of Jenin was reported almost universally as a war crime involving hundreds, even thousands, of innocent Palestinian victims. (In fact, in an area of about 100 square yards, 52 Palestinians had been killed, of whom 30 were in militia uniforms.) Anti-Israel outrage knew no bounds. All over Europe, attacks on Jews, synagogues and other Jewish institutions followed.

According to the same source, anti-Semitic incidents over the period 2001–2005 increased in Germany from 1,424 to 1,682; in France from 219 to 504; and in Britain from 310 to 455, leaping to 594 in 2006. The incidents themselves, the EU report finds, have ranged from verbal aggression to physical assault, and most of the perpetrators have been Muslims. The report does not identify specific crimes. To take one example, though, in 2003 a young Algerian in Paris killed his Jewish neighbor, a disc jockey of about the same age. With hands still bloody from the deed, the assailant told his mother: "I killed my Jew, I will go to paradise." In January 2006, also in Paris, a mostly Muslim gang abducted the twenty-three-year-old Ilan Halimi, a sales assistant. When they failed to extort ransom, they tortured him, set him on fire and left him to die.

The war with Hizbollah in the summer of 2006 provoked another massive increase in anti-Semitic speech and deed. Some of the hostility was inspired by repeated denunciations of Israel's "disproportionate" defense of its citizens by European governments and media. Speaking for many, the Norwegian writer Jostein Gaarder, author of the international best-seller *Sophie's World*, wrote in August: "We no longer recognize the state of Israel.... To act as God's chosen people is not only stupid and arrogant, but a crime against humanity."

A well-researched report by the European Jewish Council has documented the anti-Semitism on display over the 33 days of last year's war. In Britain, for instance, there were an unprecedented 132 incidents. In France, there were 61, as contrasted with 34 in the same period the previous year. A group in Germany counted more than 1,000 anti-Semitic acts in June and July (though most were related to Germany's hosting of the World Cup). While taking note of both neo-Nazi and extreme Left elements in the attacks, especially those in Central and Eastern Europe, the report concludes that primary responsibility rests with Europe's Muslim population. It might have added that the flames of anti-Semitism have been fanned by the universities, the media and the EU itself.

This past March, the historian Benny Morris published an essay under the title, "The Second Holocaust is Looming." Iran, Morris wrote, has clearly demonstrated its willingness to risk the future of the entire Middle East in exchange for Israel's destruction. One bright morning, not too long from now, the mullahs in Qom will meet in secret session under a portrait of the Ayatollah Khomeini and solemnly give the go-ahead to President Mahmoud Ahmadinejad, who has sworn to "wipe Israel off the map" and has been avidly pursuing the nuclear means of doing so. "With a country the size and shape of Israel," Morris concluded, "probably four or five hits will suffice: no more Israel."

335

Would anybody care? Morris's tone is one of almost elegiac resignation. Europeans, he writes, did little or nothing to save their Jewish fellow-citizens in the 1930's and they would be no more willing to come to the rescue now. He might have added that in the past years they have busily been preparing the ground for their exculpation by insisting that Israel has brought it on itself.

A counterpart to Morris is the German writer Henryk Broder. In a recent book titled *Hurra, Wir Kapitulieren* ("Hurrah, We're Capitulating"), he charges that fear, cowardice, and concern for trade have combined to push Europeans beyond appeasement to the point of outright surrender to Islam. Each and every Islamist aggression is now answered by pathetic calls for "dialogue." Resistance is considered provocative, and a resort to force superfluous (if not illegal). As Islamization renders the continent progressively uninhabitable, illusion, denial, and defeatism reign supreme. In an interview, Broder advised young Europeans to leave while they can.

Whether one prefers Broder's sardonic scorn or the pessimism of Benny Morris – both of them, it may be, exaggerated for effect – Europe is now on the brink of another "terrible transformation." Jews, whether Israelis or Europeans, are testing out the extent to which European civilization really has become hollowed out from within, and unable to withstand assault from without.

Commentary
July–August 2007

Various Arab armed forces these past decades have resorted to military means to eliminate Israel from the world's map. All have failed. More than that, the wars each time strengthened Israel, and the Arabs have thus achieved the very opposite of their ambitions. This opens the way to the alternative approach of psychological warfare, a familiar element in all modern wars. PW, in the shorthand the experts use, mobilizes allies and undermines enemies. What is required is a master idea, and people to propagandize in words clever enough for the general public to accept it as the truth.

The master idea in this case is simplicity itself: Jewish nationalism, or Zionism, is an absolute evil, Palestinian nationalism is an absolute virtue. To establish this, the Jews must be shown to be wicked and wrong in every matter great and small, so that Palestinians appear victims through no fault of their own, innocent people in special need of redress and rescue. With skill and persistence, the Palestinians and their Arab supporters have built up a worldwide PW lobby with helpers in the United Nations, the European Union, the Red Cross, the churches, the universities, the media and so on. One step at a time, they are subverting the legitimacy of Israel. Their multiple voices and pressures have persuaded the worldwide Left to believe that Israel is a state that ought to be dismantled forthwith. At the very least, they sap Israeli will to survive, and fortify Palestinian will to prefer armed struggle to the necessary compromises of peace.

Like much else, the Palestinian master idea is rooted in the Cold War. Backing the Arabs, the Soviet Union suffered a major defeat in the Six Day War of 1967. Trying to recover, the Soviet leadership immediately began to equate Israel with Nazi Germany, its deadliest foe. Hitherto tending to sympathize with Israel, the Left everywhere and unanimously swung against it. Here was a manipulation of opinion of the kind immortalized by George Orwell in *1984* as a Two Minute Hate. The Marxist lexicon – "imperialism," "colonialism," "occupation," "settler society" – was deployed to curse Israel. By 1975, the United Nations was declaring that Zionism is racism, and a state built on racism can only be a focus of outrage, the proper target of sanctions and boycotts. Successful American pressure on the United Nations rescinded that resolution. The Left's inherent anti-Americanism then joined forces irrevocably with the pro-Palestinian PW.

It has been commonplace to portray Israeli leaders like Moshe Dayan and Menachem Begin as Nazis. Self-appointed bodies, including the BBC, have proposed – and sometimes staged – a trial of Ariel Sharon as a war criminal. Posters in Paris today declare, "Hitler has a son – Sharon." The *New York Times* openly implies that Israel's measures of self-defense are war-mongering, quasi-fascist in spirit. Over half of those questioned in a recent poll in Germany equated the Israeli Defense Force with the Nazi army. José Saramago, winner of the Nobel Prize for Literature, considers that Israelis are treating Palestinians as Jews were treated in Auschwitz. A Nobel Peace Prize winner, Mairead Maguire, compares Israel's nuclear arsenal to Hitler's gas chambers.

Smearing Jews by attaching to them the label of their chief persecutors and ultimate murderers is not as recent a phenomenon as one might think. The very first person to compare Zionism to Nazism seems to have been the French ambassador to Warsaw in the Thirties, when the government there was already practicing an anti-Jewish policy. Jews then and after tried to emigrate to what became Israel in the hope of surviving the Holocaust, but Gen. Sir Edward Spears, Churchill's war-time representative in the Levant, and the historian A. J. Toynbee were among prominent British personalities who blackguarded these unfortunates as Nazis.

The deadlock between Palestinian nationalism and Zionism led from the 1980s onward to a new set of comparisons, this time between Israel and South Africa. This was PW of a malign brilliance. Politically and socially, the two countries had nothing in common. Apartheid does not exist in Israel where Arabs are represented in parliament and in the foreign service; Druze and Bedouin serve in the army; there are no pass laws or anything like them, and all Arabs enjoy freedom of speech and assembly, indeed more political rights than Arabs anywhere else in the Middle East, except possibly in the new Iraq. Visiting Israel in 1989, Bishop Desmond Tutu secured this new comparison in all its falsity, saying that what he had seen was "much like what happened to us black people in South Africa." Its triumph was the U.N. gathering at Durban in September 2001, when 3,000 assembled non-governmental organizations passed a resolution calling Israel "a racist apartheid state."

The white population of South Africa could see no way either to reform or to stay in power. To significant numbers of Palestinians, including both Fatah and Hamas, the simple and unconditional surrender of power by South African whites is an example for Israel to follow. Nelson Mandela always made a point of supporting Yasser Arafat, and excusing Palestinian terror. Once their will is sufficiently sapped, runs the argument, the Israelis will disappear on the ships that once brought them, and a pristine Palestine will rise up in their place. More than anyone else, Edward Said, the prominent Palestinian spokesman, fashioned this wish-fulfilment into a PW weapon with the claim that Palestinians have a moral monopoly, and therefore are bound to be the ultimate victors. Less sophisticated than Said, other Palestinian publicists, preachers, and educators incite violence directly when they describe Jews as bloodsuckers, descendants of pigs and apes, treacherous and much else of the sort. Israelis are held to be masters of America, and simultaneously its hireling tools, just as once Jews were simultaneously capitalists and Bolsheviks. When they defend themselves against terror, they are accused of crime and even of committing a massacre as at Jenin when no such thing occurred – a PW coup if ever there was one, given that gullible Western journalists were spreading the fiction.

The burning of books and the boycott of Jewish businesses organized by Hitler and Goebbels are models of PW designed to rally supporters and intimidate enemies. The approaching violence was evident, and so was what Einstein at the time called the "psychic illness of the masses." Yet some Jews preferred their form of rather pathetic wish-fulfilment to the terrifying reality. Felix Jacoby, for instance, a historian at Kiel University in Germany, opened his 1933 lecture course by declaring that he had voted for Hitler since 1927, and could only compare him to the emperor Augustus. Dr. Hans-Joachim Schoeps even tried to form a movement of Jews for Hitler (though other Jews replied with the grim joke that his real slogan was *Raus mit Uns*, or "Out with Us").

The same psychopathology is at work in Israel today. By and large, Israeli intellectuals have succumbed to Palestinian PW, and do whatever they can to weaken the will for national existence. Appealing for mobilization against Israel in a *Raus mit Uns* spirit, they speak at international conferences and publish in chic outlets as though they believe with the Palestinians that the Zionist state is a misconceived project to be brought to an end as soon as possible.

The Association of University Teachers in Britain has just voted to boycott the Israeli universities of Haifa and Bar-Ilan (and to scrutinize the Hebrew University of Jerusalem for its correctness) and a wonderful microcosm it is, too, of how this particular PW campaign operates. Supposed injustice to Palestinians under occupation has precedence over academic freedom. A few years ago, Hilary and Stephen Rose, both of them Jewish and academics, were calling for a boycott of Israeli universities. "Cooperating with Israeli institutions," they claimed quite typically, is "like collaborating with the apartheid regime." Sporadic attempts followed to boycott Israeli researchers and students. Someone called Lisa Tariki, described as "Coordinator for the Palestinian Campaign for the Academic and Cultural Boycott of Israel," contacted the AUT, and in particular a lecturer at Birmingham University by the name of Sue Blackwell, described as a former Christian fundamentalist now turned socialist. (Her web-site was found to recommend a link to the site of a neo-Nazi activist.) At the AUT meeting, Blackwell wore a Palestinian-flag dress, and spoke for the boycott motion. Israeli academics were not allowed to address the floor. Nobody mentioned that Arabs constitute almost a third of the Haifa student body.

In itself, such a boycott is gesture politics of no great significance. Those who voted for it are merely useful idiots in someone else's cause, puffed up with moral indignation that costs them nothing but that fortifies their self-righteousness and vanity. And yet the delegitimization of Israel takes many forms in many forums, and in their way the AUT boycotters are helping to confirm the primacy of the Palestinian cause in today's political sphere. Under cover of that cause, irratio-

340

nality towards Israel is diffusing into irrationality about Jews generally, sweeping one country after another. Palestinian psychological warfare has already created conditions for a fresh eruption of the psychic illness of the masses.

341

National Review
June 6, 2005

DENMARK IS A REPUBLIC with a monarch as head of state, belongs to the European Union, and keeps its own currency. The Danes do things their own way, then. When I was asked if I would accept an invitation to take part in a panel discussion in Copenhagen with the title "Fatwa or free speech?" I said I would. Also on the panel would be Lars Vilks, the Swedish artist who has been one of the most contentious individuals in the world ever since the publication of his cartoon of the Prophet Muhammad with a bomb for a turban. Extremist Muslims make fairly regular attempts to kill him. Helle Merete Brix has set up a committee to defend him, and she is the organizer of this event. I felt I had to ask her about security. Armed guards would be on the watch round the clock.

On the day I left London, the newspapers were carrying reports of the first British-born Muslim to be a suicide bomber. He'd rammed a truck loaded with explosives into the entrance of the main prison in Damascus. In the town of Crawley in Sussex, he'd left a wife and children. Some in the family or the community said that they would have stopped him if they had had any idea of what he intended to do. They were either covering up or short on curiosity, for it turned out that the bomber had been the regular driver of a preacher of hate so virulent that he'd had to flee from Britain to Beirut to escape arrest.

That day was also the twenty-fifth anniversary of Ayatollah Khomeini's fatwa condemning Salman Rushdie to death for his novel *The Satanic Verses*. A head of state calling for the assassination of a particular named citizen from a state not under his jurisdiction has no precedent that I can think of. Khomeini was sweeping aside centuries of diplomacy and the innumerable treaties and conventions that have established the conduct of nations by acting on the claim that Islam gave him universal power over life and death. Following this example, growing numbers of Muslims in one country or another attribute to themselves these self-same powers, imagining that they are "soldiers of Allah." The Rushdie fatwa serves its purpose as a declaration of war.

343

Psychological anxiety and perhaps physical intimidation have made it taboo to criticize Islamist assumptions of superiority, or still more of a challenge, to hold them up to ridicule. Anyone like Lars Vilks who tries to do so comes up against the accusation of Islamophobia, a coinage with no real meaning but which ingeniously confuses rational comment and analysis with irrational racism and blasphemy. For the past fifteen or so years, one or another Muslim country has called on the United Nations General Assembly or its Human Rights Committee to condemn Islamophobia and penalize those deemed guilty of it. The fifty-seven countries comprising the Organization of the Islamic Conference (OIC) have set up the so-called Istanbul Process to press for a law that would allow critics of Islam to be prosecuted for blasphemy. Put straightforwardly, the OIC wants to have privilege and protection through international censorship. Hillary Clinton and Catherine Ashton, on behalf of the United States and the European Union respectively, were present during this flagrant attack on free speech. They were accepting that the Istanbul Process had some merit when they should have had nothing to do with it.

Rushdie acknowledges that he intended his novel to stir up a hornet's nest, and I at first supposed Vilks to be a similar, deliberately provocative character. In his late sixties, a retired professor of art, soft-spoken and fluent in English, Vilks passes in the crowd, evidently an easy-going bohemian like pretty much all Scandinavians. He lives in the south of Sweden in a house off the beaten track. He was once shot at by a would-be murderer, but he just had time to make it into a safe room. Colleen LaRose, otherwise known as Jihad Jane from Pennsylvania, is now imprisoned for her part in a plot to kill him. University students attacked him in the course of a lecture he was giving. Only a few days before, two Albanians had a go breaking one of his windows and throwing in chemicals, but they got it wrong – the chemicals burnt them badly, and they landed in hospital. He's too recognizable a figure to go to art exhibitions and galleries as he would like. At the conference, the security guards hang around with nothing to do, and he thinks up things to keep them occupied.

Guards frisked everyone entering the hall for the meeting. "If you say I'm a defender of free speech you have already said too much," Lars Vilks starts to explain. Today there isn't time to think slowly, he goes on, you have to do what's simple and easy. Politics today, according to one of a number of striking observations of his, is "a fast-food landscape." Some years ago, someone made the likeness of a dog out of scrap, and placed it as a public ornament on a roundabout in Sweden. Others copied the idea, cobbled up dogs out of bits of glass, plastic, tins, anything to hand, and set them up on roundabouts until Swedish roads were a sort of outdoor museum. Going one better, Vilks modelled in white clay quite small roundabout dogs, each with the turbaned head of an Arab fitted in such a way that it can nod from side to side. Muslim disdain for dogs has not escaped this conceptual artist, and you can read what you like into that Arab head. Later on, he tells me how walking one day he came upon a more or less inaccessible beach on the southern coast of Sweden. Driftwood had piled up here, so he constructed out of it what he calls *The Piece*, as long as it is high, for adults and especially children to clamber upon at risk to themselves. The land on which *The Piece* stands is stolen, he says, not boastfully but as a matter of fact. Art, in his words, makes him "an equal opportunity offender."

The European Union has already reinvented blasphemy. Anyone who offends someone else's group identity is treated in the same way as offending God once was. Recently Bob Dylan said something about Croats and became a victim of this revived medievalism. In his book *New Inquisition*, the libertarian John Gower Davies lists thirty-five Acts of Parliament, fifty-two Statutory Instruments, thirteen Codes of Practice, three Codes of Guidance, and sixteen European Commission Directives that deal with various neo-blasphemy crimes within the E.U. To borrow from Orwell, freedom is slavery even in the absence of a one-party regime.

Karl Kraus, the Viennese satirist, wrote *The Last Days of Mankind* under the shadow of Hitler, and the title of Henryk Broder's latest book, *The Last Days of Europe*, waves a hand in that direction. A prolific author and television journalist, Broder disturbs Germany almost as much as Vilks disturbs Sweden. A master of sarcasm and put-down, he can be thought of as the German equivalent of Mark Steyn. In the view he expresses during the panel discussion, it's not fatwas or any imposition of censorship that make Germany so bland and boring, but the self-censorship that everyone with anything to say automatically adopts. Nobody breaks the politically correct consensus that Islam is a religion of peace, capitalism is bad, climate change is man-made, and Auschwitz is best forgotten. The E.U. is a bad idea, he thinks – so bad that it is certain to vanish, and this book can hardly wait for the return of democracy and freedom.

The rest of the evening was spent in a café with people

from the audience, a good few of them journalists who wanted to make sure that I had heard about Yahya Hassan. A poet and rapper, the eighteen-year-old Dane of Palestinian origins gave an interview last October with a title that comes straight to the point: "I'm fucking angry at my parents' generation." The sensation was immediate, phenomenal. In a population of about five million, a Danish poet can expect to sell a few hundred copies at most. Hassan has sold over 100,000 and made himself quite well-off in the process.

One of my informants is an editor of *Jyllands-Posten*, the paper that published Vilks's cartoon, and he tells me that Hassan's poems have the single subject of hate. In the voice of an angry insider, Hassan really and truly hates and denounces Islam, the Prophet, the customs and the food and the hypocrisy and the family relationships and the racism and violence of his fellow Muslims. This devastating portrayal of Muslim self-deception attracts death threats, twenty-seven of them according to one count I saw. Like Rushdie and Vilks before him, Hassan has to be accompanied everywhere by armed security guards.

The poems are being translated at the moment. These lines are all I could find in English, and they speak for themselves:

> You don't want pork meat,
> may Allah praise you for your eating habits.
> you want Friday prayer till the next Friday prayer,
> you want Ramadan till the next Ramadan
> and between the Friday prayers and the Ramadans,
> you go and ask people if they have a problem,
> although the only problem is you.

His is a unique position in that his integration into Danish life came early and now is completely cross-cultural, if that's the right euphemism. At school, he had an affair with one of the teachers, and is open about it. In her thirties, she justifies herself in public on the grounds that she had been in love with her pupil. Women are stoned for that in parts of the Muslim world; in Copenhagen she has not even been fired from her job. Rap artist that he is, Hassan evidently couldn't care less what others think of him. When he was awarded a prestigious literary prize for the book, all he said by way of thanks was, "I'm going home now."

You get the feeling from everybody here of a national resistance movement. The odds appear stacked against them, but they aren't going to be pushed around by anybody, not when they can do things their own way.

The New Criterion
April 2014

AU PILORI was a magazine once published in Paris in very different circumstances from *Private Eye* today, yet their similarities in style and spirit are astonishing and instructive. In both cases, the invaluable and undisputed right of the press to comment on everybody and everything was taken to extremes. Neither polite convention nor the law acted as restraints. Both magazines shared the same fantasy that there is nothing admirable in the world, no brave or generous men, only scoundrels and back-sliders who have to be exposed with mockery and punished without mercy. The role of the press as guardian of the public realm, as the fourth estate, has thereby been inverted as these magazines turned themselves into engines of persecution. "Who made thee a prince and a judge over us?" was the question asked of Moses when he sought a morally unjustified position of authority over others. It is the question of every citizen facing a self-appointed persecutor.

Au Pilori was founded shortly before the Second World War, in the days of Léon Blum's Popular Front. Even in the none too fastidious world of Paris journalism, it soon acquired a reputation all its own, as it sought to show that those prominent in public life were rich, crooks, Jews and Freemasons, all terms taken to be more or less synonymous.

The German occupation of Paris in June 1940 freed the paper from all previous restrictions of law and of taste. The prejudices and whims current in the *Au Pilori* office conveniently happened to coincide with those of the German authorities now in power. No need for censorship there. *Au*

Pilori accordingly went to town. A raucous satirical spirit among its writers and cartoonists produced an impression of fun which also obscured the deadly effect of a magazine telling tales about people whom the authorities were seeking to attack and eventually destroy. Nobody could afford to ignore *Au Pilori*. Circulation rose to 250,000 or more copies. Though primarily concerned with assertion of themselves and their opinions, the owners of *Au Pilori* were not sorry to earn a great deal of money as well.

Many of the "scoops" were designed to keep government up to the mark: Admiral Darlan was revealed as the son of a prominent Freemason, if not one himself; Pierre Laval had addressed Masonic Lodges in the past; Cardinal Gerlier, no collaborator, had been promised the Papacy in the event of an Allied victory; the Abbé Glassberg, a converted Jew, visited detention camps in order to free inmates to drink champagne with him ... Regular lists were published on Freemasons in all walks of life, or of Jews who were Vichy bureaucrats, or aristocrats with crypto-Jewish ancestry. Accusations of fraud and black-marketeering were printed in virtually every issue. Those wrongly accused of being Freemasons, Jews or crooks, could not sue. Their indignant letters to the editor were published, occasionally with an apology, more often with a sneer.

Nothing proved too small for attention. The lavatories in the station of Saint-Germain-en-Laye were found to be repulsive. The mayor of Garches used a room in his *mairie* for "private discussions" with a secretary. Minor officials were a favourite target. A man had knocked together 26 wooden crates in his garden in the Rue Méchain (what was he carrying off?). In the Avenue Niel a grocer preferred customers who could pay above-market prices, "and if that proves true, we can only recommend this grocery to our national-socialist friends."

"*L'Art Kasher*" was a regular feature purging the art world. Books were examined, not always predictably, as when Albert Camus's war-time novel *L'Etranger* received a nod. But nothing inspired so much good humour in *Au Pilori* supporters, and fear in everyone else, as unsigned columns with the titles "*Micro et Confessions*" and "*Ici on Scalpe,*" "*Tir de Barrage*" and "*Nous Clouons Au Pilori.*" All served the same purpose. One pithy item after another drew the attention of the relevant authorities to grounds for hounding those named, whose addresses were sometimes added for good measure. Democratic politicians, owners of businesses, doctors and lawyers, were easy to pick up; but *Au Pilori* covered the full social range down to the postman at Courneuve. Nor were there any illusions about what happened next. *Au Pilori* took the greatest pleasure in the death of enemies. When Marx Dormoy, Minister of the Interior during the Popular Front, was murdered by gunmen in the pay of the Germans, *Au Pilori* had the characteristic headline, *Et D'un! A Qui le Tour du Plomb Dans la Tête?* ("One for Us! Who's next for lead in the head?").

Readers were invited to provide stories for these columns, and paid money if they did so. A network of informers was thus set up. The novelist Céline wrote in to encourage denunciation because it led to the Stake and the Rope, as he put it in his blithe way. Editorial advice was clear. "Many readers ask us which organisation they should address themselves to in order to point out Jewish occult activities and fraud. It is enough to send a letter or a signed note to the *Commissariat aux Questions Juives*, or else to our office for transmission." By means of *Au Pilori*'s energetic and successful campaigning, tens of thousands of people were delivered to the authorities, whether French or German, who could then further claim that public opinion was demanding the ensuing persecution.

In a democracy, systematic denunciation of this kind does not carry the same penalties as under totalitarian rule. Citizens of democracies need suffer nothing worse at the hands of the press than a career wrecked, followed perhaps by arrest, or a reputation lost, a marriage shattered, a personal hurt revealed. Our *Private Eye*, it is true, gloats over the death of those considered its particular enemies, but fortunately in no way could it cause those deaths. Supporters may argue that those who choose the limelight have only themselves to blame for whatever is then exposed. But what about hitherto obscure people, suddenly hoicked into public view in one or another of its several unsigned columns for lapses, often at the level of keeping dirty lavatories or having "private discussions" with a secretary? Self-appointed to the role of prince and judge, such columns are out for revenge, from motives which are undeclared but can only be malicious. (Perhaps this is the point to record that I myself have been mentioned in them hardly more than once or twice, always in a context of amusing make-believe.)

Personalities, not principles, preoccupy Patrick Marnham in the dispiriting little account he gives of the magazine* as though its office quarrels mattered.

Exposure for the sake of exposure, and never mind the cost to anyone, is not questioned.

Zeal to identify and persecute makes *Private Eye* the spitting image of *Au Pilori* – though specially delighted to catch Jews, of course it spreads wider the net.

> The investigators at the Department of Trade and Industry (if such there be) might like to look at the report of the Assistant Official Receiver.... There is a provision in the Companies Act to prohibit people like [him] from

---

* *The Private Eye Story*, by Patrick Marnham. Deutsch, £7.95.

taking part in the management of a company where several liquidations and failures have been proved, but obviously the Department of Trade has not yet caught up with him…. This should be of interest to planning officers as this property has planning permission to operate only as rental accommodation… [These activities] look like attracting the interest of the Inland Revenue…. Meanwhile the VAT men watch with interest…. The Director of Public Prosecutions should take note.

Each of these phrases is a quotation, and almost any issue of the magazine will provide equivalent examples of such straightforward tip-offs to the relevant authorities, who can ignore them only at their own peril.

As in Paris under occupation, a whole seething underworld of informers is sometimes startlingly revealed. Their unsigned denunciations are apparently acted on, instead of being thrown into the waste-paper basket. "Mr William Hamilton MP for West Fife … received an anonymous letter from Scotland which directed his attention to the Ninewells Teaching Hospital in Dundee [and] Mr Hamilton passed this letter on to Mr Robert Carr who is expected to launch an urgent and immediate inquiry into allegations…. An anonymous letter to the *Eye* asks why Dr Gerald Vaughan, the Minister of Health, is still being paid by Guy's Hospital…. Despite Commander Ron Steventon's denial – 'I would never question a detective on the basis of a story in *Private Eye*' – this is just what he did." *Private Eye* readers are paid small sums of money for information submitted and printed.

To act the informer is quite as much a source of pride for *Private Eye* as it was for *Au Pilori*. "Our revelations about [his] unusual business practices in the last issue of the *Eye* appear to have sparked off great interest among the various law-enforcing agencies of this country…. One day after the publication of our story about [him] the Obscene Publications Squad raided all the business premises."

Suppose for the moment that every one of those fingered in *Private Eye* is a villain and a scoundrel and that the facts are correct (which is not the case – Marnham gives a figure of 2,000 writs over a period of 21 years). A good proportion of those denounced in *Au Pilori* were indeed Freemasons, Jews and Allied sympathisers, and some were rich, but that was not judged a valid defence of the magazine at the liberation. The democratic state has its investigation and enforcement agencies, and remains in full control of them, rather too full a control in the opinion of those who believe that tolerance is an aspect of justice. There is rarely any call to go beyond the due process of law. If for some reason journalists burn to place fellow citizens in the pillory or behind bars, then there are normal civil and civilised ways for them to play their part. They might even prefer to enrol as officials of the state.

353

One suspects that under the masquerade of moral passion are personal ambitions, envy, and contempt for things human. Otherwise how could the world always be depicted as a scoundrel's playground? When insufficient constraints are formed either by good manners, or the law, as in *Au Pilori's* Paris or *Private Eye's* London, there is no protection against this type of self-assertion. The way lies open for those who are at the prey of their prejudices and fantasies to impose them on everyone as nastily as they please. Redress of abuse and injustice is one thing, nark's work another; and to confuse the two is to devalue free speech altogether.

Encounter
February 1983

ACKNOWLEDGMENTS

Roger Kimball has made publication with Criterion Books a   355
source of pride and satisfaction. More than a feat, it is a triumph of free speech and I am immoderately grateful for it.
Benjamin Riley is one of the editors who has worked on this
book and Robert Erickson is another, and they both have
my special thanks. Superlative is actually the word in order.
Recovery and transmission each chapter was in the
problem-solving hands of Joanna Bonner and George
Andraos.

INDEX

A NOTE ON THE TYPE

OPENINGS & OUTINGS has been set in Kingfisher, a family of types designed by Jeremy Tankard. Frustrated by the paucity of truly well-drawn fonts for book work, Tankard set out to create a series of types that would be suitable for a wide range of text settings. Informed by a number of elegant historical precedents – the highly regarded Doves type, Monotype Barbou, and Ehrhardt among them – yet beholden to no one type in particular, Kingfisher attains a balance of formality, detail, and color that is sometimes lacking in types derived or hybridized from historical forms. The italic, designed intentionally as a complement to the roman, has much in common with earlier explorations in sloped romans like the Perpetua and Joanna italics, yet moderates the awkward elements that mar types like Van Krimpen's Romulus italic. The resulting types, modern, crisp, and handsome, are ideal for the composition of text matter at a variety of sizes, and comfortable for extended reading.

SERIES DESIGN BY CARL W. SCARBROUGH